# Coming Home

## Taking Refuge Within

Reverend Master Meiten McGuire

Published in Canada by the Vancouver Island Zen Sangha
www.vizs.org

**Library and Archives Canada Cataloguing in Publication**

Title: Coming Home: Taking Refuge Within / Reverend Master Meiten McGuire.
Names: McGuire, Meiten, 1926-2018, author.

Identifiers: Canadiana 2022045275X | ISBN 9780978482930 (softcover)
Subjects: LCSH: Zen Buddhism. | LCSH: Spiritual life—Zen Buddhism.

Classification: LCC BQ9265.4 .M44 2022 | DDC 294.3/927—dc23

Printed in Canada
First Edition

Design by Marina Nagibina with Marian Lowe

# Dedication

To the wonder of the Dharma itself –
the Truth of Oneness everywhere flowing to embrace us all.

# Contents

# Introduction

It is an honour for us to write an Introduction to this compilation of Reverend Master Meiten's writings, a new edition that includes her previous three books, as well as another 25 chapters of unpublished material. *Coming Home – Taking Refuge Within* is being published by the Vancouver Island Zen Sangha as part of Reverend Master Meiten's legacy, in celebration of her life and work.

Reverend Master Meiten died peacefully in Victoria at the age of 91 on January 2nd 2018. As we reach the fifth anniversary of her death in 2023, this new offering is a tribute to express our profound gratitude to her for bringing the Buddha's teachings into the lives of so many people.

We would like to express our gratitude to Reverend Master Oswin Hollenbeck of Shasta Abbey for his sensitive and skillful editing of the new selections.

We each met Meiten – the more informal name that she asked us to call her – at different times in the last fifty years. Terence and Nancy met her while she was living in an ashram in the early 1970's, soon after the death of her son. Pamela met Meiten in 2003 when she 'returned to the world' after 25 years of monastic life. It was a Dharma gift for us to be both students and friends to Meiten over the years, and to be part of the Vancouver Island Zen Sangha, which Meiten founded in 2006 and has continued to blossom in the years since then.

Each of us had followed different spiritual paths before realizing that Meiten offered something very special that resonated within us – her unique ability to bring the Dharma alive, while firmly rooted in the Soto Zen tradition of her teacher, Reverend Master Jiyu-Kennett, and nourished by many years of spiritual practice. In her gentle and yet firm manner she kept "pointing the way to the moon", a metaphor used in the Shurangama Sutra to indicate the essential role of the spiritual teacher, encouraging us to take refuge in our own Buddha Nature.

Throughout her teaching, counselling and writing, Meiten demonstrated a remarkable ability to bring the teachings down to earth, weaving the deep wisdom and compassion of the Buddhadharma with day-to-day experiences that we all encounter. Over and over again, the importance of the Buddhist Precepts and of Meditation are emphasized in the path of Zen, and in this book, Meiten skillfully offers ways in which these practices can help us to reduce suffering and increase compassion – both for ourselves and others – in daily life.

We hope that this compilation of Reverend Master Meiten's reflections will be of value to everyone who reads this book. We encourage you to read them slowly, and to take time to reflect on their meaning in your life. From our own experience, we know that 'returning to basics with beginner's mind' and being reminded of what is most important in life is a profound gift. As it is written in the Dhammapada, "The gift of the Dharma surpasses all gifts".

With bows of deep gratitude to Reverend Master Meiten, and to the Buddha, Dharma and Sangha.

Nancy Carroll, Terence Buie, and Pamela Bruce

# Reflections on the Path

## Zen Training in Everyday Life

Reverend Meiten McGuire

# Contents

# Foreword

A human heart may sing a song of faith, love, and understanding in many ways. My reaction as I read Reverend Master Meiten's words is that I am reading such a song. I believe that this song will be appreciated by everyone who has been privileged to witness over many years the steadfastness of Reverend Master Meiten's faith and resolve.

Our master, Reverend Master Jiyu-Kennett, said many times, "All paths lead to the Goal. Walk the one that is right for you." In the following pages, Reverend Master Meiten offers much encouragement to those who would follow the path of Soto Zen Buddhism as it has been transmitted to us by our master. This is a path of faith. What is its purpose? To help us to be true to our own True Self. This is not some distant goal, but a moment-to-moment, here-and-now goal. It so often seems that we are doing it all on our own. The truth is that we are being helped, led, even carried every step of the way. "True Self" is not an abstraction and It is not a remote deity. In our pain and confusion we may think that we are separate from It, yet It never suffers from that delusion. It is infinite Love and Wisdom, and our finite minds are never going to understand the infinite. Yet when we come one day to the point where we cry out to It with our whole being, we know with our whole being that It is, and that "I am not It, It is all of me."

It is our Refuge in life and in death. Infinite Love is incapable of turning away from us. Infinite Wisdom is incapable of doing less than the best for every being. The deeper meaning of meditation is simply that we allow this infinite Love and Wisdom to circulate within our own body and mind without willful obstruction. In the following pages, Reverend Master Meiten often exhorts the reader to have faith and be willing to step into the unknown. Answering and following the call that comes from the infinite Unknown is the greatest joy in human life.

I pray that these teachings may bless the lives of all who read them.

Reverend Master Koshin Schomberg
North Cascades Buddhist Priory

# Discipline

When we truly recognize that at least part of the unsatisfactoriness we experience in life comes out of the way "I" am, and when we are sincere in our desire to change, then the groundwork is laid for a spiritual solution to the problem of suffering. We aren't going to get anywhere as long as we wriggle out of this recognition. Discipline is the key.

The first discipline enters with dignity and simplicity: we must be willing to stop, pause, and look at our priorities as they are expressed in how we occupy ourselves in our daily lives—what we are doing with our precious time and with our equally precious self dwelling hidden beneath the surface of our lives. Most of us have been running for so long on old habit tendencies that this first discipline is a real challenge, far more difficult than sliding along with the old status quo no matter how unsatisfactory it can be at times. The first discipline requires that we set some limits so that we can find periods of "alone time" for simply being. We don't want to set ourselves up for failure; we have to look realistically at the demands in our lives to find a window for spiritual practice. Someone gave me a quotation by a Christian mystic who comments that "most of the time one-half hour was sufficient for quiet contemplation, unless one were too busy to fit this in. Then one hour was needed." The excuse that we are "too busy" won't wash here. One Buddhist master taught that if you have time to breathe you have time to meditate.

How can meditation, mindfulness, and self-knowledge be *that* important, as important as breathing? The truth is that we are more than simply this body/mind we identify with. The longing of the heart knows this—that longing for the deepest harmony and peace that come from digging beneath the surface of life. No matter how much we turn away from looking at it, we can't escape the inevitability of impermanence. No matter how hard we try to hang on to a person, a position, a possession that supports our sense of worth and self-esteem, it's not going to last. *We* are not going to last—the "we" that identifies with the physical body and mind accompanying us into this life. They are the vehicles for learning the lessons needed to grow in spirit. We must see that in clinging to them we are holding on to temporary supports that cannot provide the security promised. Thus the first discipline keeps bringing us back to being without distractions so that we can begin to see how our reliance on this or that leads us down roads of suffering. We simply have to be willing to find space/time within our lives to return to the Truth of who we really are, which is elusive and remains hidden because of our busyness.

My first spiritual teacher used to say, "The pearl of great price has a price." The pearl of great price brings "the peace that surpasseth understanding," the quiet or exuberant joy that comes when we touch the place of spiritual truth—the reality that is the very source of our being. It is indescribable, ineffable. As one of my teachers said, "It can't be taught, but it can be caught." The great spiritual teachers can only point the way because it is right within our body-mind that the confusion and the solution lie. This is the second discipline, maintaining or sustaining our spiritual practice no matter how daunting it can seem. It builds upon the first discipline, and must keep building upon it. It is said in our tradition, "It is hard to keep the initial intention/humility to the end." The body/mind seems to have an agenda that takes precedence over the spiritual. Our desire for comfortable, easy, and familiar lives will keep challenging the clarity of our initial intention to scrutinize our old ways of being. We are moving from the known into the unknown, which may appear murky and unclear, uncomfortable and not easy. A half-hearted effort brings half-hearted results at best. The old patterns, karmic patterns registered on this body/mind, have a power that *seems* independent of us. This is simply not so, but we won't really be able to extricate ourselves until we build the growing faith to keep at our spiritual practice.

Such faith and practice do not require us to blindly follow a dogma. So the third discipline is our willingness to put down pride and self-protectiveness, and take refuge in a teacher and spiritual community. Taking Sangha Refuge offers us support, guidance, and fellowship with like-minded practitioners. A spiritual teacher is a tremendous help because he or she has done the training, and gone down the path with its obstacles and perplexities. No one can do this work for us. However, the guidance of a teacher can help us keep going and see where our blind spots have taken us off course. The Christian teaching that "the Truth will set you free" would certainly be echoed by the Buddha. That Truth is not intellectual, not conceptual, not graspable; and it can be caught—though perhaps "touched" is the better word. The miracle of training is that we can move beyond our current limitations and change in ways that bring less suffering to ourselves and others. The Truth lies at the very core of our being, and every time we have the determination to choose to live the spiritual life of a disciplined practice, we come nearer to finding it for ourselves. As Bodhidharma taught, “It is not so very far away.” It is *right here,* the very source of life—not just “my” life, but all life. It is the Truth of Oneness that embraces the diversity and multiplicity we get caught up in. Nothing has to be excluded, while the clarity of our continuing practice will throw light on where we want to change, and give us the courage of faith to try out new ways. Keeping up the three disciplines is an endless training of continuing riches and surprises.

# The Path of Surrender

Those of us who have embarked upon a spiritual journey have probably at some point confronted the feeling that our lives are not satisfactory, the sense that something is missing and that external solutions haven't worked. Life has taught us that much, either gently, which is all the prodding some people seem to need, or ruthlessly, through great loss. That is the teaching of helplessness that is at the very core of our human condition. We all know that we started out that way—as helpless infants at the mercy of those around us for survival. Yet all of us have been given tools to get along in the world: we grow up and become self-sufficient—or so we think.

At the beginning of *How to Grow a Lotus Blossom,* Reverend Master[*] paints a picture of where she started – where all of us start – at the head of two roads going off to either side of a dark, cave-like interior. These are the roads of adequacy and inadequacy. As a generalization, she suggests that traditionally men have been conditioned to believe they follow the road of adequacy, proving their worth through their work, position in society, wealth. Women, on the other hand, tend to believe in their own inadequacy and seek identity-affirmation through husbands, home, children, friendships. This is a seeming choice we make out of our conditioning, going one way or the other or perhaps switching and combining options. It

---

* Please note that wherever I refer to "Reverend Master" or "my Master," I am referring to Reverend Master Jiyu-Kennett.

is an oversimplification that we don't want to get hung up on. Her point is that neither of these two stances will ever satisfy us in the long run because they depend upon our relationship with the outside world for our sense of security and worthiness. We begin our spiritual quest only when we recognize that we don't feel secure or worthy in spite of these external supports. Somehow we must sense this before we are going to take the entrance into the darkness of something else, which is where she has all of us standing at the beginning of her book.

We have to be willing and able to recognize our human predicament, the existential predicament that we humans come into this life to resolve: as isolated, seemingly independent beings facing a far larger world of others and of nature, we are utterly at the mercy of forces over which we have no control. We are confronted by the fact that we don't even have control over what happens to our bodies when illness strikes. It was this recognition of impermanence that led Prince Siddhartha to give up the life of the palace with all its apparent security and appeal, and begin his spiritual journey leading to Buddhahood. The story is told beautifully in the literature. The prince had been raised in luxury and protected from every kind of distress because his father, King Suddhodana, didn't want his son to follow the second of the two predictions given by seers at his birth: that he would either become a great king or a Buddha. So it was relatively late in life, at the age of 29, that he was inwardly prompted to see what went on outside the palace. Although his father had ordered that all unpleasant sights be hidden, it is said that four divine messengers appeared successively before the prince: an old man, a sick man, a dead man, and a mendicant monk. The prince was disturbed by the first three because he had never been exposed to such sights. He asked his attendant, Channa, if this came to all, and when Channa said "yes, my Lord," he immediately recognized that he too, though strong, healthy, and so very alive in his manhood, would be visited by these afflictions, as would his beautiful wife, Yashodhara, and all others that he loved. The fourth sight, the mendicant monk, hit home under the heaviness of this sobering recognition, and he knew that he must follow that path, so he renounced his former life and turned to the life of the spirit.

At some point these divine messengers hit all of us in the gut in the same way they did the prince. Even if we are not as advanced spiritually as he was when coming into this life, we have all been exposed from far younger days to these realities, so we've got our defense mechanisms well in place to deny and reject the unwelcome reminders of our essential helplessness. We are fortunate that life persists in reminding us that all of these external preoccupations and comforts still leave something to be desired—that nothing is ever enough. That is the nature of desire and craving. We long for something more, and every culture develops a religious formulation to ease this unsatisfactoriness. The problem—for us as it likely was for the prince—is that until we take these religious truths into our own hearts as real, they don't provide the succor, the sustaining reassurance we need. As it is said, "The painting of a rice cake cannot satisfy hunger." At some point, we know we have to embark on this journey for ourselves.

Although most of us come at this recognition cautiously, we really are on the path of surrender. We are surrendering our comfortable—

or not so comfortable—"knowns" because they are not satisfactory anymore. Until we reach that point, we're going to cling to this shore and not even consider that there is a large distance to travel to the other shore. But because every single human being experiences how insecure this life is, we are all on the path of surrender. Happily, we seekers have had the good fortune, the good karma, to have faced this mundane truth squarely and found a spiritual path that offers us a way out. So it can be said that our whole journey is simply a returning to the recognition of the terrible sense of helplessness each of us experiences as a separate "me," so that over and over again we can turn to something that eases this distress. In other words, when we slack off, life will continue patiently to teach us that truth. In Buddhism, the First Law of the Universe expresses the teaching this way: *The Universe is not answerable to my will, my whim, my wish*. Well, we say "of course not, I know that." But we repeatedly forget what we really know and, hence, suffer for it. Buddhism regards the karmic consequence of suffering as compassionate precisely because, whether we know it or not, the wakeup call moves us along spiritually.

There is an unfortunate natural tendency toward laziness that must be counteracted. The Buddha recognized this inner obstacle so clearly that it is part of his definition of "wisdom-knowledge": *The removal of the passion for pleasant things, seen, heard, or cognized; the rejection of laziness; the resistance to worry; and the purity of perfect, balanced mindfulness built on the basis of seeing the way things are—this is wisdom-knowledge, this is the end of ignorance.* We have to work at taking our spiritual practice into our very blood and bones so that we can train as if our hair were on fire and surrender to the unknown more and more readily. Our training counteracts this resistance, this inertia. Because our body/mind complex is directed outwards via the sense doors, and our self-consciousness tied up with all the phenomena that support it as separate, surrender is the way back to being united to that which all great spiritual teachers have known and pointed to. As Sir Edwin Arnold writes of Shakyamuni's enlightenment in *The Light of Asia,* "Forgoing self... the Universe grows I."

Here is the surrender we make: that of *forgoing self.* Every time we sit in meditation and bring that light of awareness into our everyday life, we are forgoing self. Why? Because "self," that which we take as "me," is *no-thing:* it is an appearance, an idea built out of just those experiences of thinking, feeling, desiring, judging, hating, etcetera, that we learn to let go of—to surrender. It can sound scary, and yet it is so simple. My Master* would say, "All we're asked to give up is our suffering." How very strange that we all tend to cling to the known, which is comfortable in its familiarity even when distinctly unpleasant. It is strange, isn't it? We are funny, frightened little beings. Bottom line—that's the way it is. When we are finally willing to recognize this basic insecurity, then our next step in surrendering is easier. We just keep offering up our fears and worries to that which is our True Home, the source of our being, supporting, protecting, guiding, and loving us, while we flounder about in the dream world of separateness. It is our ongoing spiritual work for which there is no substitute. So we learn, blood and bones, to keep going, to keep building on that deep faith and growing certainty that there is something that won't let us down. The surrender is our emergence with the certain knowledge that *forgoing self... the Universe grows I.*

# Being Comfortable

That everyone likes to feel comfortable is probably a safe generalization. Being comfortable has two aspects, it seems to me: we work to hold on to what brings us comfort, and we seek to remove that which makes us uncomfortable. The rhythm of our lives comes out of responding to that comfort-discomfort continuum. In psychology, needs and desires are distinguished, a distinction Buddhism also makes as a middle way between asceticism and self-gratification. The Buddhist mendicant is allowed only four requisites, the basics needed for sheer survival in this world. They are shelter, clothing, food, and medicine when sick. For monks, life can be simple because their needs are few. It's a good reminder for all of us that we really don't *need* a lot, though we do need a few things. This recognition can help us move toward simplifying our lives, and as we rid ourselves of some of the outer clutter, the mind has a chance to become correspondingly quieter.

All of us need to look dispassionately at what motivates us in our moment-to-moment choices, our daily and monthly ones, and then in our bigger view of how our lives have been molded by choices made over the years. At some point, we're compelled to do this when the comforts we've depended upon no longer do their job or when life pulls them out from under us. Initially, many of us struggle to readapt by again securing those comforts that were taken from us. So we eat more, work more, play more, drink more. We take drugs; we seek entertainment; we travel, etcetera. When these things no longer satisfy us, we have the golden opportunity to find true comfort in the only sure place: right within the heart.

One of the koans in Zen is "Why did Bodhidharma come from the West?" Bodhidharma was an Indian monk, the twenty-eighth ancestor in our lineage and the first ancestor of Zen. He came to China from India in the early sixth century, at that time a hazardous adventure to say the least. The journey is said to have taken him more than three years. Why would someone do that? I used to puzzle over this koan and wonder what its significance might be for me, instead of seeing it as an intellectual problem. It raises the question of why we take on tasks that are decidedly uncomfortable and uncertain from the point of view of our little self, this body/mind with which we identify. What prods us to do this? Indeed, in Bodhidharma's case, as in Prince Siddhartha's, why even embark upon a demanding religious life? Why did not Siddhartha stay in the security and comfort of the palace with his status as a prince? The answer is embedded right in the question: we are *more* than just this body/mind that wants to be comfortable and taken care of. We want and need for our growth to challenge our complacency. Life, of course, is quite unrelenting in providing challenges. Perhaps Bodhidharma was as fearful as most of us would be in facing an unknown, hazardous journey; still, he chose to say "yes" to that which was calling him. Perhaps he was more sensitive than most to that inner voice beckoning and whispering that there is more to life than just satisfying bodily and emotional urges—than simply eating, drinking, and being merry because tomorrow we may die. But how many of us are so fortunate?

It is only when we really know that the old status quo will no longer satisfy us that we are primed to look within for a spiritual solution to life's unsatisfactoriness. We have to be convinced on this key point before we put real effort into a spiritual practice. Now that I'm "out in the world" after years of monastic life, I have been privileged to meet people who are searching spiritually. I see some who just put their little toe in the water of training while holding on to the belief that they don't really have to do it, who cling to the view that there is some external fix-it-fast mode of living. I don't see these people much at our meditation meetings and, if they do come, often they quickly disappear. That's not a problem. They are just not ready yet to make a commitment to train; the time isn't right for them. They'll eventually cotton on because "the karmic consequence of suffering is compassionate," even though that can sound puzzling initially. The inherent unsatisfactoriness of skimming only the surface of life will finally prod us to look more deeply into our lives to find life's meaning. Sooner or later we begin more clearly to hear the call of the heart that guides us toward what is truly good to do and what isn't. Until we are ready to hear it, we aren't going to because we could well be asked to do that which is not comfortable to little self, which clings to certainty and comfort.

Bodhidharma came from the West because he was answering this inner call to take a journey into the unknown. He could have died on the way. He didn't because something greater was at stake. The Buddhadharma was to come to China and he, answering his own call of the heart, brought it. If he asked "why me?" or balked because it was too uncomfortable or because he feared he wasn't good enough or because his little mind couldn't understand its significance, we wouldn't have Zen today in the form we know it.

We can bow to Bodhidharma's great example and find how to follow it in our lives this very day. Every day we can put ourselves on the line and bow to that which points us to the way we can best serve all beings, rather than just stay stuck with what makes us comfortable. When we are sincerely doing our training, we know more and more that simply looking for what makes "me" comfortable is not good enough. We have too long cheated ourselves in the service of the ego and its comfort. *Now* is the time to move beyond that limitation. And the only way to do this is simply to *do it*—to rise to the challenge of moving into unknown territory. We aren't going to refine our lives except by choosing to live differently from moment to moment, bringing to bear the sincerity of our spiritual practice. We all *can* do this. This is the promise of the Buddha. We can all respond to a bigger picture than our little conditioned self-images that want the safety and comfort of that which is familiar.

It always comes back to our letting go, in good faith and with confidence that the process of our longing finds fulfillment in the doing. We have to honestly and carefully examine ourselves and our motivations in order to understand where it is we are clinging. We bring up to the light of our awareness that which lies buried a little under the surface of our busy lives, and we examine it closely. Then we will see! Because what surfaces may not be comfortable, we don't always want to do this. But with training we learn that to ignore this potential discomfort is something we do at our own peril because it brings that uncomfortable sense of being out of harmony with our own heart. *This* is what is *really* uncomfortable. Of course, many of us may not be called to do something as challenging as Bodhidharma. We simply have to put aside our ideas about what is big and important—those ideas that are simply about self-gratification. Our spiritual journey is often about little, seemingly insignificant, moment-to-moment choices that confront us. Our training commitment requires that we not be ruled so much by the consideration of the comfort-discomfort continuum and instead respond to that which is good to do, that which needs to be done *now.* Then we let it go, ready to move on to whatever comes next. We always ask our heart, our enlightened nature, *what is it good to do, what is the next step,* and we follow. Then we live in life's simplicity and shed gradually the burden of self.

# Carving a Buddha

There is an Indian story about a sculptor famous for his statues of elephants, each elephant being life-like and absolutely individual. The king, long-impressed with the elegance and authority shown by the sculptor, visited him and asked how he was able to create such masterpieces. The sculptor, recognizing the sincerity of the question, answered:

> Great king, when huge stones are brought to me from the quarry, I choose one and begin my work. This work is sitting day by day with my focus on this huge and unwieldy lump before me. With patience, gradually I begin to see the elephant which lies within and, when that becomes clear to me, I begin to chip away all that is not elephant and the elephant then appears. That is how I do my work.

This theme is clarified by a Buddhist story. A disciple goes to the master and asks, "Can I carve a Buddha?" The master asks, "What do you think?" The disciple says, "Yes, I can," and the master answers, "Yes, you can." Another disciple later comes to the master and asks the same question. Again, the master asks the disciple what he thinks. This time the disciple says, "No, I don't think so," and the master's response is, "No, you can't."

Dogen emphasizes this same point in *Gakudo-yojinshu* (*Important Aspects of Zazen*):

> One who would train in Buddhism must first believe completely therein and, in order to do so, one must believe that one has already found the Way, never having been lost, deluded, upside-down, increasing, decreasing or mistaken in the first place: one must train oneself thus, believing thus, in order to make the Way clear; this is the ground for Buddhist study. By this method one may... turn one's back upon the road of learning: in such a way as herein described must trainees be guided. Only after such training can we be free of the opposites of body and mind, enlightenment and delusion.

In the same passage, Dogen remarks that such trainees are rare. We must have faith in our Buddha Nature since at the beginning all we have to go on is the inkling that there *might* be something more to life. Confidence or faith is one of the five qualities needed for our inner journey, along with energy or determination, mindfulness, meditation, and wisdom. But even from the beginning, wisdom is there. It is what calls us, and is expressed in Buddhism's Fifth Law of the Universe: *Everyone has an innate knowledge of Buddha Nature.* Sometimes this is put beautifully as "One calls, one answers." One master expressed this same thought another way when he noted that our practice is "the Self fervently making the self into the Self." This is a powerful truth that is present from the beginning of our practice, though not understood by the little conditioned mind; it is known only by faith and comes to fruition through dedicated practice that reveals the Truth.

As in the story of the sculptor, we patiently sit still before the unwieldy lump we think of as "me," then use our sculptor's eye—the meditative eye, our wonderful awareness—to let the fragmented bits of "me" drop away, little by little. It is a chipping away of our attachments, of that which we've been hanging on to through our old conditioned habitual tendencies. As the unreal drops away, the real, our Buddha Mind or Buddha Nature, reveals itself. It was always there, obscured and hidden by our ignorance.

We come to see how powerful are the habitual forces of body, speech, and mind, and how they color every aspect of our lives in countless ways. Like the sculptor, we have to be willing to see, by being patient with ourselves and building our faith. This is the challenge of training. And this is something we all can do. It takes faith, determination, mindfulness, and meditation built on Right Understanding. What a precious gift is this vehicle of body/mind through which we train and keep going, purifying and refining our lives. Life repeatedly presents us with just the experiences we need to grow spiritually. The important thing is that we *just keep going,* through what appear to be easy times as well as the most difficult. From the point of view of our spiritual growth it is all good, all to be bowed to, all to be learned from. And then we let go, over and over again, not holding on to anything. This is the path of training through which we carve the Buddha within ourselves.

# Crumbs from the Toaster

The teaching is everywhere when we are willing students of life. Great Master Dogen reminded us of this when he wrote that to live by Zen "is the same as to live an ordinary daily life." In other words, we don't have to go off to a monastery or do something special in order to train: we can bring our mindfulness into our ordinary daily life and appreciate how rich it is in enhancing the spiritual—we don't need to split our world when we remember that everything is teaching us, everything is an offering worthy to be paid attention to. This is the quality of regard we cultivate by our practice of staying right in the moment, in this present here and now that we have been given.

This morning I was given an excellent reminder of the above when I noticed a couple of crumbs by the toaster. This led to my pulling the toaster out from the wall, revealing more crumbs. A sweep of the hand sent the toaster crashing to the floor, throwing open the tray that catches toaster crumbs. Now there were crumbs on the floor as well as on the counter, plus crumbs revealed on the tray. With an inward disapproving grunt, I picked up the toaster, put it back on the counter, and swept the crumbs from the floor. I decided not to get into the more formidable cleaning of the toaster at that time; I left it on its poor little side with the tray out lest I forget its plight—as I might if it were put back upright in its usual spot. After an hour or two, the right time to tackle the job arrived (I simply couldn't keep ignoring it each time I went into the kitchen!).

Prepared for the task, I carefully cleaned the tray and the bottom of the toaster in its upside-down position, blew on it a little bit so that more crumbs could fall, and then with satisfaction put it upright. To my dismay, this led to a shower of crumbs falling onto the counter, plus still more crumbs when I gave it a little thump or two. Where did they come from? Toaster put back, counter cleaned thoroughly, crumbs gathered into the garbage, I let the teaching flow forth.

The crumbs are like the karmic baggage we carry around—baggage that becomes significant only when we take time to notice it. Being on renewal and feeling rested, I was cleaning the counter perhaps with more care than usual and could see the crumbs that I wouldn't normally. We don't always see where old patterns are planted, so to speak, if we are too rushed or tired—at least this is true for me. Once we have seen them, we still have the choice of whether or not to respond to them. It doesn't help much in the long run when we simply stop noticing them. I think all of us stop seeing at least some of our personal crumbs, or we know people who enjoy simply describing aspects of self that are seen as foibles or faults, laughing at them comfortably without considering their deeper significance. At times it is good to address these little crumbs, and this process may lead to an awareness of less obvious crumbs hidden from view. For me, a very useful skillful means has been to take the time to clean some little thing that has come to my attention, as a reminder that I can cleanse the inner dust in the same way.

It is extremely important to remember that our sincere practice allows us to see more of little self's proclivities than would be the case if we didn't pay attention. "When we're willing to see, we *will* see" is a useful teaching because it helps to keep us from getting down on ourselves when the karmic crumbs are strewn before us. We need to remind ourselves that they are the result of many, many experiences leading to choices that over time became habitual and hence unnoticed. With this understanding we can appreciate one monk's heartfelt comment, "If we had known better, we would have done better." Our practice takes a lot of courage, patience, and faith so that we can look at occasions when we didn't know better and didn't do better—and to do so without getting down on ourselves. This is a description of *sange,* the Japanese word that conveys the regret and remorse we naturally experience when recognizing mistakes we have made. We can clean up the karmic crumbs that fall in this moment, right before our eyes. We don't have to distract ourselves or justify ourselves or blame anything: things are just the way they are. And *it is all good* because how could the repository of karma (the toaster with the accumulated crumbs) get cleansed if we weren't exposed to its display?

This karmic repository is our body/mind, which we take as "me," as "self." This body/mind is what we're training. And as we progress in training we come to appreciate the lines in *Sandokai,* Sekito Kisen's enlightenment poem:

> As you walk on, distinctions between near
> and far are lost
> And, should you lost become, there will arise
> obstructing mountains and great rivers.
> This I offer to the seeker of great Truth,
> Do not waste time.

The "obstructing mountains and great rivers" refer to the inner hindrances and fetters that prevent our being in touch with the truth of who we are—the "seeker of great Truth" who is not daunted, because he or she understands that these seeming obstacles are opportunities to train and cleanse the heart of karmic jangles. Those crumbs that spilled from the toaster, now removed, are part of the compost. Just as the composted crumbs become nourishing soil, our spiritual crumbs—these nuggets of old karmic tendencies—gradually transform from desire, anger, and confusion into compassion, love, and wisdom. This is the inevitable karmic effect of our willingness to do our own training, bringing forth the "carefree peace" that Dogen assures us is the product of serene reflection meditation. Although we can't make it happen, by training we enter the stream that carries us to the other shore. What a tremendous gift we give ourselves and others when we choose to bring our spiritual practice to the very center of our lives, paying the price of momentary discomfort for long-term inner peace.

# Disturber of the Peace

One of my teachers said that "our very nature is peace. The fool goes around always disturbing it. The wise person doesn't do that." This is a succinct way of expressing why we train spiritually, and why it must be recognized as true before such an unusual and strenuous effort can be undertaken. We recognize the truth only by being willing to train in the truth. Hence, we emphasize that Buddhism is a *practice.* Reverend Master stated it this way: "Buddhism is a religion for spiritual adults." Another way of saying the same thing is "*Do your own training.*" We are reminded over and over again that our peace of mind depends upon us, not upon the changing conditions that life presents to us. Again my teacher said, "Life is movement; life is going from here to there," reminding me that my concern about moving was not a problem in itself. Reverend Master would talk about the mysterious, wonderful "*flow* of Immaculacy" of which we are part even though we're not able to grasp it.

Of course, all of the above is another way of talking about the basic teaching of the Buddha—the Four Noble Truths. When asked about his teaching, the Buddha answered, "I teach only two things—suffering and its end." Suffering is the "first insight" and is taught in the first two Truths. The end of suffering is taught in the last two Truths, which he called the "second insight." When we really understand these insights, we go beyond this human mind and are free of suffering. This is the Buddha's promise, which he asks us to make true for ourselves. He assures us that this is a teaching for here and now, and always urges us to get on with the training in these two insights. That is the purpose of a religious life of practice: to make the Truth true for ourselves, to go beyond ideas, opinions, beliefs, feelings, etcetera. Zen, taking this admonition to heart, is at times referred to as the "Transmission outside the scriptures." At one of our temples, a large banner was put up with the words, "That which is true is greater than that which is holy"—a reminder that we not cling to the formal teachings and forget the Eternal to which they all point.

All of the above is preliminary to our coming back to emphasize an important teaching that is very hard to "get" because our conditioned mind has a basic, unquestioned premise for living. It forgets the First Law of the Universe according to Buddhism: it implicitly believes that the universe should be answerable to our wishes. This "me-centered" point of view is patently absurd, and we are given many reminders of this fundamental error. In this sense we are all foolish, or crazy in the way Einstein defined that word: we go around doing the same old thing while expecting different results, somehow not learning from what life is repeatedly teaching us. What is life teaching? It's teaching the first two Noble Truths, that, when we attach or cling to any experience, inevitably at some point we will suffer or experience disappointment because everything changes—and there is nothing we can count on because nothing (*no thing*) we experience remains fixed and permanent. As the Buddha said, *One time I too sought for a place of shelter, but I never found such a place. There is nothing in this world that is solid at its base and not a part of it that is changeless.* When we insist, when we cling, when we implicitly expect that life be a certain way and not another, we *will* suffer to the extent of that insistence and for its duration. That is just the way it is. That is the predicament of Einstein's fool and my teacher's.

So obviously the solution to our suffering, to our being out of the flow of harmony and peace, follows as the Third Noble Truth, which emphasizes the need to give up attachment, relinquishing our insistence that circumstances conform to our wishes. This means addressing directly our particular spin on greed, hate, and delusion—those energies that so successfully obscure our ability to live a life of inner peace and harmony. What a tall order this is, and the Buddha kindly spelled out the way to the end of suffering in the Fourth Noble Truth. This ancient Path was discovered by the Buddha as he sought to resolve his koan about suffering and its end, and he is very clear that this Dharma, these Laws, exist whether Buddhas appear in the world or not. The vitality of his teaching comes out of their great relevance to the human condition rather than out of mere theoretical, philosophical musings. As these Truths become increasingly part of our blood and bones, as Reverend Master would insist they must be, we gradually know in a very deep way the basic principle of training that we must come back to: *Everything that happens is for my good*. Or as she was taught in Japan: "All-acceptance is the key that unlocks the gateless gate." There is no barrier except our own refusal to "look up" in situations that trigger our particular karmically-played-out sense of vulnerability and inadequacy.

Over and over again, when our peace is threatened either by some external condition or by an inner state, we can recognize that this is an opportunity to train because truly our very nature *is* peace.

This is the good news that can urge us on in our training when we flounder in confusion and distress. It's always here because it *is* our very nature, our Buddha Nature, the place of oneness with everything. Here we truly understand that there is nothing (no *thing*) we need be threatened by or afraid of. As the Buddha taught, *There is nothing we need hold on to and there is nothing we need push away.* On the level of experience, it is all passing through and we must look at what we are holding on to or pushing away—*that* is the attachment we can let go of once we learn from it. So we can use the three "L's" of training to help us remember: *look* [or *listen*], *learn, let go.* If we try to do the last prematurely, which I believe we all do because unpleasant feelings *are* unpleasant, it doesn't work over the long run. The ghosts from the past, which linger as latent karmic tendencies, are simply buried for awhile until conditions ripen again.

Our certainty about the necessity to practice grows as we see the benefits of our doing it. The wonderful "perk" for doing this (if I can use such a term) is an immense gratitude that fills our heart and then naturally flows out to all. When we discover the peace within our very self that truly "surpasseth all understanding," and know its independence of the conditions moving through as our experiences, we relate to the world of our senses differently. The recognition of its preciousness helps us return repeatedly to attentiveness, mindfulness, and a keen awareness of how we are, which guides us to act more appropriately in this world where on its surface there are so many challenges, difficulties, and sorrows. We learn that we really can live the promise given at the end of the Buddhist ordination ceremony, whether for a lay person or a monk:

"We live in the world as if in the sky, just as the lotus blossom is not wetted by the water that surrounds it. The Mind is immaculate and beyond the dust. Let us bow to the highest Lord." We move toward equanimity little by little, mostly without recognizing it, from being a "fool" to being a "wise" person. It's up to us to fulfill the promise and the blessing of this human birth—right here, right now. There is no other time.

# Do Not Waste Time

I take my title from the advice Sekito Kisen gives to "the seeker of great Truth" in his enlightenment poem, *Sandokai.* In the poem's last line, the words "do not waste time" emphasize the urgency of the message stressed throughout the poem. One translation of the word "sandokai" is "the harmonization of the appearance with reality." If we bring our lives to this inner harmony, peace, and equanimity, then we are not wasting time. That we are so often pulled from doing this tells us how challenging our spiritual work is. *Appearances* are what we know from the conventional, mundane point of view that we've all been taught to believe since we first took our mother's milk, so to speak. The karma that brought us to this rebirth is our mistaken tendency or belief that "out there" in the external world is where we'll find real security, contentment, and satisfaction; so we have a good fit—nature and nurture combining to beguile us into clinging to a mistaken point of view. Wrong view, according to Buddha, is the very last of the Ten Fetters that hold us back from the inner harmonization where true peace can be found.

Those who turn to a spiritual solution to the basic unsatisfactoriness of life must struggle with a belief system challenged by our inward search. You could say that we are victims of a vast array of habitual tendencies, some so engrained that they are the very premises by which we live. Our spiritual practice is to patiently chip away at the habits that hold us back from the truth of our own being. We *must* go beyond the mundane appearances to which our habits are tied and be willing to challenge the apparent comfort they bring us. Otherwise, we fall back into old behavior patterns and simply reinforce them. This is a way to understand karma. We aren't bad and evil; we are blinded and mesmerized. One Buddhist master put it this way: "The same old person comes telling the same old lies and we continue to believe them." Our practice is to question and examine our lives from the point of view of Right Understanding, which is the first factor of the Noble Eightfold Path. A simple way of expressing that understanding is that we have "got it wrong"—we're deluded or ignorant in the most basic way, believing that we are separate, independent, isolated selves and that the things we encounter are also separate from ourselves.

"Things" in the previous sentence refers to *everything* we encounter. Reflecting on this fundamental point helps us to understand Tozan Ryokai's observation in *The Most Excellent Mirror—Samadhi:*

> Because delusions in the trainees' minds
> were topsy-turvy,
> All the sages true did match there to their teachings;
> Thus they used all means, so varied,
> Even so to say that black was white.
> *Delusive thought, if lost, abandoned,*
> Will all satisfaction bring.

My italicization of the second-to-last line emphasizes again what our spiritual work is. It's just this one point, and obviously we have to address what is delusive thought within our own mental processes.

Though we can find definitions, metaphors, and examples galore, our practice can deepen only when the penny drops and we directly target the error in our thoughts, feelings, and impulses. This is our ongoing work. Obviously, it isn't easy. Just how difficult it is becomes apparent only when we actually *do* the practice. Most of us prefer to theorize and speculate, brush uneasiness aside and find escape routes, so it is exceedingly important to keep returning to the fundamental point. In *The Scripture of Great Wisdom,* it is put this way: "going on beyond this human mind, he [the Awakened One] is Nirvana." The *Scripture* also reminds us that the "allayer of all pain Great Wisdom is./ It is the very Truth, no falsehood here."

As the proverb points out, "Sow a thought, reap an action; sow an action, reap a habit; sow a habit, reap a character; sow a character, reap a destiny"—a good reminder about how the law of karma is inexorable. *We* create our own destiny through our moment-by-moment actions. Because we are usually on autopilot in our ordinary daily living, we fail to investigate the choices each moment offers and their impact on us and on others. We must cultivate an attentiveness that goes beyond the mental habits of which we are usually unaware. This lack of awareness is sad because we continue to perpetuate unsatisfactoriness for ourselves and others. So Sekito's offering—"This I offer to the seeker of great Truth, / Do not waste time"—is an urgent reminder of both the importance and seeming magnitude of our spiritual work. And it directs us to the *only* place we can address our efforts: right here, right now. Our best opportunity to work with a hindrance is when it manifests itself. If we miss that opportune moment, then we have the opportunity to investigate how we were caught, and discover what the internal and external triggers were that brought together the conditions causing us to fall into old karmic patterns built on greed, hate, and delusion. *Mindfulness* and *investigation* are the first two of the Seven Factors of Enlightenment. They are spiritual faculties and tools that we can perfect through our dedicated practice. When we forget and slip back into old ways, there will arise "obstructing mountains and great rivers," as Sekito puts it. In other words, suffering will stop us, and if we are truly "seekers of great Truth," we'll use this suffering to alert and help us to move toward the end of suffering.

This is our life's work and does not in any way prevent our living an ordinary daily life. Indeed, as Dogen teaches, "to live in this way is the same as to live an ordinary daily life." It is right within the mud of our lives that the root of our practice begins; it is the nourishment that allows the stem of the lotus to grow out of the water. Then the lotus, our Awakened Nature, gradually blossoms for all to see. The flower experiences the wonders of sky and sun. It's always here, never hidden, ever present. We just have to get our heads out of the mud of obscurations and stretch up to the sky of Truth. *This I offer to the seeker of great Truth; do not waste time.*

# Enhancing Our Lives

Not long before his death, the Buddha taught his followers: *Be an island unto yourself; be your own refuge.* In this teaching, the Buddha invites us to take charge of our lives and not to depend on anyone else to do our spiritual work for us. It isn't surprising that at the end of his 45-year ministry, this was what he told his community of monks, because, as the Buddha so often taught, the very nature of the human condition predisposes us to look outside ourselves for the solution to our *dis-ease* and longing. This is worth reflecting upon because, until we truly let this teaching penetrate, until we understand that the answer to the deepest longing of our heart for fulfillment and security will never be satisfied by external things, we will be held back on the exacting and exciting inner journey. As a Lakota chief put it: "The longest walk you can ever take in this life is the sacred journey from the head to the heart." "Head" here refers to all our accumulated knowledge that helps us function in daily living. In the *Scripture of Great Wisdom,* we find this line, "And, going on beyond this human mind, he is Nirvana." We must go beyond the head if we are to come to Nirvana, the end of suffering—the "heart" referred to in the quotation above, and the heart of the Buddha's teachings too.

If we can remember that the Truth that frees us lies within, then we are well on our way through the "thick and thin" of living a spiritual life. Experiencing this truth of the heart enhances every moment of our lives by bringing to bear on each moment our spiritual understanding, our choiceless awareness. In this way it is possible to transform our daily lives. Obviously, it's a discipline and a half, requiring courage, commitment, energy, faith, patience, and willingness. Gradually, when we find that we truly have embarked upon this journey of the heart, we discover that moment-to-moment conditioning no longer drags us down. The practice takes hold and increasingly becomes our guide over both the "good" and the "not good" times—"good" meaning comfortable, "not good" uncomfortable or threatening in some way to the "me" that I take myself to be. This understanding is truly a miracle, and has to be experienced for oneself. As the Buddha taught, *Do not believe anything because I say it to you. Make it true for yourselves.* We learn this through practicing, not simply by thinking about the teaching. The cliché "practice makes perfect" aptly applies here. That we can touch the perfect is the gift we give ourselves when we train wholeheartedly. Again, this is something no one else can do for us. As the Buddha said, *You yourself must make the effort; Buddhas can only point the way.*

Thus Right Effort, the sixth factor of the Noble Eightfold Path, is all-important to the Buddha's Middle Way—his prescription to help us bring the purity of awareness into every corner of our lives. Awareness is another term for meditation, mindfulness, concentrated focus, right attention, heedfulness, carefulness. As Dogen writes in *Rules for Meditation,* "the means of training are thousandfold but pure meditation must be done." He is saying that we must make the right effort to break through the shackles of the conditioned mind by seeing them for what they are, something we can do only by means of the mindfulness the Buddha spent forty-five years teaching. The shackles are three, according to Buddhism: greed, hate, and delusion. We really can't free ourselves from suffering until we see how it arises from conditions that trigger these deep-seated habitual reactions. So the Buddha said that his teaching, the Buddhadharma, was simply to see the way things are. We don't want to do this as long as we are blinded by our attachments to beliefs hidden from our view—attachments that form the very premise on which this life is built. Our wonderful practice allows us to chip away at that which obscures our being in touch with the truth of who we are, the great truth of oneness in which everything is embraced.

This truth can only be experienced, not taught, because words and ideas are for the convenience of living this life. This is not to say that words are not useful. They are. But our mistake is to let the rationality of words and ideas take over every aspect of life. We burden ourselves trying to understand that which goes beyond what the heart *just knows*—the Unborn that is beyond language and ideas. Our training allows us to move with greater ease from the worldly known, the place where little self functions conditionally and often blindly, to the unknown center that always supports us, protects us, and quietly embraces both our pain and our pleasure. It is the beyond that beckons us to the other shore, the Third Noble Truth, the end of suffering that is Nirvana. As we continue on this journey to the heart, we come to see how our own choices and subsequent actions in the midst of daily life enhance the quality not only of our own lives, but of those around us. In this way, the gift of doing our own training becomes the great gift we offer to others.

# Experiments in Time

One helpful way of looking at the inevitable challenges in one's life is to think of them as mini-experiments in time. Right Understanding tells us that our birth and death are on a continuum of time in which we have the opportunity to cleanse the inherited karmic tendencies that required a rebirth to play themselves out. We miss this opportunity when we forget the bigger picture and simply fall into old habit patterns automatically, reaping both the good and bad consequences that are the inevitable outcome of our choices. When we live on autopilot, there is little opportunity to connect choices with consequences, and we are blind to the basic training that allows us to mine gold from the dross of circumstances. When these circumstances build up to a critical mass—and for some of us that critical mass is huge—we "get it" sufficiently to try an inner, spiritual solution to the problem of life's unsatisfactoriness. This turning of our attention within is the key to a resolution. Most of the time, and especially at the beginning, we have to take this truth on faith. We may not have much appreciation of how living a spiritual life is the most important undertaking that we can possibly make. But by being willing to give a wholehearted effort to our spiritual practice over and over again, we soon perceive signs of spiritual growth we couldn't have dreamed of. Faith leads to a kind of knowing very different from all the conditioned knowledge we have accrued, and that knowing strengthens our faith to keep going, keep trusting, keep moving into the unknown territory of spiritual growth and commitment to training.

As we tune in to the bigger picture through the openness our practice requires and allows, our lives come to resemble a series of frames like those that make up a movie, one frame connected to the earlier one and leading to a later one. In other words, life is a series of transitions. When we cooperate with life, we become willing partners to the inevitability of change and learn to move more easily with the flow that carries us toward the other shore, Nirvana, the great peace and equanimity that can be present in the midst of daily life with all its shifting, changing themes. Reverend Master called this "place" the *Iron Man,* the place of meditation. We learn to carry our zendo or meditation hall right within our heart, not only when we are sitting in formal meditation. This is the freedom of Zen, freedom from being at the mercy of our old karmic experiences that current conditions repeatedly trigger. Scenes shift and change, and we can increasingly sit serenely still within the certainty that something is working for our evolvement so that we increasingly live the spiritual truths that inspire us. This is, indeed, very freeing. It is worth every effort, and we can all do it. This is the Buddha's promise: *Mine is a teaching for here and now.* Our part is to be intelligent, diligent, and careful in following the Buddha's Way, the Noble Eightfold Path that leads to the end of suffering.

Doors open and close, open and close. We keep getting the special messages of our heart, but it's hard to interpret their meaning when the old conditioned mind holds on to what is known and comfortable while the thorns jab beneath. My Master would say, "We all tend to prefer the devil we know to the devil we don't." Through our practice we can more readily sense when a door is closing, be alert to the implications of the current frame shifting into the next. Our faith in the process of life will allow us to know that the closing door is also an opening into a wonderful unknown that is the continuing of our life's journey home. We don't have to wait until the door is slammed shut or jump the gun in fear that the bottom is going to fall out from under us. We can cooperate by simply keeping alert to our inner life while responsibly living in the present moment.

This is the challenge of training: being willing to let go of the known and trust the unknown, learning the skill of listening to the inner voice and following its guidance. Then when there is a knock on the door telling us that it is time to move on from the current familiar that once was the scary unknown, we can let the messages reveal themselves by virtue of our spiritual practice. Thus this experiment gives its results and moves us to another frame, another phase of our lives, helping us to continue growing into the very truth and purpose of this life. "There is nothing to fear but fear itself" is the way Franklin D. Roosevelt put it to America at a scary time in its history, and this message of hope revitalized the nation and helped it to move on. We can repeatedly give ourselves this same life-affirming message and mobilize ourselves by putting our spiritual understanding on the line in our current situation. The Buddha's teaching is for here and now. As one influential Zen master of the last century put it: "Pay attention to where you are. Pay attention to yourself. There is no great ocean apart from single drops of water. Wake up to the fact that you yourself, your every act is filled with wondrous, marvelous features." This exhortation opens us to an extraordinary life within the very midst of ordinary living with its constant changes. Life is truly an experiment in time where, frame after changing frame, we learn how to live more fully within the Unborn.

# Humpty Dumpty Had a Great Fall

We all know the nursery rhyme that goes

> Humpty Dumpty sat on a wall,
> Humpty Dumpty had a great fall;
> All the King's horses and all the King's men
> Couldn't put Humpty together again.

Like Humpty Dumpty, we have all taken a tumble. The mystery of how we fell from grace, unity, totality, the Absolute, the Eternal, God—whatever way we refer to the oneness that is beyond all words and concepts—cannot be grasped by the little mind of separation. We start with the aftereffects of the great fall, and have to do hard training to return to that oneness within.

That's just the way it is; and if all the king's horses and all the king's men—all our powers and resources—can't put us back together again, we're in trouble. This is our essential human predicament: at some point, we recognize that there is something very wrong with our splintered, fractured lives and that our old ways of trying to fix the problem don't work anymore. We have to learn this—and believe it—before we will be ready to embark on a spiritual practice. That is the radical awakening spiritual seekers come to know for themselves, sobering and perplexing though it is. We realize that we're helpless here and must start from a new understanding, a new beginning. This means moving into the unknown, whether we want to or not. On hands and knees, with tremulous bows, we have to find that humility that allows us to ask for help from something greater than our little selves.

When moving into the unknown, we have to be willing to let go of what we think we know—our beliefs, convictions, old ways. Though he lies shattered on the ground, this much Humpty Dumpty can do, and it is the most important action he can take. For many of us it is only when we have had a great fall that we find the humility to take this vital step of asking for help. And we have to keep remembering to do it over and over again. Our spiritual practice is the path, and we have to keep renewing our willingness to follow it, and not fall back into old ways when there is an easing off of the acute sense of bewilderment. Training does its work when we do our little part—when we are willing to ask for help, to acknowledge that we don't know the answers, and to keep moving into unknown territory in good faith that our intention to heal, to return to the place of oneness and peace, will protect us.

It's an exciting, exacting, and at times a scary way to live, where the benefits (though they far exceed the costs) often remain hidden from our eyes. We have to keep going in faith, be willing to make seeming mistakes, and learn by remaining open. And at the same time, we always have to take that one next step of doing what seems good to do now. When we try to look any farther ahead, we're back in little mind, in the splintered, uneasy state. Drifting back to the false security of what has passed, we again cheat ourselves of being present to this moment. So, over and over again, we just have to let go by keeping our mindful awareness sharp and tuned up. Here in this present moment we can feel the assurance of grace that our deepening faith allows us to recognize. We didn't make it or create it—but we can be open to it. And that changes everything.

This is the challenge of our training—just to keep at it without any other assurance than that which comes out of our innate knowing that there is something greater than what we have known. Humpty Dumpty can't heal himself, can't make himself whole. But he—and we—can be healed. This is the gift of our human birth and good karma, which bring us to this wonderful spiritual practice. Our part is very little, but we must do it. As my Master would say, "the Eternal does not insist." And as it is often heard in Buddhism, "We must make the effort. The Buddhas only point the way." Similarly, the Buddha's last teaching to his disciples was a reminder that *all conditioned things arise and pass away. Work out your salvation with diligence.* The miracle of life is that we can do it. Whether slowly or with passion—however it comes about—at some point the mess of Humpty Dumpty's splintered self has to be cleansed. And it will be.

## It Didn't Have To Be This Way

A mantra that has been helpful to me in the last little while is the reflection *It didn't have to be this way.* The discipline of maintaining awareness as we let our day unfold can bring this useful teaching to the fore of our consciousness in ways that help us appreciate each moment as it arises. This first started coming up for me when I noticed a sense of well-being with things as they were. This recognition was so simple when it struck that I often felt surprised. What clicked was a fruit of the practice: my ability to recognize when there wasn't anything wrong. Our ordinary stance is to notice when things *do* go wrong—when we are jolted by some person, event, or thought that we take as unpleasant or unsatisfactory. At such moments we generally go on autopilot with a habitual reaction—an attempt mentally to push away the offending person or situation as quickly as possible. Without our spiritual discipline we simply stay on a repetitive cycle, perhaps sensing that something is wrong but not able to put our finger on what it is. Our spiritual practice helps us to observe whatever comes up, using the eye of mindfulness that is gradually weaned from our conditioned judgmental mind. This is helpful. As we learn to embrace the conditions that appear, our awareness naturally expands and grows. With time this new tendency of sustained awareness manifests its consequences—happy, happy, happy ones!

The sober truth is that our volitional actions—the choices we make—have consequences that take us down the road of satisfaction or dissatisfaction. This unfortunately (or fortunately) being the case, it is important that we look before we leap, so to speak. The cost of reality, my Master noted, is that we must keep letting go of self, of our habitual desires with their accompanying annoyance and anger, by the discipline of mindful awareness of our reactions. We learn this by doing it. Over and over again we return to this present moment in awareness both of the circumstances or conditions that arise, and of the self-awareness of the inner vibrations that have been triggered by them. This is the work that allows us to see the potential suffering of succumbing to habitual conditioning. This seeing is also a fruit of our practice. We gradually come out of sleep-walker mode and awaken to the precious opportunity that each moment in life brings. The proof of the pudding is in the eating, meaning that we learn by doing the practice. And it is a surprisingly good pudding we begin tasting as we start living our meditation in daily life. We don't want to leave it behind on the meditation cushion, and increasingly we wake up from the old thought patterns that take us out of the present. The time to wake up is *now,* dear friends, and, as the Buddha promised, we all can do it. We must make the effort; Buddhas can only point the way.

In other words, the student must make the effort and then the teacher can help. This has been my experience through the ins and outs of many years of training—years in which, believe me, I sometimes didn't have much of a clue as to what was going on. The longing of the heart, when it gets sufficiently strong, won't let us rest with the old status quo where we slide along on life's surface. Increasingly, we become dissatisfied with the Eight Worldly Conditions that beckon so enticingly in one way and repel with its opposite: honor and shame; loss and gain; pleasure and pain; praise and blame. This is well worth pondering because it is vital to see how we are at the mercy of these conditions. No matter how "good" we are, at times we'll experience one or other of the conditions that is unwelcome and brings discomfort. Our practice takes us to the place where there is "nothing special," as one of the great Zen masters of the last century taught. We move toward calm and equanimity, toward maintaining our center—the mind of meditation—in the midst of conditions. We are strong when conditions don't rule us, Dogen observed. We come to see that working with these conditions is the work of a lifetime, or longer, and that it doesn't really matter. As Dogen succinctly teaches in *Rules for Meditation,* "the means of training are thousandfold but pure meditation must be done." That means that whatever form our training takes, we must be mindful, aware, and appreciative of the challenges and conditions of the moment. This requires that we learn over and over again to step back from our sleep-walker stance and *wake up!*

It is so simple, so simple, as one of my teachers used to say. And we have as our birthright all that is required to make the journey. In Buddhism it is considered rare and precious to be born in the human realm and to have heard the Buddhadharma. We are fortunate also in having the intelligence and sufficient life-stability to bring the teaching into our life—*this* life, *this* body/mind. We have all the gear we need to get home. Let's exercise the spiritual faculty of faith and confidence with as wholehearted an effort as we can muster *right now.* Let the ever-present fact of impermanence, the sheer unreliability of life work for us as a spur to get on with our training. It doesn't matter how long we have dallied along the way. Our seeming lapses don't matter. Right now we have the precious ability to choose which direction we take. In one of the *Upanishads* we are told that there is a path of pleasure and a path of joy. The former appears enticing at the beginning, luring us until we hit its barrenness. The path of joy, by contrast, seems at first not too appealing as we navigate through the rocks and thorns of spiritual discipline. Its smooth terrain appears only when we have the courage and faith to continue. Eventually, it brings the wonderful recognition and appreciation of the sheer goodness of life. And then we remember—gratefully—that *it didn't have to be this way* as we bask in the deep contentment of experiencing nothing special. This is the wonderful gift of training open to all.

# Karmic Streams Intermingle

The Buddha in his first discourse, "Turning the Wheel of the Law," states that the cause of suffering is attachment, without any qualifications. Anything (any *thing*) that is held on to has the potential to bring unsatisfactoriness in its wake. Of course, all of us attach to things all the time. As Sekito Kisen writes in his enlightenment poem, "Here born we clutch at things/ And then compound delusion, later on, by following ideals [another variety of *thing* that we attach to]." The metaphor expressed in the title, if understood as connecting attachment with karma, can act as a helpful antidote to free us from our grip on aspects of our lives. On the first watch of the night of his enlightenment, the Buddha got in touch with his myriad past lives in great detail, perceiving how he was born in this environment with this name and these characteristics, seeing what he did and how at death another life followed, over and over again. He found too that these lives were without beginning, and that they could not be traced back to a source. This is worth pondering upon, as is the teaching that came to him in the second watch of the night—that beings pass away and are reborn according to their deeds, which of course is a statement of the law of karma. Our actions have consequences that may appear in the present life, in the next, or in some future life. This is the karmic stream that we have each inherited from beings in our particular stream. In this way, we are given this opportunity once again to clarify the great matter for which we train.

The view that emerges from this teaching is dynamic and positive, bringing fire to the training for those of us who have been touched by it. It rests on the Right Understanding expressed in the Four Noble Truths. We simply do not need to perpetuate the churning desires, anger, and confusion sullying the karmic stream that is who we take ourselves to be—this "me" distinct from "you." The beginning of our spiritual practice is built on the understanding that there is something more than clinging to the old habits and beliefs propelling us into this existence. The deep spiritual purpose of our lives is to alter the course of our karmic stream in order to return to the inner knowing of our Awakened Nature. Repeated opportunities are presented for this process in daily life with the appearance of other karmic streams. After all, every little karmic stream runs alongside countless others. Sometimes they intermingle in exchanges that are agreeable—in relationships, in jobs, in recreation. This only becomes a problem when we grasp at the pleasant and push away the unpleasant, forgetting to our detriment that streams must also flow apart, however satisfying or unsatisfying their time together has been. Every meeting ends in parting.

When we embrace all life as a magnificent movement of myriad streams, we free ourselves from suffering because we perceive beneath the surface level of convention, knowing that everything is changing, that the present is a shifting scene. It's all just passing through. *We* are just passing through. As this knowing deepens, more and more it can become the guiding principle for living. Karmic streams come together, move side by side, intermingle, and then separate. When we understand this, our hold on life lightens. In the Buddhist discourses, followers drawn to the Buddha say to him, "Your face is clear, your countenance serene." This serenity arises out of the dispassion of knowing that inevitably "all that arises also passes away." This is the truth we can keep bringing ourselves back to in our interactions with others. The process of our training then allows us to appreciate each moment—our karmic stream touching now this stream and now that—in all of its fullness because we are open. Our face can be clear and our countenance serene because we are not hanging on to the past or fearing the future: we live *now* in the purity of our intentions as expressed in the three Pure Precepts: *Do as little harm as possible; do as much good as possible; and do good for others by our willingness to keep up the inner work of the heart.*

We begin to catch the moment, so to speak, when an attachment appears. Such times, the literature tells us, are best for training—when the hindrance has arisen. This gives a dynamic fire to our training. When we are willing to look, we see these inner movements, and we can release their tension by remembering that we can't hold on to anything. This allows us to learn from the experience. Our karmic stream has met another within a flowing space of time. In Dogen's "Uji" ("The Theory of Time"), Reverend Master translates the word "time" as "existence, time, flow." The vast flowing that is life becomes *our* life as we cease to resist or grab at whatever momentarily arises. It is a flow of Immaculacy, Reverend Master taught us, and we all partake of it. Our sincere and ongoing spiritual life of meditation gives us the opportunity of knowing it for ourselves. And then we bow and bow and bow in this wonderful freedom—our birthright to participate in the life of the Eternal, the Unborn, the True Source of our being.

We "enter the stream" of Buddhism as we are willing to let go of our clinging to this phantom "me" and "mine" and move to the other shore. To have the courage to embark on and continue the journey home, we shift our faith in this little self to faith in the Buddhadharma—though not fanatically—just willingly to "come and see," to find the truth of the teaching for ourselves. And as we continue to train, we recognize increasingly what a radical shift we have made in the inner direction. We truly find we can more easily move away from our usual course of "me-centeredness" to be a willing partner within the vast flow that includes us all. Through this we give ourselves the opportunity to learn from each intermingling of our karmic stream with another, letting go when they move apart. As one influential master of the last century taught, "Let go a little, a little bit of peace. Let go a lot, a lot of peace. Let go completely, complete peace." This is the Buddha's promise, the Third Noble Truth that there is an end to suffering—Nirvana. Our entire training is learning how to release attachments that hold us back from fully participating in the dynamic flow that is life.

## Know Where You're Coming From

One way to think about karma is to note how it is built on an assumption that there is "something out there" that can eliminate the unreliability and unsatisfactoriness of this human condition. The Buddha taught that a new birth is propelled out of the ignorance or delusion of beings in our karmic stream. We are the inheritors of this ignorance as well as of the karmic tendencies energized in our efforts to ease the painful insecurity that comes from this false view. A sense of the self as a separate individual wraps around our whirling energies and, as the comedian Jackie Gleason would say, "Away we go!" Here we are, this body/mind that must be cleansed or purified. Out of the basic ignorance of something greater—the Eternal, Unborn, God, Oneness, Love—over and over again the sad drama in myriad variations is played out: we want, desire, and crave certain aspects of what comes to us; and we feel aversion for, and anger, frustration, and uneasiness with other aspects. We want this and we don't want that, without recognizing that they are simply opposite sides of a single coin. This is the beginningless cycle of samsara, the wheel of birth and death, the wheel of suffering. We have to recognize this truth before being willing to look for an inner solution to the problem of suffering. Thus the basic karmic tendency, expressed in many ways, is built on this assumption—this conviction—that there is something external in the world that can truly satisfy the loneliness, uneasiness, restlessness, and boredom that all of us at times experience. Yet the search for it is repeatedly frustrated because, as the Buddha put it, its very premise is based on a false belief or wrong view.

That wrong view is the belief that we are separate, independent selves, a "me" and a "you." The existence of separate things that seem so palpably real is expressed in terms of opposites, mental constructions that pull us into liking and rejecting, a seesaw of misguided movement. This is where we habitually come from in our life activities. Without awareness we swing up and down, perhaps just little movements of the seesaw—but perhaps gigantic ones—feeling pleased and not pleased, gratified and frustrated. In Buddhism these opposites are expressed as the Eight Worldly Conditions: honor and shame, loss and gain, pleasure and pain, praise and blame. These conditions convey the vulnerability of separateness, and I think we can all relate to this relentless seeking. What we learn through a deepening spiritual practice is just how endemic it is—and how disturbing to our peace of mind. We're told in our tradition that "training is endless." I've heard that many times since beginning monastic training. Now I can say with the English poet A. E. Housman, "Oh, 'tis true, 'tis true." Housman is referring to his own simple ignorance when, at 21, he fell hard in love. Disappointed at 22, he knew love's fragility, its unreliability. Of course, such knowledge never stopped any of us from repeated attempts to possess what we desire.

Little mind/self, ready to defend its territory, rises up to resist the understanding suggested here, to protest that there is true love, satisfying and lasting. And, of course, there are marriages that seem to have been made in heaven, though I'm not sure that there are many. Shakespeare's insight that "the course of true love never did run smooth" seems the far more common experience. Witness the sad number of divorces or couples that stay together only out of a sense of duty or habit. But I'm getting off track. The key point is that whether we are talking about relationships, jobs, books, music, sports, alcohol, drugs—whatever the form of satisfaction engaged in—everything changes, nothing can be counted on, all is passing. The law of impermanence mandates that whatever is clung to will bring suffering, with unsatisfactoriness in its wake at some point. This is so obvious that we all tend to sweep it right under the rug: we don't want to see it! So the Buddha described his teaching as *just seeing the way things are.* This is such a stunning teaching that we become bemused and stopped in our tracks if we reflect upon it. The wondrous Truth is right before our very eyes all the time. It is so vast, pervasive, close, and simple that we can't grasp it, don't notice or see it, and can't believe it.

There isn't any *thing* we need hold on to and there is nothing we need push away. The Buddha assures us that the stillness, the pure awareness that is always present, remains when the sad, compulsive seesaw motion stops. *That* is Buddha Nature, the Truth that can set us free, "the peace that surpasseth all understanding." It is so simple that we keep missing it because we are out to get the next big thing that comes along or rid ourselves of a current state. It's no wonder that restlessness is the fourth of the Five Hindrances and the ninth of the Ten Fetters. We are driven folks who at some point get tired enough to be willing to stop, look, and—finally—see the Truth. Then our work is cut out for us. My Master taught that "we stand against the world in order to train in wisdom." This is the world of our minds, of the mental constructs and beliefs and attachments that perpetuate a reality that is not real. Our starting place then has to be a willingness to place a temporary hold on what seems real, releasing ourselves gradually from the first fetter of believing in separateness—in an "I" independent and alone. In order to do this, we also have to let go of the second fetter, a disbelief in the Buddhadharma. In other words, we have to be willing to start walking that path the Buddha assures us will lead to the end of suffering before we can find it to be true for ourselves. With these two working for us, we come to realize that pretty external solutions, patch-up band aids, and quick fixes to feel better will not in themselves do the trick; and the third fetter—belief in the efficacy of rites and rituals—is let go of. Then we buckle down and *do it.* There simply is no substitute for keeping up the spiritual practice once we have entered the stream.

The essence of our practice is meditation, that which the Buddha prescribed as the medicine to the suffering of the world. Meditation is an unusual effort, different from our usual ways of working with a problem or challenge. Hence, it is a challenge and a half. Instead of *doing* something, we are told *not to do* anything. We simply "sit" with awareness. We turn upon ourselves the light of awareness to reflect within upon who we take ourselves to be, and advance directly along the road that leads to the Mind, to our Awakened Nature, our True Self. Once we know ourselves, as Dogen says, we can forget ourselves. At present, we've got it the wrong way around: we forget ourselves and then figure we know ourselves. This is truly putting the cart before the horse. Only those of us who are sincerely committed to deepening our practice can know just how very difficult the challenge is—and how truly freeing. The freedom of Zen is not in any ostentatious external display. It is freedom from old conditioned ways that so habitually rule us we actually don't know where we're coming from, don't know what propels our actions, and hence don't know the sober truth that the problems in our lives are not "out there." It is as Shakespeare's Cassius says, albeit in another context, "The fault, dear Brutus, is not in our stars,/ But in ourselves, that we are underlings." There is no worse tyrant than this little conditioned self with all its confusions. So let us patiently, patiently just keep going. The miracle is that doubts and confusion gradually lessen and clarity shines into more and more areas of our lives—and we have the wondrous opportunity over and over again to know just where we're coming from: Buddha Nature expressed in compassion, love, and wisdom. What more could we possibly ask of life?

# Loving

There is a line from *The Scripture of Avalokiteshwara Bodhisattva* of particular importance for our ongoing training: "Great Kanzeon views all the world in Truth,/ Free from defilement, loving, knowing all/ Full of compassion." I find it interesting that "loving" is put before "knowing." The same teaching is given at the beginning of *The Scripture of Great Wisdom:*

> When one with deepest wisdom of the heart
> That is beyond discriminative thought,
> The Holy Lord Great Kanzeon Bosatsu,
> Knew that the skandhas five were, as they are, in their self-nature, void, unstained, and pure.

"Kanzeon" is the Japanese word for Avalokiteshwara, the Bodhisattva of Compassion. In other words, Great Wisdom, the pure knowing of who we truly are, comes out of a compassionate heart, not from the intellect. It can't be "figured out." Rather, we have to be willing to let go of the judgmental mind in order to find it. How we do this is at the heart of our practice, and we all know what a challenge it is.

Reverend Master taught that little children are naturally in tune with this deepest wisdom of the heart, Buddha Nature. It is our birthright, the life force that finds form in body/mind. She would say that we have this knowledge educated out of us so that we distrust the deep Truth within. And, of course, our inherited karmic tendencies propel this "self," conditioning the particular form of body/mind—and away we go! This is expressed in the profound teaching of Dependent Origination or the Conditional Arising of a new being. Our training gradually allows us to stop this wheel of becoming, birth/death after birth/death, releasing into the vastness beyond the human mind that which it cannot grasp. How could it understand when it is part of that great unknown the Buddha referred to as "the Unborn?" The calling of the heart that propels us into spiritual practice is answering that which is always here. And faith, not intellect, is the faculty that supports our ongoing efforts to train.

The nagging question "How then can I know?" expresses our dilemma because we simply cannot know in the ordinary way. Our training helps us to recognize over and over again how conditioned we are by a mistaken view of reality. Kanzeon beholds the world as oneness. From that perspective, self is an illusion, a wrong view that colors pervasively our being in the world. This misrecognition is the existential human predicament that needs to be resolved by this rebirth. It is, indeed, the purpose of rebirth. Thus, Right Understanding—the first factor of our path to the end of suffering on the Noble Eightfold Path—may be articulated as our need to ground ourselves in this right view of things as we navigate life's challenges. Then we come to know the dangers of judging, blaming, hating ourselves or others. We learn to be alert to the conditions, either internal or external, that arise, and to let go of our seeming need to find fault. One monk summed up the teaching as simply *to stop finding fault.* For me, when little self starts grumbling inwardly, the valuable counteraction comes up as a question: "Why take offense?" Just asking the question helps me to recognize that I don't need to go in that direction, which can be so enticingly easy. Once we take offence, we are heading down a comfortably familiar but exceedingly unhelpful old road of bouncing between blaming self or other.

Although it is easy to see how unhelpful such a stance is, all of us who are sincerely training know how very difficult it is to correct. The determination to change these old patterns is one way of characterizing our practice. The Precepts are important because they help alert us to potential pitfalls when we feel threatened. With time we become more willing to recognize how vulnerable we really are to old conditioning. All too often the vulnerability is cloaked in self-righteousness or self-criticism. It's a strange thing how comforting it can be to go into an inner diatribe about one's faults and inadequacies: *You should have done this; you shouldn't have done that; how could you have been so insensitive, unkind, stupid,* and so on and so on. We are definitely closed off from Kanzeon in such a stance. The stance itself obscures the wonderful compassion at the very heart of Being. As *The Scripture of Avalokiteshwara Bodhisattva* states, "Great Kanzeon views all the world in Truth,/ Free from defilement, loving, knowing all,/ Full of Compassion; He must always be prayed to," which means to me that Kanzeon or compassion must always be *turned toward* by us. What a wrench it can be simply to stop the blaming and just be still.

This is our training. As we move through the challenges of daily life, we must use the precious awareness cultivated in our daily formal practice. We are as sitting ducks, vulnerable to potential hunters that can destroy our birthright of peace when we drift along unmindfully. Hence, the Buddha emphasizes the importance of being heedful, mindful, and attentive to both the circumstances that come to us and the inner movements of our conditioned mind. This is the foundation of our spiritual life that allows us to move beyond the old conditioning. First we must *see,* and then we must cultivate the discipline to *pause* before immediately reacting, to consider whether our response is wholesome or not. This is tricky because it means going beyond our old automatic self-centered evaluations, which are often so much a part of us that they are not necessarily even noticed. Our willingness to train allows us to recognize more readily when we are moving down old ways that potentially may lead to suffering. Then we have the opportunity to make another choice, which may be simply not to do anything. This is always tricky because our practice is not one of inaction: it involves making choices, each of which has its own consequences—even our choice not to do anything. The Buddhist way is a *practice,* and making mistakes—or what seem to be mistakes—is part of the package. The answer, of course, is that we *do the best we can,* letting the Three Pure Precepts be our guide more and more as we become acquainted with little self's flutterings.

It is in the purity of our intentions, refined through practice, that the "loving, knowing all" of Avalokiteshwara flowers, and we learn how to love ourselves! This may seem like a tall order—and little self in its arrogance can add confusion to the pot. When I first entered monastic life, junior monks were told to "turn the stream of compassion within." Senior monks could find this as difficult to do as we beginners did. To appreciate just how difficult it is, I like to use the metaphor of a little child crying at a busy street corner when we come walking by. Most of us would pause—even if small children make us uneasy and we are in a hurry—kneel down, ask the child what is wrong, and comfort her with reassurance that everything will be all right. That little child feeling forlorn and frightened cannot comfort herself—no way. When we are that little tearful child, feeling inadequate, blaming, and fearful, we can learn that there *is* something to help us. Our part is to be willing to open to the love within that is ready to embrace and comfort us. We have to be willing to experience being lost and floundering—to give up our arrogance and false pride—which allows us to turn toward that love. In other words, in stillness we surrender to that which we cannot know in old ways because these old ways are the problem. As Reverend Master wrote, "Man stands in his own shadow and complains about the dark, but only he can turn around."

There is a love that "surpasseth all understanding." It is always here for us. The Buddha told his followers not to believe anything just because he said it, but to make it true for themselves, adding that his was a teaching for here and now. Great Master Dogen said that the Truth is at the very place where we stand. It isn't far away. The work of the heart is to cleanse those impurities that prevent our knowing for ourselves this truth of who we are. It simply cannot be found in books. It is in going *beyond* the human mind that we find what we are truly looking for. When we open to it, this flowing love is ours. In *The Light of Asia*, Sir Edwin Arnold, writing of the Buddha's enlightenment, notes that "forgoing self... the Universe grows I." This "I" is not the little-self sense of "me," which is what must be given up. Renunciation can seem so threatening that the ordinary mind obscures its meaning by referring to job, possessions, relationships—obscuring the intended spirit of renunciation behind our very real obligations in order to make renunciation appear impossible. True renunciation is a quiet, inner resolve to leave behind the greed, hate, and delusion that foster the continued delusion of separateness. There are many layers of these three poisons, from obvious to subtle and more subtle. Hence, the emphasis is upon dedicated, ongoing training, the gradual uprooting of the weeds choking our inner peace, as we become aware of them. The reward of training comes in the doing of the training. Increasingly we understand Dogen's insistence that "training and enlightenment are one." The loving heart flows to all and we give a heartfelt bow to training for training's sake, bowing for bowing's sake. We don't ask for more because we come to know that truly we are given all that we need.

# Poignancy

This morning while I was sitting quietly, *Flowers Fall,* the title of a commentary on one of Dogen's seminal writings, came into my mind, followed by the affirmation "yes!" and by a sense of the preciousness of each passing moment. It was one of those bitter-sweet moments when the poignancy you feel can almost be held in the hand. It was as though all of life had stopped for a moment. Perhaps this is what a Zen master meant when he taught that *Eternity in the moment is the only important practice.* There is no stress, no fitful need to "fix" anything; it is just the precious *being* that our practice allows us to touch and know.

It isn't as if this happens only at rare moments. The rarity is that we don't recognize the specialness of each moment. As the poet William Blake writes, "He who kisses [a] joy as it flies/ Lives in eternity's sunrise." Substitute "each and every moment" for "joy" and you go some way to capturing the poignancy of such moments in words. But the more poignant question remains: how many of us are able to capture the moment itself—to kiss *this* special moment as it flies by? Our practice allows us to do this by bringing the light of our precious awareness to the present moment—right here, right now—without splitting it up in any way. This happens when little mind/self is dormant. I say "dormant" because, as we all know, little self is always right in there just as soon as something triggers its activity. Still, we can, in a manner of speaking, capture the moment's poignancy before little self's arousal. This is the gift that we give ourselves by committed practice, the gift that makes our spiritual practice the foundation and ground of our lives. It is a dedication to grow and expand and move beyond whatever limits still hold us back.

The wonder is that this awareness is possible at all. We can't see it happen because it is a process of growth more subtle than learning any physical task. It is a blossoming within as we learn to let go of the shackles that bind us. Five hindrances to our awareness were carefully enumerated by the Buddha: sense desire, ill will, sloth and torpor, restlessness and worry, and doubt. These five are just another way of expressing our being dominated by greed, hate, and delusion. They are the forces that propel us into a new round of existence as a "you" and a "me." It is useless to get down on ourselves for being selfishly driven, angry, lazy, restless, or eaten with doubt. What's the point? That simply strengthens Mara, Buddhism's personification of the destructive inner forces that pop up so effortlessly and insidiously on the screen of our mind, blocking our awareness. The Buddha was visited by Mara seven times after his enlightenment. Mara visits us too—with thoughts, feelings, impulses, and desires that have many manifestations well worth pondering. Our practice allows us to be aware of them within ourselves and to see the conditions that trigger their arousal. Awareness gives us the power to choose not to be dominated by these inner movements.

Over and over again, we learn we can say "no!" and choose to go a different way. In the *Katha Upanishad* we are told that there is a path of pleasure and a path of joy. In the beginning, pleasure invites us with remembered enjoyments and gratifications. How alluring! Shakespeare in one of his more rueful sonnets writes, "The expense of spirit in a waste of shame/ Is lust in action." The whole poem addresses this disillusionment, concluding, "All this the world well knows; yet none knows well/ To shun the heaven that leads men to this hell." We can say in response, "Bill, it doesn't have to be that way; these experiences can be the way to extricate ourselves from the snare of lustful desire." As we live our practice more and more, we find we really can take that other path, the path of joy. At the beginning it seems uninviting—repugnant even—requiring discipline and self-control to resist the snare of craving. Most of us had so much of that stuffed into us during childhood, imposed by parental and societal standards, that we recoil and rebel. The difference is that now we can internalize values that are true for us—true to our heart—rather than feel we "should" do this or that and "shouldn't" do something else. As soon as we hear little self applying that formula to judge action, our practice again allows us to see that that is a conditioned and limiting admonition from the past to be examined in the light of our maturity. We *can* put away childish things just as we can shameful pleasures.

We must bring the full force of our training to *this* moment and develop the wise discernment to see what is appropriate *now*. This is a chipping away of old tendencies, old karma, and it can be done. Is it difficult to do? Well, yes it is. But so what? Life is difficult; life is a challenge. Life will teach us over and over again the virtue of the examined life lived with mindfulness and restraint, not as imposed by old conditioning but chosen because that is what we want, knowing we can follow the path of joy that leads to Nirvana, the end of suffering. As the Buddha taught his followers: *This is a teaching for here and now, not to be believed because I tell you. Make it true for yourself. Come and see.* This is a call to freedom from self that something in us yearns to follow. When we are open, the heart responds with quiet joy and appreciation. We have to put our shoulder to the stalled wheel of inertia, habit, and over-adaptation to an unsatisfactory life, and just *do it.* Our intention allows us to appreciate those exquisite, ordinary moments that are so much of our life and to feel the poignancy of knowing that all this is passing away, with nothing to hold on to. Then we truly live in "eternity's sunrise." This is Nirvana, "the peace that surpasseth all understanding," that doesn't depend upon some particular event or person or circumstance. We can live free and independent, supported by our wonderful practice/training.

# Refining Your Life

The title conveys a way of viewing our practice, of bringing our lives into harmony with that which underlies the phenomenal world we find ourselves in. Obviously, before we feel the need for change in our lives, there must first be some dissatisfaction or sense of incompleteness—a feeling of the unreliability of this world of "self and other" that so many of us are caught up in. Most of us need to have some experience of life before its unsatisfactoriness becomes sufficiently noticeable for us to think about it on more than a superficial level. Only then do we catch a glimpse of the constant factor embedded within all our problems. It's "me"! The world I experience is not the problem—"I" am. Yet as much as we may admire the infant who looks upon the world with the eyes of innocence, I doubt that anyone would really want to return to that state of dependency and inexperience. Becoming adult in the fullest sense means, as St. Paul reminds us, putting away childish things. He also points out that we "see through a glass darkly." That darkness is the veil of ignorance that, according to the Buddha, propels another birth. Through spiritual practice, we have the opportunity to refine our lives by living in the light of truth—the light of our True Self hidden or obscured by the encrusted experiences that form the conditioned mind.

Right Understanding is the beginning of the path of training for us as Buddhists. It reveals the nature of the work required of the heart/mind to free us from suffering, to truly refine our lives beyond the superficial. As we immerse ourselves in our spiritual practice, we become students of life's lessons. When studying science, we learn about the scientific method; when studying ourselves through our spiritual practice, we come to see ourselves as the experimenter rather than simply as the subject of life's experiment. At this point something rather exciting begins to shift in our approach to living. As Reverend Master noted, this shift is an attitude of mind based upon right effort toward true spiritual perfection. In other words, we begin to perceive that the problem isn't "out there." In our approach to what we take as the world, we learn how to follow the path of training that leads to the end of suffering. So what is the nature of the experiment? Just as scientific experimenters must have sufficient information to recognize where more data are needed, so spiritual trainees must come to see how the patterns in their behavior reflect their conditioned mental activities. I have noticed that people who are not training may recognize patterns—"I'm a restless person who has to be up and doing something," "I'm bossy," "I get hurt by what people may say to me," "I get angry when criticized by the boss," and on and on—but in and of themselves these observations don't bring change to the patterns. Awareness brings precious insights, but we have to go beyond mere self-observation. Observation without action simply expresses a kind of passivity or helplessness—the hopeless feeling that "I can't change; circumstances need to change first."

The attitude of mind that puts us in the role of experimenter brings an opportunity to test a hypothesis that forms around our Buddhist understanding of training. We begin with the law of karma, which states that our actions have consequences that potentially can bring suffering in their wake. Fortunately, we have the Precepts as our guide to alert us to behaviors we need to be wary of. For me, the three Pure Precepts convey the teaching most simply: do as little harm as possible, do as much good as possible, and purify the heart/mind to truly do good for others. The variable being tested here is whether by following these simple guidelines my life will really improve in ways important to my inner well-being. Scientists test what is called "the null hypothesis"—the hypothesis that the variable being tested will make no difference. Like the scientist, the trainee must begin by examining the spiritual variables to see if they make any difference, to see if our lives are improved by changing our behavior according to the Precepts. Now comes the pivoting point: we must take charge of lives—refine ourselves—to prove or disprove the hypothesis. We know the undercurrent of unsatisfactoriness that propelled us to begin a spiritual practice, to undertake our Dharma experiment. Now we use the light of our beautiful awareness, cultivated through our practice, to deliberately choose not to follow old habit patterns. We must pause in flight, so to speak, to see where we're going and then, if it is good to do so, refrain from that old pattern. This is not easy! It involves stretching ourselves and going beyond our comfort zone of mindlessness.

The miracle is that the combination of the two tools, awareness and choice, changes the very fabric of our lives. The conditioned mind wants dramatic results, and certainly the modern mind expects answers right now. Instead, the work of the heart goes on, quietly chipping away at these old sad patterns built out of a great many experiences that often are not even remembered. The trainee/experimenter is encouraged to keep checking the results.

This is an ongoing practice, so we must keep applying our spiritual understanding to each situation as it arises. Gradually, we begin to understand how this very life can be the Bodhisattva's playground: we're here in this life to let go of old automatic patterns, and through the eyes of training we do the best we can in this moment, both for ourselves and others. In doing this, we follow in the sure steps of the Buddha himself. Our confidence in the practice grows as we continue to apply the beautiful light of our awareness to how we live this precious life right now. The longing deepens to fill our heart/mind with the goodness that is our birthright, to live naturally from the Buddha Nature that flows with compassion, love, and wisdom. This gradual conversion of desire, anger, and confusion is the consequence of our choice to keep up our training. If we persevere, the ongoing experiment is always a success, and we continue to disprove the null hypothesis—the view that our training makes no difference. It does! We just have to keep on going, alert to the danger of complacency or laziness that lulls us into a false security and causes us to forget the great experiment. As we come to learn, the great matter for which we train is an exciting experiment that never ends.

# Reflection

In Dogen's *Rules for Meditation,* one of the key teachings is given near the beginning: "All you have to do is cease from erudition, withdraw within, and reflect upon yourself." Last evening after the talk on Dogen's *Rules,* someone asked how you go about reflecting upon yourself. This excellent question brings us face to face with a paradox of training: we cannot answer the question without going beyond the question. Why? Because it is precisely this activity of the conditioned mind—this mind asking its questions—that we are confronting when we turn within and reflect upon ourselves. *The Scripture of Great Wisdom* explains that the five skandhas that constitute the conventionally perceived self (form, sensation, thought, activity, and consciousness) are, "in their self-nature, void, unstained and pure." This is the very heart of the teaching: that which each of us has implicitly believed and taken as our "self" is a misperception, the conventionally perceived self being *sunyata,* a Sanskrit word often translated as "emptiness," but which Reverend Master translates as "purity" or "the Immaculacy of Nothingness" to avoid negative and nihilistic connotations. We are so caught up in our false reality that we cannot see through it, beyond it, or over or above it to what is unborn—that which comes *before* all this apparent reality we cling to.

This is one way of expressing the Right Understanding that forms the beginning of the path to the end of suffering. Also translated as “Right View,” Right Understanding ties the whole teaching together for me. Ignorance, that which propels a new birth, is a wrong view that beings in our karmic stream have embraced. The belief in a self that is separate, apart from, and seemingly independent of the world “out there” is a mistake, with consequences that inevitably lead to suffering. Why? Because the belief itself gives rise to a sense of inadequacy in us. Our experiences are colored in such a way that we bump against much that is unsatisfactory, unreliable, and unwanted. We look to what seem to be external phenomena to support and bring security to the self. Confusion is perpetuated because sometimes we experience this comfort and sometimes we don’t. In other words, right off the bat we have landed in the world of opposites created by our ways of viewing the world. This truth has to be penetrated, and is both simple and profound. Of course, if everything went our way all the time there would be no motivation to embark upon a spiritual practice that promises to lead to the end of suffering. For starters, we wouldn’t comprehend what suffering is. We might see others who seemed to be unhappy, but their experiences would be alien to our own; it would be virtually impossible to feel empathy for them; their experiences wouldn’t compute.

However, the realms of existence are not permanent, and the Buddha pointed to this impermanence as an important fact to be trained with. The universality of change becomes increasingly clear as we do our practice. Near the end of *Diamond Sutra* we find the words:

Thus shall ye think of all this fleeting world:
A star at dawn, a bubble in a stream;
A flash of lightning in a summer cloud,
A flickering lamp, a phantom, and a dream.

Our spiritual practice allows us to penetrate this basic teaching, letting our understanding deepen so that we no longer try to hold on to experiences that inevitably will alter. That is why our practice in a sense is so simple—we simply have to let go repeatedly of whatever we are clinging to in this impermanent realm of existence. But it is also tremendously difficult, as we all know if we are keeping up our practice, living more and more from the very center while life flows. That is why the essence of our practice is expressed by Dogen's exhortation to "cease from erudition"—cease from being caught up in the various mental activities that arise and pass—"and reflect upon yourself." How do we "reflect" without "erudition"? Dogen explains: we just sit, not trying to think and not trying not to think; we sit "with no deliberate thought"—"the important aspect of serene reflection meditation."

This is the *letting go* of our practice: we are not trying to do anything; we are simply *being* in our sitting place with awareness. We come to appreciate that this awareness is our precious birthright that no one had to help us learn and that no one can take away. More and more we learn to appreciate what we already have. It is so simple. And yet we have to learn how to *be* and to appreciate its simplicity. Although it is always here, always present, we get pulled off into the flurry of experience that is so enticingly varied and beckoning. That these experiences are to a large extent karmically driven remains hidden to us; thus we take them as real in and of themselves. This is a mistaken point of view that our ongoing practice gradually penetrates. So how can that be easy? You have heard me say many times that what we are doing is the hardest thing in the world. Why? Because it is an *inner* activity that over and over again we have to choose to cultivate and nurture. The nature of the world generally is unsympathetic, which is one reason why having a Sangha Refuge is so important. These Refuges become increasingly precious as our practice takes us beyond the known of our particular environment—family, school teachers, siblings, friends, society, culture—to the very heart of who we are and what life is. Put simply, we come to see the false as false and the true as true.

That we are not who we take ourselves to be is the Buddha's teaching. We are both more and less. To find the Truth we have to give up false beliefs that form the premise of our ordinary life. It always comes back to the astonishing understanding that belief in self is simply a point of view. As Reverend Master put it in *Zen is Eternal Life,* "as the Bodhisattva proceeds through the stages to Buddhahood, he gradually realises that Nirvana is a state of mind resulting from right effort towards true spiritual perfection." And it's true, so true. Reverend Master would say at times that we should "use greed positively," which I take to mean that we should want that which is truly valuable. To encourage us all, here are some descriptions of Nirvana found in the *Sumyutta Nikaya:* "Cessation of lust, of hate, and of delusion is the Unformed [i.e., Unconditioned]," "the End," "the Taintless," "the Truth," "the Other Shore," "the Subtle," "the Very Hard To See," "the Unweakening," "the Everlasting," "the

Undisintegrating," "the Invisible," "the Undiversified," "Peace," "the Deathless," "the Superior Goal," "the Blest," "Safety," "Exhaustion of Craving," "the Wonderful," "the Marvelous," "Non-distress," "the Naturally Non-distressed," "Non-affliction," "Fading of Lust," "Purity," "Freedom," "Independence of Reliance [on changing conditions]," "the Island," "the Shelter," "the Harbor," "the Refuge," and "the Beyond."

Friends, Nirvana is worth everything and stands not one iota against all that we hold dear. It is an enhancement of this life right now for those who are intelligent, energetic, and willing to make the effort. As always, the important thing is to keep up the practice, which includes our taking refuge in a teacher when we need to. The miracle is that we really can make the Buddha's truth one with ourselves, little by little, but not as "we" mandate or insist. As Dogen points out, our practice "is simply the lawful gateway to carefree peace"—the natural consequence of our life-enhancing choice to do our spiritual practice.

# Stretching Yourself

These are some thoughts about how to practice with the basic Buddhist teaching of *not-self*—the realization that there is no separate and individual "I" underlying the multitude of experiences we attribute to a "me" and see as "mine." If we don't bring the Dharma to an understanding that is deeper than just a book-learned one, then the real support we need in living simply won't be there when life brings its various challenges. The only sure resting place is within the true heart, our Awakened Nature, the Truth that holds together all this diversity we experience. When we sit in serene reflection meditation—the very heart of our spiritual practice—we allow ourselves to see the impermanence of all thoughts, feelings, impulses, and memories that arise, and to know that they pass away whether we want them to or not. That is their nature. That is why, as his very last teaching to the community of monks, the Buddha taught, *All things that arise pass away. Work out your salvation with diligence.* He didn't say that we might just as well give up and indulge ourselves or give in to despair. We can do the work within the heart and move from the conditioned and impermanent to that which lies beyond—the Eternal. This is the profound teaching of the Buddha's enlightenment that he invites us to make true for ourselves.

We begin with both faith and, according to Buddhism's Fifth Law of the Universe, an innate knowledge that our Buddha Nature must be true, that there must be something more than the constricted limitations of the human condition. So we must be willing to open to and explore the unknown. This is the radical conversion—the turning—that begins our formal spiritual life. We move from what we know, or what we think we know, and open to the mystery of what lies beyond. In formal meditation, we sit and are willing to allow whatever arises to pass away, and we gain proficiency in doing this by the actual practice. Book-reading, workshops, and talks can help us only so far—to the point where we are willing to embark upon an inner journey to the unknown, to the source of our very being. And those of us who are doing a sincere and committed spiritual practice know how challenging this journey is. We are willing to see what it is we're holding on to, and in that moment choose to let go—over and over again. This is cultivating the pure awareness that with increasing steadiness steps back from the passing show that one master called the "scenery of life." We are allowing ourselves to see who we have taken ourselves to be and how much we are influenced by mental activities that only arise and pass.

The important thing then is to maintain this quality of awareness when we get up from formal meditation, bringing mindfulness into every aspect of our lives. We can do this by developing a double consciousness, so to speak. Ordinarily, without this discipline, sensory experiences grab us repeatedly and we react both inwardly and outwardly from old habitual tendencies. Sometimes, the consequences of these actions turn out fine. But sometimes they don't. We can literally be left reeling when we don't connect cause (our choice of action) with effect (the consequences of that action). There are blind spots in all of us, and we perpetuate the resulting unsatisfactoriness by not examining where our actions come from. So, along with the impact of sensory experience, we must cultivate another consciousness—one in which we increasingly become aware of the mental activity inwardly rebounding from these experiences. In other words, we gradually go off autopilot to give ourselves the opportunity to make different choices, weakening the dominance of old conditioned pulls. This is wonderfully freeing and is certainly one aspect of the freedom of Zen practice that we want to cultivate. It gives us more options than we think, believe, or feel when conditions threaten our equilibrium and confidence, and it enables us to go beyond the opposites that immediately arise as we move through daily life. The very purpose of this life for a Buddhist is to do just that.

The best time to overcome a hindrance is when it appears. In Buddhist teachings, the first two of the Five Hindrances are desire and aversion. Where do they arise? From within this body/mind. As long as we are alive, we have the opportunity to train, to move beyond the conditions that trigger body/mind cravings and anger. When we understand this much, then we are more willing to use our wonderful awareness to see not only the stimulus—the sense object that impinges upon us—but how little self is moved by it. Hence, in the gradual training that begins with the effort to clean up our act—training governed by the Precepts—we are next told to guard our senses. To me this means just what I've been writing about, something done so as not to get flung off-center into reactive behavior. This is very instructive, because when we don't act in those ways that are our second nature—our reactive human nature—we have the chance to act from our *first* nature, our True Self, our

Original Face. This is fertile training ground. For all too often, when something comes up and little self cringes, wanting to grab or push away, we are dominated by its demands, going along with it or withdrawing, whether we recognize it or not. At such moments, we don't grow much from our life experiences; we're playing it safe—or so it seems. In fact, we are continuing the karmic blindness of not seeing the way things are.

To move beyond, we must stretch ourselves. We need to use the awareness we are cultivating to see the flutterings of little self. This allows us to stop and consider before going down an old familiar road that leads to unfortunate consequences. We have the chance to ask what is it good to do, rather than go with what habitually has governed us—our desires and frustrations. We *can* choose to act differently. And when we do, when we leap into the unknown, we must trust something greater than our habitual modes of reacting. The plaintive question then arises—"But how do I know if I'm following Buddha Nature?" Here is where we must simply act in good faith, in the knowledge that we are not acting from "little-me" desires, that our pure intention is to grow spiritually. With all important matters, my Master advised asking the Lord of the House (our True Self) three times what is it good to do, and listening carefully because we recognize that we don't know. We can check what we're hearing with the Precepts. For as my Master taught, "Know that the Lord will never break the Precepts." We can also take refuge in the Sangha, asking a teacher or practitioner we trust. Ultimately, however, learning comes from doing. There is no way of knowing the consequences of an action before taking it. We can do our very best, which is exceedingly important, but finally we have to act; even choosing not to act is an action from the karmic point of view.

When we continue to choose the comfortable and familiar, we end up short-changing ourselves. We never give ourselves the opportunity to stretch out of our perceived limitations, our fears, our self-consciousness, so we really don't let our potential blossom forth. Life is far more than what our conditioning tells us. We find out more and more who we truly are—a part of that which embraces all—beyond all our words, ideas, and concepts. It isn't so very far away, and when we are willing to turn toward it, sincerely letting go of the obscurations that bind us, we open to a bigger picture that is always here. My Master would say, "The Eternal can wait; it is eternal. How long do we want to wait? How much more suffering will it take before we're willing to live in deep, good faith?" She would add, rather sadly, "It takes as long as it takes." Eventually, we'll all "get it" because it is our birthright, the source of who we really are. We gradually learn that we can give up the shadows for the light. But it's up to us to stretch ourselves and reach to the light.

# The Doorway In

One of the monks in my Order, a student of iconography, gave some talks about a mandala. To get to the center—the oneness represented by the mandala as a whole—there are four entrances, symbolically representing our greed, hate, envy, and what he called "the pride of inadequacy." Although we all possess elements of each of these, he explained that for each of us there is a dominant one that represents our particular entrance into spiritual life. Envy/jealousy was the entrance to the north, greed east, hatred west, and this strange kind of pride south. These entrances are another way to look at the three defilements or poisons that in Buddhism are understood as the forces propelling a new birth: greed, hate, and delusion. The last, which would include both envy and pride, is essentially the ignorance of who we really are as we experience ourselves (our *selves*) as separate and distinctly independent entities. This ignorance is the first of the twelve links of Dependent Origination or Conditional Arising, the sobering description of how a being's past actions produce consequences to be enjoyed and suffered subsequently. Thus it is said that we create our own destinies—something we come to understand for ourselves with ongoing practice.

The mandala entrance for me pretty clearly was and is this strange "pride of inadequacy," the delusion that there is either something to be proud of or inadequate about. It is the denial of the oneness that is the source—Buddha Nature/Buddha Mind—and is essentially a form of delusion. One of the great masters of the last century was asked by a student how he could get in touch with delusion. The student said that when doing the practice he recognized greed and hate arising but not delusion. The master gave the profound answer, "You're riding a horse and asking where is the horse." The very nature of this notion of individual selfhood is what carries us through this world of birth and death, joy and sorrow. The Wheel of Life we are so helplessly revolving on is based on our own clinging to a belief in our separation, which leads to our looking outwards for fulfillment and wholeness. Myriad past lives show the futility of such a search: the particularities of these tendencies simply give us our individuality, strengths, and weaknesses. This is the "horse" each of us is riding without recognizing it.

One stumbles over the notion that inadequacy might be at the root of pride. Of course, they are just another pair of opposites, and opposites lean on one another, being the two sides of one coin. When I look back over my life, it is clear that the pathetic need to be something I was not (a persona of pride to hide behind) was a veneer covering a sense of fragility and insecurity. *Pride,* we are told, *goeth before a fall.* Pride would lead me on to, well, being proud or haughty, like one asking "Who are you to be telling *me* what to do, interfering with *me?*" And that often inevitably led to a "fall" when life would call me on this bluff. My bold statement of self was so blatantly false that part of the veneer was also a false humility. When I studied abnormal psychology, one of the traits I could see in myself was a passive-aggressive personality. This is a destructive pattern for sure, and one I was stuck in for a very long time. Only by repeatedly experiencing the consequences of reacting from one or other of these conflicting patterns have I gradually lessened their hold. I don't have to take this stance in being in the world, in relating to others, habitual though it has been. Life challenges one's defensiveness and out comes the aggressive reaction. That doesn't work and back one falls into a position of timidity so unsatisfactory that once again the old arrogant tendency to hit out pops up. Relationships are damaged over and over again. And one of the most damaging parts is the subsequent disappointment and uneasiness experienced.

I don't know if more clarification is needed about the link between pride and inadequacy. It seems so clear to me now. And truly it was and is my doorway in, because the unremitting unsatisfactoriness of living with a sense of loneliness, isolation, and always needing to prove I was something I wasn't (more adequate, more on top of things, more the leader) took the heavy toll of chronic depression lifted by momentary "successes" that, of course, never could adequately support this feeble structure of self. Now I know that I'm no big deal and that there is no need to be. "I am what I am" is the way one of my teachers described his own stance in the world. This is, strangely enough, what we have to grow into: this is what we find when we reach the center of the mandala. We're all right just as we are; there was never anything wrong in the first place. Simply *being* can be so pleasant. When we drop the phony pride or persona of adequacy, we simply are adequate. We don't have to compare; we don't have to judge ourselves. This is the big ongoing challenge of our training. We have to keep coming back to the drawing board, refining away all those false self-images, those deeply grooved tendencies that bring suffering, to uncover and discover that there was nothing wrong in the first place. Then we move to what Reverend Master would call "the third position." It is an adequacy that is beyond the adequate-inadequate continuum. It is the adequacy of wholeness, of learning to be just who we are without defensiveness or comparison.

The Buddha taught that there is this place where ideas of "I am superior or inferior or [even] equal to" don't apply because these measures have no meaning. Then the myriad differences are simply the rich panorama of life. We don't have to be threatened, nor do we have to push our way to the top. Where we are is just fine. This is the nature of contentment, something that had escaped me for much of my life. This is the very real gift that comes more and more as I continue my spiritual practice. In a sense, I still cannot understand it. Nirvana, described positively, is "the peace that surpasseth all understanding." It surpasseth understanding because it cannot be explained in concepts or words. It is our Buddha Nature, our True Self that has never gone anywhere, that has always been right here. As we allow the lid to be blown off the delusion that fosters pride and fear, we discover for ourselves the true adequacy of simply *being*. This is worth every effort and is the endless journey into the unknown. Our task, our practice, is simply to keep going in faith and trust in the unfolding process of our spiritual life. The fruition of the training arises in every step. As the Buddha would tell his followers: *This is a teaching for here and now that dedicated, intelligent seekers can make true for themselves.*

It is up to us, and when we are willing to go through the doorway at the entrance of the mandala, which signifies our willingness to look at ourselves, powerful help becomes available to us, whether we recognize it or not. Usually it is only in looking back that we can see that help. That is precisely why faith is the essential requirement: faith in ourselves, faith in the teaching/practice, faith is those who live a dedicated spiritual life. This is expressed in the Three Refuges: "I take Refuge in the Buddha; I take refuge in the Dharma; I take refuge in the Sangha." It is fundamental for living a Buddhist life, and in the time of the Buddha the repetition of these words was the way one became a Buddhist. These Refuges describe a total commitment to living a spiritual life, and this dedication needs to be renewed each day or whenever we begin wavering. It is not a question of stepping back from life. We must put our energy right within the burgeoning challenges of daily life. Then training truly becomes its own reward, which we find out for ourselves simply by keeping at it both when things are going well and when things are going badly. It becomes the sustaining support for a life that, gradually, becomes a natural expression of the Three Pure Precepts: *Do as little harm as possible; do as much good as possible; and purify the heart/mind to truly do good for others.* Within the challenge of our daily life, we are over and over again "lighting a candle instead of complaining about the dark." That's it! And it is so simple, so simple.

# The Unreality of Thoughts

Living without awareness, we are dominated by our thinking, our beliefs, and our wishes. When we give allegiance to this apparent reality, we strengthen it and increasingly stop questioning whether that which flows through our minds has any substance. This is the trap of our conditioned little self that has lost touch with the ground of its being—Buddha Nature. Many, many times, little self has led us a merry chase down painful alleys of disappointment, regret, anger, and longing as we act upon the myriad ideas we have implicitly taken as real. This is the plight that lies behind our spiritual search. Increasingly, we come to know that something is wrong here, usually without recognizing that the problem is right within our point of view.

Our spiritual practice brings us into confrontation with our mental activity as we learn to sit still beneath little self's noisy demands for involvement. This "sitting still" with awareness—in formal meditation—is the heart of Buddhist practice, the medicine that the Buddha *qua* physician prescribed for the suffering people of the world. We are dominated by our ideas, and language is what gives those ideas form. Once one sees this truly, our meditation practice becomes an important wedge driven into the seemingly solid reality of our thoughts. However, that initial seeing is only a small inroad; and, once seen into, little mind has more tricks up its sleeves to shore up its seemingly impregnable fighting lines. If we tell ourselves that meditation sounds scary or impossible, we are simply giving little mind new fuel to run on. Is it any wonder then that, all too often, we wish the insight would just go away!

So we have our work cut out for us. Yesterday, the group talked about the profound uneasiness brought on by this awareness of what thought is and by this stepping back from involvement with thoughts. One can commiserate while pointing out that this is just the way it is. There is a cost to reality, a price attached to the pearl of great price. If we don't want to pay that price of self-awareness, then we put aside our training, go back to old ways, and in that heedlessness reap the consequences of our decision. Eventually, all of us must answer this call of our True Self, our Buddha Nature. Unreality cannot support our growing hunger for something more satisfying. It's just a matter of time. So why not act now? Well, I'm too busy, I don't feel well, I'm kind of restless and need distraction, my friends will think it strange, I have to keep up with the news, I need to respond to others' needs—and on and on. We have to pause within our busy pursuits and really take a hard look at our lives, at the priorities that have grown like weeds and are now habitual. This hard look allows us to shift those priorities a little and see where there is some time for serene reflection, for looking into our unexamined lives.

A commitment to do the spiritual practice is vital. We must learn to persevere in the face of the discomfort that comes of repeatedly examining who and what we take ourselves to be. Our practice is to stay with the discomfort that arises and let go of the shadows that are our thoughts and feelings, looking at them dispassionately to see how they simply fade when we no longer feed them. Then the stillness we find beneath all the discomforting noise is touched and nourishes us in a way that is different from external satisfactions. We are reminded of that truth at special times—when watching a little child fascinated with a growing flower, finding unexpectedly the soft beauty of a lake at sunrise, or walking through a majestic forest. The longing calls us, reminding us that we've been missing something wonderful that only the quiet heart can see and feel. But a commitment to spiritual practice requires effort.

The Buddha described Right Effort as fourfold. First comes the effort necessary to let go of those unwholesome thoughts unhelpful to our spiritual quest for well-being. These rampant thoughts require the firmest right effort so that we don't once again succumb to old ways of acting and reacting. Simply letting go over and over again is what it comes down to, saying "No!" to them and returning to the present moment. They are not just going to go away; in fact, they don't need to go away. The thoughts themselves are not the problem. The problem is our buying into these thoughts, identifying with them, and acting on them so that we become slaves to them. The thoughts will calm down when we stop stirring them up. We can't make them be still; trying to still them is simply another disturbance of the mind. We just stop feeding the thoughts, stop buying into them, and stop acting on them. This first right effort leads to the second: to not let new unwholesome patterns take hold of us. These two go together.

At the same time, two other right efforts come into play: nurturing the wholesome thoughts that are present and encouraging the development of wholesome states that have not yet arisen. Again, it is only through our willingness to be alert, attentive, and aware that we will begin to act in ways that are helpful rather than harmful, both to ourselves and others, as we move from the confusion and demands of the conditioned life to the purity and clarity of the Unconditioned, our Buddha Nature. In *Rules for Meditation,* Dogen writes that "the koan appears naturally in daily life." Koans challenge old patterns of our little self/mind stimulated by present experience. Also in *Rules for Meditation,* he writes, "Understand clearly that the Truth appears naturally and then your mind will be free from doubts and vacillation." We have to do our part, confronting the koan when it arises. Daily life is our teacher—the mud that provides the nourishment for the lotus of our True Self to reveal itself. We don't have to get rid of anything. We learn skillful ways of meeting the koan's challenge and addressing it so that it can teach us how to let go rather than simply lead us on to more unhappiness. Then "the Truth appears naturally." It never went anywhere—it was just obscured by our running around in our heads and acting on old beliefs that were out of harmony with That Which Is.

With the appearance of the Truth, we move away from suffering into the peace and joy of Nirvana. This is "the peace that surpasseth all understanding." It is our true home, the source and ground of our being. That we ourselves can touch that place and know it with knowledge not conditioned by circumstances is truly the miracle of training/practice. We can't demand it, we can't legislate it. It offers itself to us because it is our True Self. Here is the inner unity that heals our terrible sense of separateness and allows us to sense more and more the oneness existing beneath, within, and beyond the myriad things we see and know. As we are told early in our training: *The All is One and the All is different.* Little mind will ponder this point, perplexed, because little mind is itself the obstacle that keeps us from knowing this truth, from living in the simplicity promised here. It's hard and vital work, but once we see the Truth, we keep going through good times and difficult alike. Tozan Ryokai writes in his enlightenment poem, "The night encloses brightness and at dawn no light shines." The Truth, the Light, the Water of the Spirit is always *here,* in *this* moment, present in all its majesty. It is our privilege through dedicated and sincere practice to come to know it. That is the gift we give ourselves—the gift of this priceless pearl that can be purchased only by our own efforts. We all know what we have to do. We simply have to keep letting go of little self with all its obstructions and demands and errors.

When the opposites are dropped, the Buddha Mind shines—to rephrase Dogen's warning that "when the opposites arise, the Buddha Mind is lost." We stand against the world of opposites and appearances, in order to train in the Great Wisdom of the Oneness that is the "allayer of all pain." We are part of something far greater than this little me, and "that is all/ Ye know on earth, and all ye need to know," to quote Keats in a different context. This in itself is the work of a lifetime. But what does that matter? Let the commitment deepen and fill us with resolve so that more and more we are willing simply to go on, always becoming Buddha.

# Thinking

During the discussion after one of our recent meditation meetings, someone noted how she has difficulty maintaining mindfulness when she is making plans. Her practice has developed to the point that she remains mindful while engaged in a specific activity, such as making a meal, but her mind might slip away when planning the meal. This important self-observation reflects the potential confusion we face when trying to understand how the heart of the serene reflection practice is, as Dogen's *Rules for Meditation* tells us, "neither trying to think nor trying not to think; just sitting, with no deliberate thought, is the important aspect of serene reflection meditation." So where *does* thinking fit in? When is it appropriate to use our wonderful mind?

In Buddhism there are three different actions: those of body, speech, and mind. We create karma by our unskillful use of them, with mental activity being the trickiest. The verses at the beginning of the *Dhammapada* make this clear:

> We are what we think.
> All that we are arises with our thoughts.
> With our thoughts we [create our] world.
> Speak or act with an impure mind
> And unhappiness will follow you
> As the wheel follows the ox that draws the cart.

However, as the text goes on to state, when we "speak or act with a pure mind... happiness will follow you as your shadow, unshakeable." Our spiritual effort both in formal practice and in daily life is to keep the awareness as bright and sharp as possible so that we don't create unhappiness for ourselves and others, but instead maximize happiness for everybody we encounter. Through our practice we have the golden opportunity to see with growing clarity the sobering truth that "we are what we think" and that "with our thoughts we [create our] world." Here is an awesome responsibility that is good to reflect upon. It follows that accepting this responsibility requires us to cultivate right choices, which are enabled by the entire Noble Eightfold Path. This lies at the heart of our spiritual practice.

The practice is so simple: we maintain awareness and clear comprehension in our lives. The simplest situation for developing this practice is when we are "just sitting"—doing zazen. When we sit on that cushion, bench, or chair facing the wall, all of us know just how exceedingly difficult it is to maintain serene reflection in the face of the myriad mental activities that march in. We are a bundle of conditioned tendencies that have the power and magnetism to draw us into the "soap opera" of little self, which is always encouraging us to identify with what are otherwise just passing events. This is difficult to "get" because our little mind/self can't comprehend it. All that mental activity seems so real in its garb of ideas fashioned from the data of our senses. Our sleeping minds take the appearance for reality and react by being pleased or displeased at the impact. This is the mind's *dis-ease,* and our meditation is the medicine to cure it. But at times that medicine is not sweet tasting, as we all know who have dedicated ourselves to a spiritual life, and again and again we slip back into taking the unreal as real. This will not make sense to someone who has not attempted self-examination, because it brings into question the very premise on which we build our sense of who we are—our *self-identification*.

When we move from formal sitting meditation into formal walking meditation (kinhin), the practice becomes even more challenging. In our practice we walk in a circle; hence our awareness now expands to include not only the activity of walking but also some sense of the rest of the group. Of course, to some extent this is necessary; otherwise, we would bump into the person in front of us or create too great a distance between walkers, causing the whole rhythm of the group's walking to be disrupted. Also, as we move, the scenery changes, and we have the opportunity to notice how strong this visual impact is, and how easily it draws our attention. At such moments, our practice is to notice which stimuli are dominant and then return our attention to simply walking, mindfully raising and placing first one foot, then the other. As we develop mindful walking, we can use this model for living mindfully in daily life. Mindfulness grounds us in the present moment. This allows us to notice more readily when we have slipped into thinking about something—slipped from the simplicity of the present moment. The model is of mindfulness in action, emphasizing its purpose of not letting us get lost in aimless associational thinking and feeling, which is our wont. So when we are preparing a meal and chopping vegetables, we focus on this activity and bring our mind back to it no matter how many times it wanders. Then we are doing daily-life zazen in our every-minute mindfulness. In this way, our practice comes to include more and more aspects of our daily life.

As we all know, our lives are more complex than just walking from here to there or cutting vegetables. How are we to do our practice then? Well, it's the same principle, but applied with "skillful means" (that is, with intelligence) to the specific situation. This is why it is so very important to do daily reflection, to investigate with dispassion those times when we slipped out of mindfulness and were left with the consequences of a "niggle," an uneasy feeling about whatever the situation was. How does this apply to the Sangha member's perplexity when using mindfulness while planning? When you make planning your choice of activity, then you just plan. If I'm planning a meal for lunch, then perhaps I'm looking at a cookbook or into the refrigerator, or writing down what will be included in the meal. This is what I'm doing and there is no problem. However, the little restless mind's tendency to build associations from the vast reservoir of conditioning can pull us from our chosen present task. Then, without realizing it, we've gone off into worrying about the end result of the meal, the punctuality of the guests, and so on. In other words, we have gone into "deliberate thought" about the future. When we notice we have done this, we come back to simply planning the meal, which is done in the present moment: we write down a recipe, we decide the order of the meal; whatever is appropriate to the present situation is done with mindfulness. This is an important point because it is necessary to use our brains in planning. Again, we learn through repeatedly doing our daily practice as purely as possible that our tasks are done better when done mindfully. We're more efficient because we haven't allowed ourselves the seeming luxury of distracting ourselves from whatever task we have decided to do.

Mindful living requires our increasing ability to move with the events of our lives. There is a fluidity here that is beautiful; we don't get stuck so often because we are not ruled in the same way by our opinions about how we and everything else "should" be. When we are grounded in the present moment and willing to be aware of little self's habitual modes of perceiving and reacting, we are bringing our formal practice into daily living. We're at the heart of the practice; it isn't just something we do to find equilibrium while in formal meditation away from the hurly-burly of life. We can develop more and more what my Master called a "kaleidoscopic" mind because we are less and less caught up in perpetuating an illusory self. The life of the trainee becomes less dominated by feelings and thoughts. Dogen wrote in his "Tenzo-kyokun" ("Instructions to the Chief Cook") that our aim is to find balance in every activity. We don't get caught so much in "one-sided" thinking. It isn't *not* to think when it is time to do our income tax or play bridge: the activity becomes the focus that we're grounded in and hence is what gives us the opportunity to see when we slip off into past or future, into feeling frustrated or smug, or whatever. Our mindfulness allows us to choose wholesome ways to respond to the simple or interactive events that make up daily life. And gradually we see we have changed and life indeed becomes more simple because we learn the art of letting go and of acting from the still center of our being. This is the wonderful gift of our training.

# Mental Poisons

It isn't difficult to understand *why* we have developed ways of coping that keep us busy and preoccupied, moving in our heads from past to future, future to past. Not until we sense that something is going wrong can we recognize or perhaps just get a glimmer of what the problem is. I know that before I turned to a committed spiritual solution, my life was in such a turmoil of confusion that all I really knew was that I was suffering a lot without understanding why. That there could be only *one* problem would never have even occurred to me. That problem is in the very makeup of our own little mind with its monkey-like chattering incessantly going on. To begin to see that this is so and to let that seeing mature provide fuel for our practice. Otherwise we could go on forever reacting in conditioned ways to this stimulus and that. This is the dilemma we all feel when sitting for some time with the mental poisons that color our lives.

How then are we to put behind us these poisons and get to the "other shore" that the Buddha speaks of? The Paramitas, the Buddhist perfections, offer us one model of self-purification. There are six in Mahayana Buddhism: generosity (giving of ourselves), discipline (living by the Precepts), patience, energy (Right Effort), meditation, and wisdom. When we turn to a dedicated spiritual search for the Truth, the Transcendent (so-called, but in fact it is always immanent) requires a wholehearted commitment to move beyond the deep-seated tendencies that stand in the way of our cultivating these perfections. Somehow people expect it will be easy. It isn't. But then life isn't easy. Dogen has a lot to say to us about the hard work entailed in our practice/training:

> as yet I have heard of no one who became wealthy without much study nor of anyone who became enlightened without undergoing training… Enlightenment can only be realised as a result of training. Some means of study are shallow, others deep, some are interesting and others boring, but treasure is derived from much study… If enlightenment can be realised without training, the teaching of the Buddhas cannot be perfected… The Buddhas do not force you; everything comes out of your own efforts in the Way. When you train, you are beckoning to enlightenment; your own treasure is within you, not outside; training and enlightenment are their own reward… In returning to our True Home, we are transcending the status of the Buddha.

Later in this same passage from *Gakudo-yojinshu* (translated by Reverend Master as *Important Aspects of Zazen* in *Zen is Eternal Life*), Dogen writes:

> One who would train in Buddhism must first believe completely therein and, in order to do so, one must believe that one has already found the Way, never having been lost, deluded, upside-down, increasing, decreasing or mistaken in the first place: one must train oneself thus, believing thus, in

> order to make the Way clear; this is the ground for Buddhist study [practice].

When we *know* that our spiritual practice is the true medicine for easing the suffering and unsatisfactoriness we experience in our lives, there is only one thing to do. It really doesn't matter that it is challenging and difficult: there is nothing else to do but commit to our spiritual practice. This means that we must be willing to experience the suffering that leads to the end of suffering, rather than simply perpetuate the suffering that just leads to more suffering. This is an important choice we need to make—and we must make it often and repeatedly, because it is not easy! So we keep at it in the growing faith that this moment's uneasy spot can help us move beyond to a richer, more satisfying life. We don't get stuck and we don't give up. We train; we cultivate the perfections and drain off the poisons. We train when things go well and we feel all right, and we keep training—not getting lured into distractions—when things aren't going well and we don't feel all right. The big teaching here is that feelings don't matter, that they are not the true measure of how things are. Instead, they are signals of karmic patterns that can be explored as we move along the path of awareness, seeing the way things are, heading toward That Which Is Eternal—to the other shore that is right within our own heart. The important thing, as *The Scripture of Great Wisdom* reminds us, is always to keep "going, going, going on beyond."

# Shedding Skin

A snake shedding its skin is an apt image for what happens in our spiritual training, whether we realize it or not. I don't know if the snake feels any discomfort or uneasiness when it is time for the layer of skin to be sloughed off, but when we come to those points in training where we have outgrown a "skin," our training can feel anything but good or desirable. At such moments we may wonder why we ever undertook such an activity. How are we to understand this paradox of training—that growth in our spiritual life can feel so painful when it confronts those very aspects of living that prompted us to begin our practice in the first place?

We can start by looking at what we take as "me" or "myself," seeing them as a bundle of habitual, conditioned tendencies that have been forming for a long period of time, held together by this notion of an "I." This false view, which separates "me" from what is "out there," is the dilemma we come into life to resolve. In Buddhism it is called the essential ignorance or delusion and is the beginning of a new life, a rebirth as a "you" and a "me." With the sense of separateness comes vulnerability. We are born helpless and dependent, and however independent and well-functioning we may be in the circumstances of our present lives, underlying even fortunate circumstances is a terrible sense of inadequacy and uncertainty. We cover up and hide this reality from ourselves and others under various self-images. That we aren't aware of these self-constructions only intensifies the problem.

Obviously, not all of our inherited tendencies are limiting or undesirable, and they all appeared to play a useful role in helping us to grow and survive at some point in our lives. That some or many of them now hinder our growth is the problem that sooner or later must be addressed. These are the skins we begin shedding when we make a sincere commitment to spiritual practice. But we can't do that until we are willing to see the underlying root causes of the unsatisfactoriness we have become aware of. This is the challenge of our training, and many of us falter many times along the way. Although our faltering progress may seem too bad, it is not really a problem. The important thing is that we persevere. For as long as the vulnerability of feeling separate and alone prevails, we will never cease from our search for something to relieve it. "Here born, we clutch at things," writes Sekito Kisen in *Sandokai,* and we all know how an infant's fingers do just that. As we grow older, our clutching at externals becomes more sophisticated and refined than the child's, yet it still reflects that vulnerability we all faced as babies.

The question we must ask ourselves over and over again, when our training allows the awareness to see it, is this: Do I still need to act this way in this situation at this time, or is this another skin of conditioned behavior that needs to be shed? I suspect that we don't stop to ask ourselves this very pointed question because it might require that we change some aspect of ourselves or our situation. Many of us have to be pushed to the very edge of endurance in some way or another to be able to leap beyond the fear that challenges the status quo. This edge takes many different forms: the death of a loved one, the sudden breakup of a marriage, the loss of one's business, a fire that has gutted everything we owned, the threat of a terminal illness. They all lead us to the same place: to where we are simply stopped in our tracks and can't just shrug it off or ignore this crossroad. This is the suffering of the First Noble Truth the Buddha wants us to really look at. Often misunderstood as "pessimistic" or "nihilistic," the truth of suffering is in fact simply "realistic"—the way things actually are. When suffering arises, life offers us the wonderful opportunity to make some deliberate, intentional changes that are fundamental rather than simply skin-deep.

This is the beginning of our spiritual life and can change everything. We don't have to give up anything; instead, we'll find that some tendencies, like outgrown skins, simply won't fit any longer as we get to know ourselves and who we have taken ourselves to be. Some things will fall away relatively painlessly; some will take years of training for us to address. When we really come to see that living a life of selfishness creates problems for ourselves and others, we then see the layers and layers of its manifestations becoming increasingly subtle. The Buddha advises repeatedly that we let go of selfish desire and the anger that its frustration brings, because these are what stand in the way of our spiritual growth and happiness. We do this letting go as we come to see the truth of the teaching, and as we come to know that our practice is the sure means to the end of suffering. It is endless training because each shed layer of skin helps us to see the next, more subtle layer of skin that constricts us. As with any training we are committed to, we become more skilled as we practice letting go of our old skins. It isn't that it's easier in the sense that it doesn't hurt. It can hurt a lot. Only now we know that this is salutary pain signaling where another barrier within is holding us back. Through our ongoing practice, gratitude, joy, and humility flood our lives more and more, while the pain of separation recedes. And as we go on letting go of successive layers of ignorance, we are “always becoming Buddha.” This is the life of training.

## Siren Songs on the Journey Home

Homer tells us that when Ulysses finally set sail on his homeward voyage from the Trojan War, his ship had to pass a place noted for its danger—the island where the Sirens sang so sweetly and enticingly that sailors were lured to find them, only to meet their death on the island's dangerous shores. Ulysses had his sailors put wax in their ears to protect themselves; but he, curious to hear the Sirens' song, had himself firmly tied to the ship's mast so that he could hear without endangering himself or his crew. The experience just about drove him crazy, and he pleaded with his men to release him so that he could follow the Sirens' song, but the men had been forewarned to ignore him, and in the end they all made it through safely.

When we sit in meditation, we invite the Sirens to sing for us the song of our own habitual tendencies. These tendencies often lie hidden so deeply that we don't really know them for what they are. Inviting them to reveal themselves is what our meditation is about: when we sit "neither trying to think nor trying not to think, just sitting with no deliberate thought" (as Dogen tells us in *Rules for Meditation*), we relinquish control over what we are aware of—we *just sit with awareness.* Now, like Ulysses with the Sirens' song, we believe that we can experience whatever comes up—hear the lure of our old habit patterns, our conditioned tendencies. We can confront them, but like the Sirens' song, they can be pretty compelling. And like Ulysses, we need a firm post to be tied to so that we don't follow them. The firm post is our meditation, which allows our awareness to separate itself from its usual involvement in all these sounds and sights and sheer noise. It can be quite a din!

The metaphor of the Sirens' song helps us to see what we are choosing to do when we undertake a meditation practice. We want to be peaceful, to hear the beautiful sounds of carefree peace, but all too often we find instead that we are confronted by the old stuff that has been dragging us around—that which is the very opposite of peaceful, and busy, busy, busy. The art of meditation is learning to ground ourselves in awareness itself, so that we don't mentally ground ourselves on the Sirens' rocks by becoming too absorbed in their latest tune. For, like the ship returning home, we too are on a return journey home—one far longer than Ulysses' and in many ways just as perilous. The sailors helping us are determination, faith, right effort, willingness, courage, and awareness. We must be willing, as Dogen tells us, to "look inwards and advance directly along the road that leads to the Mind." We develop the sheer grit to keep going, and our growing faith in this inward search sustains us. If we do our part the ocean will carry us, even though we touch the other shore only at its pleasure. All we can do is go on in trust. Impatience, doubt, uneasiness, grabbing on to the pleasant—these all are passing. We just need to hold our course, relying on pure awareness to show us the passing phenomena singing their Siren songs.

Our part then is to keep up our practice. The Sirens have been enticing us for a very long time, and on many occasions we have let them take us off course into suffering, unsatisfactoriness, even disaster. One great Master told a disciple who said he couldn't get in touch with delusion, the third defilement: "You're riding a horse and asking where is the horse." Delusion, the horse, and the Sirens' song are all one. We have serious work to do here, and in doing it we free ourselves little by little from our reliance on that old horse and the song alike. That we *all* can do it may seem an overstatement. Yet that is the Buddha's promise. As he stated, his is a teaching for here and now that we can prove for ourselves. We are tested by the lure of old patterns of seeing and believing in numerous conditioned experiences. By resisting the temptation to be carried away by the Sirens' song, we strengthen our pure awareness and thus discover that we can make different choices. We venture into uncharted waters, the unknown that we have always been so leery of, to find that the land we come to is far more appealing, peaceful, and joyous than we could have believed. Then we move on, over and over again, always going into the unknown, navigating the treacherous waters with our growing awareness, our Buddha Nature where all is well.

It's a wonderful journey home, back to the Source of our Being, where "All losses are restored and sorrows end," to quote one of Shakespeare's sonnets. And miraculously our sorrow's end—like the journey home itself—is right within our heart. To paraphrase a Tibetan way of describing this intimacy, *It is so subtle, like space, we can't grasp it; it is so pervasive, like the air around us, we don't notice it; it is so near, like the nose on our face, we can't see it; and it is so simple, we can't believe it.* So, what are we waiting for? Just don't waver. As the old saying suggests, "When the going gets tough, the tough get going." It takes fortitude to continue the journey home because we all have Sirens singing within us, and the destructiveness of their song is defused only when we are willing to confront them or let them confront us. With growing faith we see that we are given exactly what we need at every moment in our lives for our continuing spiritual journey. *When we are willing to see we will see.* This is the fundamental change in attitude that turns us from drifting toward the Sirens' perilous shores. It is a very different point of view from the ordinary one and, again, takes a great deal of faith and determination to cultivate.

Always we come back to the central teachings, one of which is that "All-acceptance is the key that unlocks the gateless gate." Probably none of us has any problem accepting what is pleasant, comfortable, and agreeable. The problem, of course, is that life also dishes out to every one of us the unpleasant, uncomfortable, and disagreeable. So it is right here that we must train in acceptance, believing that, whatever the circumstance, we can handle it, learn from it, grow in our understanding through it, and *leave it behind.* In Buddhism, the human realm is considered the best of the Six Realms of Existence for spiritual practice precisely because it has both happiness and suffering. Happiness supports and reassures us, and brings stability, while suffering prods us to learn the life-lessons needed for our spiritual growth. We must navigate the waters of training, willing to learn from all of our life experiences, willing to let the light of our beautiful awareness shine on those old conditioned tendencies that have been singing their Siren songs to us for so long. We don't have to be lured onto the rocks. We have choices. We steer our ship this way or that—it's up to us. All of us can return to our True Home.

# Reminders on the Way

## Zen Training in Everyday Life

Reverend Meiten McGuire

# Contents

# Meeting Loss

I read about a performance given by Itzhak Perlman, the great violinist who is paraplegic. At a Carnegie Hall concert, he struggled to the stage with braces on his legs and used canes. After carefully sitting down, putting the canes aside, and taking off his braces, he signaled to the conductor to begin the violin concerto. This was a familiar scene to music lovers who had attended his other concerts. Then something different happened. At the very first violin note, one of the four strings on his faithful violin broke. The audience gasped. They assumed that the violinist would leave the stage as he had come—no one could play with only three strings. However, what then followed made this particular concert more memorable than others. After a brief pause, Perlman signaled the conductor to begin again and played exquisitely with the three remaining strings. At the final note there was an explosion of bravos and applause, after which Perlman finally signaled the audience to stop. Then he said these memorable words, "You know, sometimes it is the artist's task to find out how much music you can still make with what you have left." The person writing about this conveyed awe at the magnificence of the human spirit so vividly demonstrated.

The dramatic event that tested the skill and courage of this acclaimed performer happens all the time in less spectacular ways in everyday life. Loss is at the heart of life. The Buddha taught that one of the main characteristics of existence is impermanence, *anicca*. In the First Noble Truth he pointed out that change itself is not the problem. Change is simply the way things are. As we train, it becomes clear that it is our clinging or attachment to moving phenomena that creates problems for us. This is the Second Noble Truth and most of us need to penetrate it repeatedly. So the second characteristic of existence that the Buddha emphasized is *dukkha*, the inherent unsatisfactoriness of life as it is ordinarily lived. The third characteristic he enumerated is less obvious, though it is gradually revealed with continued spiritual practice: since everything shifts and changes there can be no permanent, independent and separate 'me,' *anatta*. I think Perlman demonstrated these important aspects of existence and showed how to go beyond them. Our Right Understanding allows us to live a Buddhist life of spiritual practice that is equally magnificent to Perlman's performance, even though it may not be appreciated as such. As Dogen wrote, "To live by Zen is the same as to live an ordinary daily life."

One of the great Zen masters of the last century pointed out that the Buddha-to-be walked the way of *loss*, renouncing palatial life with all its pleasures and security. The disturbing prod for him came when he was faced squarely with the truth of impermanence by being exposed to four sights: an old person, a sick person, a corpse, and a mendicant wanderer walking by without agitation or distress. These are referred to as Divine Messengers because they gave him the impetus to move beyond. His mission was to find the spiritual solution to the end of suffering. This was his koan. He could see that although he was young, healthy and alive, he too was destined to experience old age, ill health, and death. *To live the way of loss* does not require the kind of literal renunciation shown by the Buddha. What he found through this momentous choice was that there is a Noble Path that leads away from our *holding onto* that which changes, thus releasing us from the inevitable suffering otherwise attendant upon living within changeableness.

To paraphrase Perlman's observation after his magnificent performance: *Sometimes life asks each of us to see how much music we can make with what we have left.* All of us have experienced loss. All of us have survived experiences of grief, fear, and grave difficulty—situations when we are forced to confront big change. Our Buddhist practice allows us to work with the less dramatic incidents of daily life that challenge our equanimity. As one influential teacher of the last century put it, "The Buddha taught us how to die before we die. Then we can live at peace." This 'dying' is the repeated letting go of the 'me' that wants and demands things to be a certain way and not another. St. Francis wrote at the end of his famous prayer, "It is in dying [to self] that we are born into Eternal life." Our wonderful ongoing practice is to keep refining our awareness about *what* we are holding onto, what we are resisting when life brings us varied experiences that challenge us to let go. The process becomes increasingly subtle. As it is said, there is no resting place where we can simply be complacent, resting upon our laurels. None of us ever really knows what will happen next. This sobering truth can help us return to the present moment. Over and over again with respect and courage, we can make wholesome choices, deepen our faith and true knowing that there *is* more than this passing moment. Just as Perlman learned when he was confronted with the loss of a string on his violin that he could make music with *what he had left,* we can also learn how to rise to the true glory of our life when we are faced with the awe-filled challenges that come.

We can learn from each moment by our willingness to train. Each moment is our teacher. We can bring to bear the fullness of this path of Buddhist training. That choice is always open to us. Then the question *how can I know?* is answered through the doing. We can bow in acceptance to the way things are and from this secure place over and over again ask *What is it good to do now?* This silent music of our spiritual practice ripples through the great universe in which we are all interrelated. In a quiet, unostentatious way we can applaud our daily mundane choices to keep up our training. We are beautifully aware that when a seeming loss appears, we too have the capacity to *find out how much music we can make with what is left.*

# An Exquisite Knowing

The Dharma was flowing in my meditation this morning, when the words of this title appeared. It startled me because impermanence was the Dharmic theme passing through, and yet it truly is an exquisite knowing that can revolutionize our lives. The purpose of our spiritual practice is to ground ourselves securely in That which knows this truth.

The Buddha's first discourse is referred to as "Turning the Wheel of the Law." It is symbolized by the Dharmachakra showing the Noble Eightfold Path that leads to the end of suffering and begins with right understanding. Right understanding is an 'exquisite' knowledge that illuminates the entire Path with increasing brilliance as we are willing to practice by keeping on with the training of the conditioned mind. This is so arduous and challenging that we must keep grounding ourselves in that right understanding. Great Master Dogen referred to it as the "Great Matter for which we train." Because the nature of the human mind is to fall into confusion, it attempts to short-circuit the profundity of life by using its rather feeble tools to grasp this Great Matter. We feel comfortable with the known. When we *can* solve whatever life confronts us with by using the conditioned mind and what we've learned over the years, we simply do it. This is living on the mundane level without reflection or depth. And it is not a problem.

Somewhere along the way we are hit with the inadequacy of living this way. This is the First Noble Truth that prompts, prods, and sometimes insists upon our going deeper. When the surface no longer satisfies sufficiently, we search for a spiritual path, a way of going beyond the mundane. We won't do that generally until life has brought us to it. This is an important—an exquisite—right understanding because gradually we are helped to really change our point of view, our attitude toward life. Can we see it? Can we see how the recognition on a deeper level of the sheer unreliability of this world is vitally important in finding a truly more satisfactory grounding in this very life? As the Buddha taught, "It isn't so very far away." Ironically, it is right "here and now"; this the Buddha promises. It is waiting for those who are intelligent, dedicated, and energetic in pursuing the path of training.

The Buddha frequently referred to the danger of indolence, lethargy, indulgence in sleep, sometimes calling this "sloth and torpor." Its opposite is restlessness, and we can sway on this pendulum for a long time. This becomes clear as one is willing to study oneself, to really crack that 'book' of self that has so much to teach us. My first spiritual teacher referred to life as a schoolhouse. We're here to learn. What is life teaching us? As willing students we have to find out for ourselves that what is being taught is how we react to the events appearing in our lives (cause and effect). It really is so simple, as my great teacher would say: Our practice is to learn to stand back from being caught over and over again in old karmic (habitual) patterns of reactivity that seem so natural because they've been grooved into self and recreate the self by that very repetition. This is subtle as well as simple.

After his enlightenment, the Buddha was reluctant to go out and teach what he had found true for himself because he saw that people have much dust over their eyes and wouldn't understand, being too caught in the opposites of wanting the pleasant and avoiding the unpleasant. To move beyond these opposites is how we move beyond the unsatisfactoriness of sometimes being gratified and sometimes not. The 'Exquisite Knowing' falls into our psyche, so to speak, at those times of bemusement, when we drop the pretences and attachments ('me') that obscure what is really happening in this very precious gift of human life as it is being lived right now.

In the Dhammapada's first chapter, the gift of choice is brought out in what are called the "twin verses." We are reminded that "hate never yet dispelled hate, only love can do that." This is a *choice* we can learn to cultivate, but we have to truly see the futility and destructiveness of resentment, anger, hating. The Buddha then asks, when people really know that "they too will pass away," how can they quarrel? We're all in the same boat, dear friends, all wasting time in old reactive, futile patterns that keep us on the wheel of suffering. Over and over again, we have the opportunity to pause even in seeming mid-air and use our wonderful awareness of how swiftly this life passes to consider choosing another response. Don Juan told Castaneda to live with "death upon his left shoulder." This is indeed the exquisite knowing that this very life is also the moment to move beyond wherever we are stuck. The opportunity to train is only ever now, so let's do it, always willing to take that next step into the Unknown.

# Regret and Letting Go
## Faith in Action

In a group discussion recently someone talked about her current dilemma with *Sange,* which is the Japanese word translated here as "regret." The difficulty for her is that she feels regret about the feelings she's having toward some important people in her life. She's not acted upon these feelings, which is often what does bring up the Sange, and yet the feelings linger and disturb her. A wonderful discussion followed about the value of being willing to be still within the feelings, about not getting caught in an intellectual and kind of analytical process about them, but rather about the work of shifting one's point of view toward the other person and situation. This frees us for the all-important movement in training to then *let go* and move into the next moment with new resolve and determination. In other words, the process may be described as the "3 Rs": 1) *Register*—really look and see what's happening, which is a double awareness of the arising condition and the inner reactivity of the conditioned self; 2) *Reflect* or *Review*—which is that important *pause* to consider from the place of meditation, i.e., pure awareness, what has happened; 3) *Respond*—from the position of taking charge of our resolve to not act in ways that are harmful to ourselves or others. One could add a fourth "R" here: 4) *Release*—which allows us to not drag the past around with us.

We only truly have this one precious moment that is right here, right now. Our practice allows us to see how rarely we are fully living with this appreciation: we have the opportunity over and over again to see how we fritter away our time in ruminating over past happenings or projecting future ones. In one of the Middle Length Discourses, this pertinent teaching is given: "Let a man not dwell upon the past or on the future place his hopes, for the past has been left behind and the future has not yet come. Instead with *insight let him see each presently arisen state.* Let him know that and be sure of it invincibly, unshakably. *Now* the effort must be made... " This is referred to later as *one fortunate attachment.* We are willing to keep up the purifying process of letting go as we learn how to *appreciate* what each moment offers us. We ground ourselves in right understanding, the first factor of the Noble Eightfold Path which leads to a more satisfactory, satisfying life. "The Buddha's words are true, not something empty and vain," as it is put in one of the Scriptures. Right understanding first of all is a deep appreciation of the Four Noble Truths, which is the "teaching that is unique to Buddhas."

The First Noble Truth, as we all know, is the truth of suffering or unsatisfactoriness, *dukkha.* This Sanskrit word literally means "hard to bear." The Buddha in his first discourse on the Middle Way enumerates a number of specific aspects of life that condition this state, which include not having what one wants and experiencing what one doesn't want. As conditioned beings propelled by the karmic energies of desire, anger, and confusion (or greed, hate, and delusion, as the defilements are more generally referred to), we will find ourselves at times in one or the other of these two places. Why does the Buddha begin his teaching by pointing out this basic aspect of life? Because until we are willing to apply a sincere spiritual practice built out of this Noble Truth that there is suffering or distress that comes from the very conditions that bring forth this rebirth, we will flounder over and over again in our attempts to grab onto what we want and push away what we definitely do not want: *greed and anger* swinging this poor little self on a pendulum of opposites. Our wonderful practice begins and grows with our willingness to *see the way things are.*

When we know more and more deeply through our ongoing practice the danger of falling into these extremes, our knowledge is also more heartfelt that *I don't want to go that way anymore,* that it is the wrong way. My sense is that this is where the trainee who raised the initial question yesterday finds herself: she's very clear about not acting on these disturbing feelings and yet has not found the clarity about how to move with them. She sees this disturbance as something to be ashamed of—*she does not want to be this way.* She feels *stuck* in important relationships/situations that are distressing and doesn't know how to change. Paradoxically, this is a critical and *fruitful* place from the point of view of training. Why? Because we clearly see the limitations of our conditioned way of being and have not yet seen how to change. The feelings themselves are the signals that some important change is hovering silently beneath the distress. The 'I' doesn't know what to do and in that posture of not knowing can ask, "Please help."

Protest from the floundering conditioned self pops right up. *We* want to be the one in charge, but that 'we' is that of the conditioned body-mind that is showing itself to be wanting. Can you see how our willingness to stay in this uncomfortable position comes out of our long-term choice to keep up this exacting practice? In other words, we're not trying to push away the discomfort through old habit tendencies or indulge by acting out of them. We are really being held securely by our good faith that there *is* Something More, a bigger picture of which we are a part as is everything else. Call *It* God, Eternal, Unborn, Beloved, Absolute, Universal Life Force, Self with a capital 's.' It doesn't matter because IT *IS.* In *The Scripture of Great Wisdom* this is expressed as, "Going on beyond the human mind is Nirvana." *Now* is the time to "stand against the world of the conditioned mind in order to train in Wisdom," as our practice has been described.

So what can she do? What can all of us do when faced with a similar conundrum? We can keep turning to those Three Refuges which are at the heart of the Buddhist teaching: *I take Refuge in the Buddha.* This is our Awakened Nature, that which is obscured by the very in-your-face 'me' or the conditioned mind that we are training through our wonderful dedicated practice. *I take Refuge in the Dharma.* This is the 'very truth' as expressed in varying ways in *The Scripture of Great Wisdom* and it is the profound and yet simple teaching the Buddha gave in so many different ways to guide us. And *I take Refuge in the Sangha.* This originally referred to the community of monks that formed around the Buddha, attracted to give their lives in that special way to learn and follow the Buddha. Now it is used as well to refer to all of us who are doing this practice and come together in just the way that our Sangha does. She took Refuge yesterday in her willingness to ask for help from the group. This helps us all because truly we're *all* in the same boat. Life can knock any of us for a loop, which was expressed when I first was at Shasta Abbey as, "You never know when old karma is going to come and hit you out of left field." It's here to teach us, dear friends, and this is *the* different point of view that can vitalize our practice. Life is not easy *and* through our willingness to practice, we can little by little make the Buddha's teaching true for ourselves—by our choices we can move toward the end of suffering. This is worth everything.

# Out of Time

The Buddha-to-be, Prince Siddhartha, was propelled by "Heavenly Messengers" to renounce the palatial life he knew and begin his spiritual search for the end of suffering. The first three of the messengers conveyed the fact of impermanence: an old person, a sick person, and a corpse. Pondering the meaning of these human experiences, he let go of the vanity of youth, the vanity of health, and the vanity of life itself, even though he himself was a young man in the very prime of his life. An urgency stirred him to look for That which doesn't change and could be a true refuge. It was the fourth and final messenger, a mendicant monk, who showed him the way. He didn't try to kill the messengers because their messages dismayed, startled, and troubled him. He'd simply never thought about running out of time because his life had been so protected up until his fateful 29th year: the time had come for him to grow into Buddhahood and be a pure beacon of light to guide others.

We too must wake up and find that kind of urgency to search within ourselves for the light of our True Self, Buddha Nature, to look for That which is permanent and secure, a safe Refuge. That there is such a Refuge is the Buddha's promise for us to "make true for ourselves." Buddhas certainly can point the way but *we* must make the effort; it's not something anyone can do for us or, perhaps more importantly, keep us from doing. As my first teacher would say, "We people aren't so bad, we just forget." We get caught up in this dream of life, in our conditioned, conventional ways of being in the world. Uneasily, not protected from the various assaults of impermanence, we go through our days, victims of our own self-absorption and beliefs. If these *always* worked for us, surely we'd stay stuck without even knowing it for a very long time. That would be like the heavenly or deva realm, and the heavenly realm is referred to as the "most dangerous" of the realms of existence because those beings, in having everything so totally pleasant over a very long period, forget that they too are subject to impermanence. They simply hadn't factored that into their timetable. Though perhaps unnoticed, the fact of impermanence is part of existence in every realm.

The Buddha taught that the human realm is the best place for spiritual growth just because it has a mix of the satisfactory and unsatisfactory. Hell is the realm of unremitting suffering. We each have our package of strengths and weaknesses: the shining light of our good karma and the dark confusion of the bad. *Good* refers to that which is wholesome, helpful, leading us out of suffering. *Bad* refers to those painful obscurations and defilements that lead to our falling into that which is unwholesome and unhelpful, thus taking us farther and farther away from the peace and beauty of our True Nature, Buddha Nature, which is calling to us all the time. It is said that the first karmic consequence these unwholesome patterns bring is a further darkening of the inner light, a heavier veil of confusion and ultimately despair. Somewhere, sometime, this stirs up a sufficient discontent or dis-ease with one's habitual patterns to stimulate the search for a spiritual solution to the end of suffering. Deep within something murmurs *there must be Something*

*More than this.* The dreary round of Samsara again announces its important message and Life has prepared us to hear it in a more viable way: we're spurred to delve *beneath* the appearances that we've taken as so real, just as happened for the Prince Siddhartha. We *enter the stream,* we're on the Path of training.

Most of us I suspect, as was the case for me, don't have much of a clue where this is all leading. Whether it feels like it or not, we're stumbling into the Unknown, that which goes beyond all the conditioned knowing we've been so caught up in and with which we've identified. And, again whether it 'feels' like it or not, we're beginning to rely on faith. The plaintive cry *How do I know?* expresses the fear that comes at times when we are willing to pursue the quiet Call within to reach out beyond our comfort zone. The Buddha said it was the greatest good fortune, good karma, to have inherited a human body which is intact enough to appreciate and respond to the buddhadharma when exposed to it. It truly is a precious human life, as the Dalai Lama calls it, not to be wasted. As Dogen wrote, "It would be criminal to waste such an opportunity by leaving this weak life of ours exposed to impermanence through lack of faith and commitment." This is the key choice that those of us who have embarked on the spiritual quest must honor over and over again. It's so easy to slide under the sway of the five hindrances the Buddha warned us of: desire for pleasure; aversion to pain; sloth and torpor; restlessness and worry; doubt. When these arise, our sincere spiritual practice allows them to be addressed, not just succumbed to.

We must keep remembering the vital importance of continuing our training whether life is going smoothly or not. It is all changing, all an opportunity to learn and grow. We can strengthen our resolve and not be daunted by the obvious fact that *time is running out.* This clear heavenly messenger urges us to train hard *this* day, *this* present moment, because the basic uncertainty is unrelentingly coming down on us. We are invited to go more deeply inward and learn willingness to simply *be* within this natural Flow that is life. As the Buddha taught, "There is nothing you need hold onto and there is nothing you need push away." Reverend Master would remind us that this is the "fullest nothingness you'll ever know." She told me once, "I assure you, there is absolutely nothing to be afraid of." This is her special legacy to me, the Transmission of a Truth for me to keep growing into. And gradually by keeping at it, by not giving up, by doing the best possible in the present moment, something shifts and one is *outside of time.* Somehow we have transcended time's limitations by letting go of those *ideas* about it that ensnare us. This timeless realm is not so very far away: it's so near that we don't see it. It's our True Home that is beyond our limited notions of time and space, here for all. Reverend Master said, "The Eternal can wait; It's eternal. How long can we wait?" When we've truly moved 'out of time,' we're not running out of time anymore and come to appreciate more and more the preciousness of the present moment. As creatures of contrast, we appreciate this magical place our dedicated training lets us touch, which is *timeless.* And strange as it may seem, right then the "obstacles dissolve" and Nirvana IS.

# Filters of the Mind

Right understanding can be expressed in many ways. As a skillful means it is using the Dharma over and over again to clarify the practice, to remove the filters of the mind. In other words, it helps us to keep going—"Going, going, going on," as in *The Scripture of Great Wisdom.* Perhaps the 'Great Wisdom' is just that willingness to keep going on beyond what we think we know, what we feel, what we desire. It is penetrating the truth of who we are beyond the shadows of the sobering mass of conditioning that influences our ways of being in the world and perceiving it. We have to keep pushing gently at the edge of our practice, wherever that may be. We have to keep letting go of judging ourselves and others, whether it be as adequate/inadequate, good/bad, or the myriad other pairs of opposites that rule us whilst we remain often unaware of their impact.

Zen has been referred to as the *Transmission that is outside the scriptures* and also as a *direct pointing.* We don't add another filter to our task of recognizing them. That is the power of "just sitting, not trying to think and not trying not to think, just sitting with no deliberate thought." Its power is subtle because it is defying, so to speak, the rule of the conditioned mind—confronting it directly. I think this right understanding can help those of us who are particularly caught up and attached to mental activity. The reminder can be an antidote to the discouragement that arises when we recognize that once again we've spun around in myriad ideas, fascinating or trivial as they may be. Just seeing their hold is a good first step forward, to be built upon by using the deliberate willingness to simply let go of the whole fabric when it is noticed. It is so easy in this respect: we see what we're doing and we choose to let go, returning to the 'just sitting,' meaning coming back to this very present moment with whatever we're doing.

That we can all do this is obvious: it requires no great special skill that we must be taught, no special aptitude that only a few possess—it is indeed *nothing special.* Ironically, its very ordinariness presents the challenge because we are so caught up in ideas and fantasies, fancying ourselves 'right' or 'wrong,' ruminating over this and that, running away from boredom, and fearing simply be-ing. This is the karmic plight of the human realm. We've moved beyond the 'single' enlightenment of other animals and infants who simply live within the moment, temporarily free of the conditioned filters: they live in oneness without appreciating its wonder because they've not experienced sufficiently the pain of separation. They aren't yet "enthralled by shadows' misty dance," as one of my Dharma sisters described the movement of life. As my great teacher wrote reassuringly to me after I became a monk, "Life *is* movement; life is going from here to there." He was admonishing me for fretting over a major move that I had made from the ashram to the abbey. At a later time, another teacher advised me *not to try to second-guess the Eternal,* another way of saying the same thing.

There is something, Buddha Nature, that in a sense won't leave us alone, hard as we may try to distract ourselves from hearing Its call. When we try to hang on to the status quo, a very strong tendency for many of us, Life itself will interfere simply because *life is movement* and doesn't allow stagnation. Often my caution to seekers is not to stay stuck. *Any* experience is valuable when viewed from the eyes of training. Our right understanding lets us *learn* from both the desired and unwanted experiences that come our way, which then allows us to *let go* and move on with clear eyes to the next moment, what is offered to us now. In doing this, we are dropping off filters whether we recognize it or not. The load of living simply becomes lighter and we become brighter in the sense that we open to the precious moment with less filtering of how it 'should' or 'should not' be. We just live doing that which needs to be done, as Reverend Master put it. In this simplicity we walk hand in hand with the Eternal because we're not holding on to the past or fearing the future. As the filters are worked with through our willingness to keep looking, to keep going, we truly "live in the world as if in the sky." This is the freedom of Zen and the foundation for a life of gratitude and appreciation of what *is.*

# Opening the Heart

Probably the biggest stumbling block in our understanding of the Buddha's teaching is the Second Noble Truth, that the cause of suffering is attachment. At our meditation group yesterday the question again was asked, "If there is non-attachment, how can one love?" Our conditioning certainly leads to obscuring the fundamental difference between attachment and love. Over and over again our wonderful practice will reveal to us how our very attachment to this person or situation interferes with our true, pure love. As we are willing to train with our expectations and attachments, we penetrate the Second Noble Truth and come to realize for ourselves the precariousness of our balance when we implicitly expect or insist that some external situation be the way *we* want it to be. Usually our attachments or expectations are as hidden ground that we believe to be firm and reliable—until we take a step or are confronted with an unexpected event that doesn't hold us up. That is when we can truly come to understand the hazard of attachment and penetrate that puzzling teaching of the Second Noble Truth.

For me, after many years of training, the above is axiomatic, an 'of course'—how could it be otherwise? Nonetheless, the strong-seated tendency to attach is something that comes up for us and challenges us to move to a deeper level of acceptance. We can come to see that *what* we are attaching to really is some aspect of 'me,' which implicitly expects the object of attachment to conform to our wishes. If this were obvious, we'd probably all have been free from the confusion between attaching and loving many lives ago. We're in this life as another opportunity to go beyond these opposites of desire and aversion (in the present context expressed as attachment and indifference/coldness). Life offers plenty of opportunities for this work of the heart. Our job is to be willing students to its great lessons: every time we confuse caring a lot about someone with the expectation that they will then conform to what we want or expect from them, the potential for unsatisfactoriness, for disappointment, is initiated. It comes back to the basic First Law of the Universe as seen in Buddhism: The universe is not answerable to my wishes.

The Buddha repeatedly emphasized that the nature of this realm of existence has three main characteristics: impermanence, unreliability or unsatisfactoriness, and thereby not-self (*anicca, dukkha, anatta*). I think that the first two are obvious while the third characteristic is puzzling. The Buddha taught that any appearance, any form—called *dharma* (with a lower case 'd') and often translated as 'thing'—is not substantial and real in the way it appears conventionally. This is what we are invited to "come and see" over and over again. Do we 'want' life to be this way? A big, fat NO, so over and over again we deny the truth that is right before our very eyes. We implicitly cling to unexamined beliefs about the nature of things—we're deluded. And then we begin penetrating this perplexing Second Noble Truth regarding attachment, as the Sangha member did yesterday. We can do this because we are reflecting on these great truths, not just skimming the surface intellectual understanding of the words. It's uncomfortable; the truth is not necessarily comforting as we struggle with our own particular mix of desire, anger, and confusion that propelled this life. *And* it truly is freeing. "The Truth will set you free," as Jesus put it. Why? Because as we little by little truly see the danger of attaching, we can *let go,* let life be as it will be.

Some of the teaching given in my early days as a junior monk ring so true all these years later. Reverend Master would say, now I believe rather sadly, "It takes as long as it takes." She'd also say, "I didn't make the rules, I just tell you about them." Another teaching I understand so much better now and can truly relate to is that we "help others to be a success *in their own way,*" not as 'I' want them to be. Can you see that this is the very heart of being unattached? Here is the place of a true, deep caring for the other as independent and separate from 'me,' while yet truly related within the great wholeness of which we are all a part. The key teaching of Tozan in his enlightenment poem is, "He is me. I am not Him. When we know this, we are instantaneously one with the Truth." Reverend Master translated this in the Scripture *The Most Excellent Mirror—Samadhi* as, "You are not Him; He is all of you." This is the Great Matter for which we train—to know this for ourselves. And truly it is worth everything as we come to appreciate how each bit of clear awareness lets us see when once again attachment has colored over our world and perpetuates the belief that our well-being *depends* upon this or that external circumstance.

As we touch the "deepest wisdom of the heart" that is our Birthright, we at times simply know, as Kanzeon, the Bodhisattva of Compassion did, that all is "void, unstained, and pure," as it is put in *The Scripture of Great Wisdom.* When we release from this basic confusion of needing the other to be this way or that, to do this or that, the loving heart, the heart of goodness, is naturally experienced. There is this *flowing love,* a truly unconditional love, which rests upon the firm conviction that something cannot be only good for me without including you in the picture too. Why? Because beneath all these myriad differences is a Oneness, a Truth, that is beyond our human conception. Again, as it is expressed in *The Scripture of Great Wisdom,* it is "going on beyond this human mind" that *is* Nirvana. That mysterious, beckoning 'Place' within this very heart truly is always here. And the Buddha promises in the Third Noble Truth that when we free ourselves from our clinging, from our attachments, we will know it for ourselves. To live in the security of our own loving heart of goodness is truly the great gift of training. It's here for us all, waiting and calling.

The *Light of Buddha is* always *increasing in brilliance.* Our work is to do the *practice* of being willing to keep going deeper and keep penetrating how in this situation right here and now attachment to having 'my' way has again brought in its wake disappointment. The work of the heart is to be willing to experience this pain and to learn from it. Then we learn also how to let go into the newness of the next moment, knowing that our choices are greater than we thought—from the heart of goodness we embrace self and other without the overlay of the confused mind that dwells in opposites. The Buddha has shown us the Way to the end of suffering and we have the great, good fortune to train together, giving support to each other, to courageously take that one next step that is good to do—over and over again. Yes!

# Little Things and Letting Go

As we go on doing our training, we have an excellent opportunity to see how this life is really made up of little things happening one after another in a patient flow. Before a meditation practice the tendency for most of us is to live on the surface of experience, reacting in predictable ways—perhaps without even seeing it—to whatever the momentary impact is: with pleasure and with pain. These feelings condition the understandable but unhelpful pattern to want to hold onto the seemingly pleasant and comfortable whilst pushing away the painful and uncomfortable. Hence, we are on a pendulum swinging between two extremes, rarely pausing in the center with its potential stillness that doesn't trigger either one. Actually, really seeing this karmic tendency of the human mind is the beginning of wisdom, the right understanding that lets us appreciate the unending impact of life changing before our very eyes whether we want it to or not.

Our very practice itself directly teaches us. The practice, of course, is our willingness to let go of whatever has popped up into the restless mental processes and to settle into being in the moment. This is every-minute mindfulness. If we don't pay attention, we won't appreciate how much the mind flits around. In the *Dhammapada* the mind is described this way: "The flickering, fickle mind, difficult to guard, difficult to control, the wise person straightens as a fletcher an arrow." This is the first verse in the section on the mind and is followed by: “Like a fish that is drawn from its watery abode and thrown upon land, even so does this mind flutter. Hence should the realm of the passions be shunned.” And here are the following two verses to drive home our human predicament: “The mind is hard to check, swift, flits wherever it listeth, the control of which is good; a controlled mind is conducive to happiness,” and “The mind is very hard to perceive, extremely subtle, flits wherever it listeth; let the wise person guard it; a guarded mind is conducive to happiness.” These descriptions become exceedingly evident as we are willing to increasingly dedicate ourselves to our practice of training the mind. One can feel mercilessly controlled and caught, and this needs to be experienced to some extent before the true need to take control over one’s life in a unique inner way is recognized.

So, what does this have to do with the title about *little things?* Because, and one can jump with joy, we get to appreciate through the very practice itself how so much of life simply passes us by, influencing us in numerous ways whilst strangely being barely noticed. This we truly can see for ourselves, and when we do, a kind of dismay can arise. Our whirling dervish activity is seen for what it is—habitual, mindless patterns that are triggered by the varying conditions passing by. That we don’t see something so obvious has often bemused me. When we do, then we can begin taking a different stance in living this precious life. There are so many little things that just are what they are. They are not ‘real’ in the sense that we implicitly take them to be: they are simply passing through. They are so many tiny movements within the vast sphere extending far beyond. Without our devotion to mindfulness they entice us repeatedly, triggering automatic reactivity, playing out a karmic theme or dance in a rather compulsive manner. Can we really see this? As the Buddha taught, *It's not so very far away, it's here and now.* We're part of a vastness beyond the conditioned mind's comprehension. We can learn to dance differently with less rigidity as we begin seeing how old dance steps can lead to unpleasant bruising.

The miracle is, friends, that as we begin to appreciate the very *little* things that make up so much of a day, we open naturally to the Bigger Picture of which they are a part. I believe that is why one of the great Japanese Zen masters of the last century taught that *our practice takes us to the place where there is nothing special* and Reverend Master wrote, "Nothing matters; Mindfulness is all." We make this truth true for ourselves by going forward wholeheartedly, resting on a vital and sincere willingness to bring our meditation more and more into our daily life, instead of leaving it on the cushion after formal sitting. It really is so simple and, as I've so often said, the most difficult thing in the world to do. The very unsatisfactoriness of living the unexamined life is the prod to keep us at it. And as another great Buddhist master of the last century put it: "Let go a little, a little bit of peace; let go a lot, a lot of peace; let go completely, complete peace." This is the Flow of Immaculacy described in *The Scripture of Great Wisdom*. We've never been separate.

There *is* a Oneness, a Whole, that is not exclusive in any way, whether It is called Buddha Nature, Spirit, God, the Eternal. We mustn't get stuck in words. As Tozan put it in his enlightenment poem: "Finally we understand nothing, for words inaccurate will be," and "Enslaved by words we fall into a hole." In other words, we've taken the mental formulations as a task-master. Rather, the conditioned mind may be recognized as a helpful servant, conveying potentially useful information, as a computer with a database. There is Something else we've lost touch with which Reverend Master, following Keizan, called the Lord of the House, our True Self, our Awakened Nature. Dear friends, there is a still, small Voice, an Inner Voice, always guiding us along our shaky paths. Reverend Master would say that the first step in the religious effort is "getting out of God's seat." Again, in Tozan's poem he points out this fulcrum Truth: "You are not Him; He is *all* of you." To know this for ourselves is to live in peace (Nirvana) with the Way Things Are, doing the best we can with this karmically conditioned body-mind to turn the Wheel of the Dharma, instead of helplessly letting the wheel of repeated births and deaths (samsara) turn us. I've heard many trainees comment on how *interesting* their lives become as they apply this beautiful right understanding as a soothing balm on the many little things that come in a day, letting go and letting go some more to appreciate the refreshment of each new moment.

# When Body-Mind Drops Away

In "Rules for Meditation" Great Master Dogen wrote, "When body-mind drops away naturally the Buddha-Mind immediately manifests itself." Having been a Buddhist monastic for about thirty years, I have read, recited, and heard the Rules literally thousands of times. My relationship to it has shifted over the years. Initially, there was puzzlement about some of it and a glimmer of understanding generally. As a junior monk, one recites this almost daily at the beginning of the midday meditation period, which became a bit much for 'me,' who had more of a chip on my shoulder than I knew. I felt bored and resentful going through the motions as was required—this is definitely not recommended but there it was, or I should say there 'I' was. After Transmission, a monk is not required to attend midday service, and it will be no surprise to those who have heard me describe my training challenges that I stopped going. However, as a senior monk I was required to go periodically as a celebrant for midday service, this time doing the bows in front of the altar and offering the incense. During this period, I was able to return to "Rules for Meditation" with a renewed respect and greater understanding. Over the many years that followed, a profound appreciation and awe for Dogen's teaching have flowered within me. There is a magnitude to this very first teaching, and snippets from it sometimes almost explode within this receptive mind which has increasingly been captivated by the buddhadharma.

Such it is with the quote at the beginning of this writing: "When body-mind drops away naturally the Buddha-Mind immediately manifests itself." A Sangha member was talking about how he didn't agree with something proposed by a senior monk, he didn't think the monk was being modern enough in his understanding of the Westerner's resistance to titles and certain words. Then he said, he'd just "dropped it," seeing that it really didn't matter, that this was his opinion and he didn't need to hang onto it. And *that was it!* That was the letting "body-mind drop away naturally" and he was back in harmony with Buddha-Mind. It doesn't have to be in the big awakening we imagine a kensho to be; it doesn't have to be when one is formally sitting in meditation, which is the groundwork of our practice. It just happens naturally every time we *choose* to let go of body-mind, to let go of this 'me' who is living the stance of separateness. It is when we gently step aside from some usual pattern to relax into the balance of this present moment that allows its simplicity to reveal itself.

Reverend Master talked of the purpose of Mara, the personification of all these karmic patterns that obscure Buddha-Mind, as "standing in the way so that we can *see* what stands in the way." Once we appreciate what it is that is in the way, then we can let go of it. In other words, it isn't 'out there' in this situation or that; it is within the very body-mind confronted by this or that. Simple or not as this may seem, it is exceedingly difficult to maintain this basic understanding. Why? Because we are attached to this body-mind as who we are, who we take ourselves to be, and it is easily threatened by changing circumstances. When we allow ourselves to step back just a little from the fray, it is possible to see more clearly what is happening in the moment. Then the golden, humble opportunity presents itself: we can *let go* of old habitual patterns—body-mind drops away naturally. Then Buddha-Mind, the Source, the Truth is naturally expressed at that moment.

This way of living is "the same as to live an ordinary daily life." That it is truly extraordinary is our conundrum, while our practice lets it happen more and more as we live through the vast variety of Life experiences that come to us. When we live this way, we are expressing another great monk's teaching: "Eternity in the moment—*this* is the only important practice." And it is *so simple:* we learn to drop our insistence that Life be the way we expect, want, demand that it be. We learn to bring ourselves, our body-mind, into harmony with a bigger picture, one in which we are included and embraced within a oneness that the body-mind could not possibly 'get.' Why? Because it is a *part* of a Whole, and the Whole is greater than the sum of its parts. In Reverend Master's translation of "The Most Excellent Mirror—Samadhi," this fulcrum teaching is expressed as "You are not Him; He is all of you." The conditioned body-mind ['you'] can truly harmonize with the Truth, with 'Him' who is all. And the great wonder of our dedicated practice is that we can know this, be in touch with the Source. It is not 'ours' exclusively and It certainly cannot be mandated to appear or grasped. It is simply *here* when we let go of our ideas and opinions, our engrained habit patterns. *When body-mind drops away naturally, the Buddha-Mind immediately manifests Itself.*

# Grasping the Will

It is really difficult to accept the way things are when life has gone awry, when one feels stuck and terribly dissatisfied. No matter how understandable our tendency is to blame circumstances and ourselves, it simply doesn't help in finding sound and lasting solutions. After her major retreat in 1976, Reverend Master emphasized the importance of *willingness* as the basic attitude we need in our spiritual work. What she had learned is that at certain points one simply doesn't *know* what it is good to do, or how to do it. This brings a salutary humility that allows us to ask for help, turning to That which is the Truth of life we're seeking. We see how *self-will* can take us in the wrong direction, because it is based upon our ego-limitations and hence a narrow vision of what is truly good to do. Many of us seem to need to experience a lot of setbacks before we face how unreliable our old conditioning is and how important it is to be willing to examine its appropriateness in our present lives. This is very difficult to do and is at the heart of our spiritual practice. It is the "going on beyond the human mind" that is Nirvana, as it is put in *The Scripture of Great Wisdom*. We just can't have it both ways, and Life is an excellent teacher to keep driving this key point home.

So, where does *grasping the will* come in? We are told of the dangers of going down the old current of *self-will,* and that can appear confusing. This is another paradox of religious life that is only resolved by the practice itself. Grasping the will indeed can be contrary to what the conditioned self-will is inclined to do. We grasp the will as we come to *know* for ourselves that certain choices we routinely make are unsatisfactory, that they take us down the road of suffering. We have to be willing to see this, and that can be a great challenge. Why? Because a strong tendency is to go into blame mode, blaming the other person, blaming the circumstances, and blaming ourselves. And this simply perpetuates the basic confusion that is at the heart of our problems. Often we need reminders that *the* problem is not "out there," however clearly we see that "out there" is not conforming to our wishes or to what seems "right" from our point of view. In my own experience, life has continually shown me that attempting to solve the external difficulty without examining the inner domain doesn't work. That just takes us right back to unsatisfactoriness, albeit in another place and perhaps in another, or even the same, form!

The mystical, contemplative traditions are replete with teaching that the core problem is our sense of separation, which is a strong, implicit belief that influences our way of being in the world in very fundamental ways. Call it little self or ego-mind or body-mind, however it is labeled we simply have to turn ourselves around to "get" it. This is the conversion that helps us find new ways of coping with these old, familiar problems. It is *not* a matter of then getting hard and critical with this 'me'—that simply reinforces the belief in being separate and vulnerable! And there is nothing like pain and distress to get our attention. We can view this as helping us or just as something else to try to get rid of. That is an important *choice,* and at some point, much as 'I' don't want to face something, it simply has to be seen. My first spiritual teacher would look me right in the eye and say with gentleness, "It isn't easy." Reverend Master would tell us, "I don't make the rules; I just tell you about them"; she also said, "It takes as long as it takes." Now I can really hear the compassion behind these words. These wonderful teachers saw the suffering we bring upon ourselves and knew that they could only point the way, holding out the reassurance that deeply changing ourselves *was* possible. And the Buddha kept assuring us that he could but point the way whilst *we* must make the effort. Again, that is just the way it is.

So here comes the plaintive ego-cry: "What can I do?" If we truly *know* as a fundamental Right Understanding what has just been written, then comes the next part: We just must begin. We begin *right here and now.* Much as seeing how stuff of the past has contributed to our plight, much as we can feel stressed about the unknown future, it is *only* in the present moment that we can begin a "new life." There is the reminder from the Chinese tradition that "A journey of a thousand miles begins with but a single step," and then we take another step and another. Each step of the way is good. Little self wants to have immediate proof of the efficacy of these steps. So we come back again to the importance of *faith* in our ability to change, and faith in the purity of our intention to move in more wholesome ways than we've been doing. Then we trust in the spiritual Path we've chosen to take. I can assure you that the Buddha's words "are true, not empty and vain," as it is put in one of our important scriptures.

Self-doubt is endemic to the conditioned mind of separateness. How could it be otherwise since the world, seemingly external, is far bigger than little 'me'? The antidote is our growing understanding that we're caught in the dilemma of holding on to an invalid point of view and need to extricate ourselves. It certainly can *feel* like trying to pull oneself up by one's own bootstraps. And it is right here that the amazing inner resource we all have enters: *grasping the will* to go beyond these self-created opposites. And friends, this is truly the work of the heart that *no one* can do for us. As Sekito Kisen taught in his enlightenment poem, "As you go on distinctions between near and far are lost. And if you lost become, there will arise obstructing mountains and great rivers. This I offer to the seeker of Great Truth, *do not waste time.*" Now is the time and we can all do this work of the heart. There simply is no other time!

# Choosing Faith

"Choosing faith" suggests that faith is an *activity,* not just a nice feeling. In the movie *Shadowland,* Anthony Hopkins plays C. S. Lewis, the influential Christian theologian. He is asked by the Dean of his Oxford College why he prays. The question comes out of the evident and radical change in this intellectual giant who though eloquent at the lectern has been slow to actually take to Christian practice. Lewis's answer is most revealing: "I pray not to change God but to change myself." God, the Eternal, simply IS. From God's point of view there is no problem. As my Master put it, "The Eternal can wait. After all, It *is* eternal." But what about us? How long will it take us to heed the inner Call of our Buddha Nature? That which is always drawing us, pointing out quietly where it would be good to look at our choices, at what we are doing, and how we are living our precious life. Our very busy lives go down old conditioned grooves quite easily, sometimes bringing satisfaction and sometimes not. These are the habitual patterns most of us carry before turning to spiritual inquiry and self-examination.

We live in a world of assumptions, premises that we often aren't aware of. This is the ignorance that the entire thrust of the buddhadharma is designed to erode or dissolve. In other words, we all have "dust over our eyes." We all start in ignorance. If we simply squander this life by living with surface satisfactions and distracting ourselves from noticing our underlying insecurity, ignorance is perpetuated. *Samsara,* the wheel of birth and death, goes on and on and on—the karmic stream to which we add our own mistakes—until we finally "get it." What is this "getting it"? It is waking up to the Four Noble Truths in our own lives. Right Understanding is the first factor of the Fourth Noble Truth, the Way to the end of suffering. At first, this is a mundane understanding. Really, all we have to do is stop and be willing to look at our lives and the First Noble Truth about the endemic nature of suffering glares forth. Birth is suffering, aging is suffering, death is suffering, not getting what we want is suffering, being faced with what we don't want is suffering—everything has the *potential* element of unsatisfactoriness. Dissatisfaction persists when we cling to what we take to be self, when we live in the ignorance of taking on an isolated, seemingly substantial identity separated from the "world."

Through this Right Understanding, which includes all Four Truths, pointing not only to suffering but also to the end of suffering, the beginning quote, *I don't pray to change God, but to change myself,* emphasizes the re-direction needed in life. We *ask for help* because we recognize the essential helplessness within our stance of separateness. Lewis overcame this isolation by falling in love. When his wife was diagnosed with terminal cancer, his sense of anguished helplessness was expressed through prayer. With growing faith he had to recognize that death was at hand and that he alone was not strong enough to embrace its inevitability. Wherever this poignant recognition arises is our *cutting edge* for training. As a dog gnaws on a bone to sharpen and clean its teeth, we too are honing in on and cleansing our awareness when we actively train at this cutting edge. We have to move off the safe but unsatisfactory approaches we've been leaning on because we can see they aren't working and we're floundering—we're suffering. Lewis wisely turned to God, to That which is greater than what we know. He understood implicitly that his suffering arose from his limitation, his being blind to the larger dimension that includes what he *does* know but goes much further than that.

This is how we awaken to faith. It is a deliberate choice to go beyond what we know. One Zen master pointed out that the Buddha walked the way of loss, which can sound off-putting to most of us until we understand it. Analogies are used, such as we have to breathe out before we can breathe in. Another comes from the Zen tradition of a professor coming to check out the respected abbot of a nearby temple. The master serves tea but continues to pour tea into the professor's cup after it is full. The professor protests as the tea spills all over, to which the master points out that when something is full there is no place for anything more. If we are arrogant and self-satisfied, there is no room for growth. Can we see this for ourselves, in our own lives? It is the very unsatisfactoriness of life when we are forced to confront our own helplessness, our simply not knowing, that again can provide the cutting edge of moving beyond the current limitations of 'me.' We *have* to recognize that we're lost in a maze of conditions which won't yield to our usual attempts to feel good about ourselves. This is emptying the cup of our opinions, beliefs, ideas that are imposed onto what we encounter. This is the position of *wanting nothing, having nothing, knowing nothing* that Meister Eckhart described as spiritual *poverty.* We don't want to go there. That which doesn't want to go there *is the problem*—it is the false, illusory sense of self that has dominated our way of being in the world.

Right Understanding is to *see* all of this clearly enough to know we must embark on a radically different approach to life. Life teaches us over and over again that this is so. Though we resist and protest, finally we are willing to get on with it. To live a spiritual life is to awaken our seedling faith over and over again, so that we can move into the unknown territory of true satisfaction, security, and love. This has to be done repeatedly—it is a *choice* we make. Finally, we find through our ongoing practice that there is nothing else we can do, because when we are willing to see, we *will* see. What will we see? The inherent unsatisfactoriness of life when lived out of the conditioned body-mind which is dominated by a desperate attempt to gain satisfaction and to avoid the opposite. And what does it mean to *live* a life of faith? It means to keep challenging our old stance of living in the realm of opposites which have ruled us for so long. And *how* do we do that? By being willing to recognize the danger signals when little self becomes all protective and fixed in old patterns. We *can* see this and when we do, the choice opens right before us whether to go down that old road again or *to pause.* What follows the pausing is the potential for doing something *different.* Hence, it is the unknown. When we are willing to recognize the *I don't know,* we are at the cutting edge of training. In just this vulnerability we can be open to hear the still, small Voice of our Buddha Nature. That is the unknown we keep moving into when we are doing a sincere spiritual practice.

The entire Noble Eightfold Path is designed to help us. This is an *Ancient Path* according to the Buddha. He promises that it leads to the end of suffering, that it is the way to end suffering. A wholehearted commitment to look right into the areas where we need to grow is our way to walk the path to peace and inner contentment. No one can do this for us, and we can take the Three Refuges as a good guide. This takes the humility to be able to acknowledge *'I' could be wrong* and the courage to try new ways consciously, with awareness. How could this be anything other than faith? There is an inner knowing expressed in the Fifth Law of the Universe that states "Everyone has an innate knowledge of Buddha Nature." This inner knowing is different from what we *think* we know. When C. S. Lewis said he was praying to change himself, what he knew deeply was that he needed to be healed, made whole by moving out of his narrow confines into the greatness of God, That Which IS. We are allowed the privilege to choose whether to do this or not. Whether it is called free will or grasping the will, we have the choice to align ourselves with That which is greater than this little 'me' or not. My Master would say, "It takes as long as it takes." To which I add that this can happen when we get fed up enough to be willing to question and let go of the known that is no longer working for us. It is our very clinging that obscures and hides That which we are looking for—true peace of mind and inner harmony.

# Beyond Hope

During last evening's discussion following meditation and Dharma talk, I had referred to being 'beyond hope' in response to a comment made. Someone said that for him hope was very important, that it was a looking up that came out of his practice. Another member later wrote me that it was hard for her to imagine a world without hope, that "hope is part of the human condition... and we can't survive well without it..." These comments and the discussion around them have led me to reflect on the nature of hope in our lives. As always I am so grateful for these sharings for they help me clarify my own understanding. They help me formulate how the Life of Dharma is showing itself to me at this particular point in training.

For me, hope is a dangerous ally. It projects into the future, and this invariably and naturally is colored by what I want, what comforts me. The 'me' that is projecting can be decidedly wrong, and at one point in our interchange it came out so strongly how often in my long life I'd been disappointed. It was just the way it was because I wasn't seeing things—me, life—clearly, bound by the karmic past which colored everything. Trying to make something better that in looking back really didn't need 'fixing,' I'd end up frequently right back (from the inward point of view) where I started from. As someone wrote, "Wherever you go, there you are." To which he added, "and what are you going to do about it?" Hoping for the next good thing without looking at where you are simply doesn't work.

This is the problem, or so it certainly was in my life, of hope.

That "hope springs eternal in the human breast," as the thoughtful Sangha member had written me, doesn't mean to me anything more than that it is part of the karmic condition which propelled us all into this present life. Well, don't we each have our own understanding of words, such as 'hope'? I'm reminded of the Mad Hatter in *Alice in Wonderland* telling Alice that "words mean what I want them to mean, no more, no less." So, I'll go with words meaning what the dictionary says, no more, no less. The Oxford Dictionary defines hope as: "expectation and desire combined." Using this definition, we can see that we're spun around by hope through desire plus the confusion of expecting something that is hidden within the future.

After one of the first public talks I gave when still in Sidney, the first question or comment made by an older and obviously not well woman was that she couldn't imagine how she could be without attachment for her children, something like that. Attaching to people and things is also part of the human condition. As Sekito Kisen wrote in his enlightenment poem, "Here born we clutch at things and then compound delusion by following ideals." Attachment and hope are both challenged by those who embark upon the spiritual solution to the end of suffering. We are born in ignorance, which is the mistaken belief in a separate self within a world of separate others, as the Buddha states in his teaching on the conditional arising of a new being (Dependent Origination). Unresolved karmic energies propel this life where once again there is a search for security and wholeness. Because of these influences, impressed upon this conditioned body-mind we take as self, the whole array of hopes, fears, likes, dislikes, and such is reactivated. Holding onto the past by either yearning for or dreading its recurrence is our sad human predicament.

Now faith is another matter. Faith is the deeper knowing that everything is all right and is working out the way it should. And, of course, we certainly have a part in this working out. Our wonderful practice helps us ground ourselves in the present moment to look at what we're doing, *how* we're participating with life, with this grand karmic play in which we all are involved. We give ourselves the opportunity to see more clearly how we fall out of harmony when conditions arise that trigger the defilements of self-desire, frustration, and blurring confusion, to see how we are tugged and torn sporadically and relentlessly by the clutch of old beliefs, memories, and longing.

At that moment of seeing, in that 'wait a minute,' we ground ourselves in a trust of our willingness to change, to grow, to be in harmony with life. And though it may not seem so at the time, this makes possible the magical moment to turn, change directions, try something different. We're in the unknown to which our trusting but not foolish heart opens us. We are willing. For me this truly is 'beyond hope' because it isn't resting on some future outcome. It's here and now, grounded in the present. We are bringing our wonderful practice to shine on what is stirring the hope or fear *now*. This is do-able and worthy of all the energy, dedication, intelligence, and zeal we can muster to our aid. We examine this hope that springs up right now. This is the eternal present which is the very ground of our training. We move away from the general to the specific for it is in the latter that we have an opportunity to be beyond hope. This is the important inner work of the heart that has outward manifestations. The work is to free ourselves from the unsatisfactoriness of the activity of desire, anger, and confusion which are disturbers of the quiet peace of the secure heart. This is the freedom of Zen.

From this place, the place of wisdom, we then "Live in the world as if in the sky," as it is put at the very end of a Buddhist ordination ceremony. In this context this means that we don't discard the conventional ways of living. So as was pointed out in the discussion last evening, we say "I *hope* you have a nice day" or "I pray for your success." This conveys both our good wishes and implicitly our essential helplessness in seeing them fulfilled. It is based on the mundane or conventional reality to which we've been born and is expressed in the language we've learned. It would, it seems to me, be pretentious to be so exalted that we can't be human in this way.

However, the "deepest wisdom of the heart" is knowing that all this passing scene is "void, unstained, and pure." *We live in the world as if in the sky.* We are freeing ourselves from suffering by over and over again grounding ourselves in the Bigger Picture, awakening to the splendid freedom of our True Nature, Buddha-awakened Nature, in which Compassion, Love, and Wisdom naturally flow and embrace everything as it is right now. Then we "rest in our own essence": we've returned to our birthright, our oneness with the Wholeness that holds us all. We were born in ignorance that led us to look outwardly in search for the security that lies within. Here hope is abandoned. It doesn't come up because, as Robert Browning put it in all simplicity, "God's in His heaven, all's right with the world." Or as Julian of Norwich found, "All is well. All manner of things are well." And from this wondrous knowing we just naturally live right in the present moment wholly and sufficiently, and hence with no need for hope.

## Part of the Solution

We are all probably familiar with the question, "Do you want to be part of the problem or part of the solution?" It is another good way to express Right Understanding, which begins the Buddhist path of training, the Noble Eightfold Path. It also helps us understand Great Master Dogen's reference to the "Great Matter for which we train." Increasingly, as we understand the purpose for which we train, our answer to the question inevitably will be "Oh, please, let me be part of the solution." Why? Because we have grasped more deeply the basic truth that our actions have *consequences.* And those consequences, according to the karmic law, are "inevitable and inextricable." This is a sobering reminder about the necessity to bring our dedicated practice into the very situations that trigger old reactive behavior. The full potential of old karmic tendencies to explode again into behavior expressing greed, hate, and delusion may be looked at from the point of view of Right Understanding. We can then *pause* before, so temptingly, falling into old behavior.

When all conditions ripen we can use this understanding to avoid old reactive patterns. In other words, our training, the dedication of our true practice, allows us to strengthen *new,* also latent, tendencies. We can listen in the purity of that simple pausing to ask for help, recognizing the danger of falling into the three defilements that obscure the very Truth, our Buddha Nature, for which we are doing the practice in the first place. The Buddha talks about *restraint* because when the defilements get heated, their power may seem undefeatable, and that is simply not so. As Reverend Master reminds us, our practice is to "stand against the world [of the conditioned mind] in order to train in wisdom." This is the wonderful teaching that can help us whenever we are faced with painful conditions that life assuredly brings to us all.

We are given the opportunity to *choose* to be part of the solution instead. How can we do this? We can do this by building on our growing recognition of little self's maneuvers and vulnerability. We allow ourselves to be honest with the inner tension we experience. As we do, we are also able to observe how it weakens through our practice. We have to *use* our wisdom faculty in the present moment. Is that easy? No! We are doing the most difficult thing in the world when we sincerely embark on the inner journey of the Heart, the Unconditioned, the Unborn—the very *truth* of who we are. This can be the ground that sustains us whenever we are tempted to be part of the problem.

It is very important to be really honest with ourselves. At times, the defilements are only a *whisper,* subtle and beguiling. Mara, a personification of the whole karmic load, has an 'army' of ten forces, which include craving, aversion, laziness, and fear. A reminder of Mara's power is clearly shown in statues of the Buddha in the earth-witness position where the right hand is pointed down to the earth whilst the left hand is in the meditation position. This symbolizes the Buddha's resolve that "as the earth is my witness, I shall not move." His merit was so great that in one night he attained enlightenment. But the *training* that gave rise to this magnificent achievement is open to all of us. It is a chipping away at our karmic tendencies. It is not necessarily dramatic at all. We can figuratively place our right hand, our *right intention,* to touch the ground of our *Buddha Nature,* which has been hidden and obscured in the intensity of *this* moment. Each time we turn in simple faith to pause, look within, and ask for help, we give ourselves once again the golden opportunity *to be part of the solution.* At the moment it may not seem like much, but we are gradually, little by little, freeing ourselves from suffering. We make true for ourselves the Buddha's Truth and, as Great Master Keizan put it, become dutiful children of Buddha. This is worth every effort and is open to us all. It's just up to us!

# Endless Training

A concern was raised in our group discussion about the teaching that training is endless, that it keeps going through periods of darkness, yielding to places of ease. It is the excellence of training that allows us to be increasingly aware of the dance of our inner life. Reverend Master referred to this as "going in and out." In a famous mondo [dialogue between master and disciple] Dogen mentioned how the master said to his questioning student, "Sometimes I make the eyes of old Shakyamuni blink and sometimes I do not. Sometimes it is good to do so and sometimes it is not." This led to the awakening of the student who was so ready to hear the teaching in just that way. As always, it is helpful to have these basic teachings raised afresh as a trainee deepens his/her understanding in which the seemingly obvious is stumbled upon as we move to a deeper understanding.

When, perhaps in a less subtle way, I was asking about the same thing, my great teacher wrote to me that "Life is movement; life is going from here to there." We could also say, don't get stuck, just keep going, which is what Reverend Master was told when questioning or wanting to hold onto a particular experience in her meditation. "Just keep going" is what is taught in the *Heart Sutra,* the basic Buddhist teachings: "Oh Buddha, going, going, going on, and always going on beyond, always becoming Buddha. Hail!" The "hail" can mean "How wonderful is this great promise given by the Awakened One!" In other words, to view 'endless training' as something negative and profoundly discouraging is just another point of view of the conditioned mind of limitation, in essence not different from any other mental state that has arisen. We could say it is just another maneuver of Mara (the personification of temptation) to lure us off the enhancing, wonderful Path to the end of suffering. That it comes up is not a problem. As always, our opportunity is to learn and let go, thus freeing ourselves from the mind of opposites.

Dogen's teaching in "Uji" reminds us that "Arrival is impeded by arrival." Do we really want to *end* the Journey? Reverend Master taught that "Heaven is the most dangerous place" because we fall into "quietism." That is *not* the "peace/harmony that surpasseth all understanding." Instead, it can be a narcotic that keeps us asleep, an addiction that we all share, to a greater or lesser degree, by being in this conditioned mind. We 'want' a fabrication that has been concocted by our mind about what 'real' peace is. The Reality is bigger than that. As the *Heart Sutra* points out, it is "going on beyond this human mind (that) is Nirvana." Any 'idea,' we need to remind ourselves, is a product of this human mind that we are converting into Buddha Mind through our practice. Any idea is just another movement to let go of, learning whatever it has to teach. Just that, dear friends, we don't have to be stuck along the way, and Mara will always be ready to tempt us into sidetracking the endless and inspiring work of our spiritual life. It is up to us to keep going, and with time, more and more we relish the movement itself. The life of training is a joyous opening to the Eternal, the Divine, to Buddha Nature. *How* can That be limited to our little ideas of how it 'should' or 'shouldn't' be?

We are taught in the Eastern mystical traditions about inactivity and activity: there is activity within stillness, and also stillness within activity. There *is* an Unborn, Undying, Unchanging. The Buddha assured us of this in an early discourse. It is our birthright. Our sincere spiritual practice points us to the Source we've lost touch with. A sense of longing for Something that is our true Refuge is the great prod for our inner work, and it won't let us down. The great teaching then is that *All* is a manifestation of the Uncreated Unborn. That we have lost touch with this Truth gives rise to the karmic dance of life. We come to understand that life's true purpose is to reharmonize with that Truth of Oneness, finding for ourselves that we never have been lost or separated from It even for a moment. This boggles the limited mind perhaps, whilst still there is an inner *knowing* that resonates with It. As T. S. Elliot wrote, "In the center, the still-point, is the dance. And there is only the dance." *How* we dance with the Eternal is the question—not that we *do* dance. We learn humility by stumbling through the karmic consequences of unsatisfactoriness *and* we develop the courage to try new steps. *This* is the ongoing training. Training and enlightenment are indeed one, as teaches Dogen.

The Buddha's promise is that our very life right now can be more peaceful, harmonious, and joyous. It doesn't *stop* being Life because we're training. We are always moving towards enhancing this precious gift of life through the particular circumstances that we have been given. Our very life becomes the Life of Buddha by our willingness to keep training whether things appear to be going our way or not. Again, as Dogen wrote in "Shoji," *When the Buddha does all and we follow this doing effortlessly and without worrying about it, we gain freedom from suffering and become ourselves Buddha*. So, that's it, folks! It has nothing to do with escaping life to reach some ideal of what the end of training would be like. Rather, it is *how* we live each moment of our life: are we inclining toward Nirvana or toward unsatisfactoriness? We take the opportunity to *choose* moving to a higher and higher level simply because we are *willing* to *go on*. What a promise! What fulfillment, right here, right now!

# Rewriting the Script

The Buddha's teaching of Dependent Origination is based on his experience of past lives and how the law of karma—cause and effect—influences the present body-mind which, before spiritual practice, we take as 'self,' as who we are. In this life we can simply play out once again this program based upon an enormous bulk of experience. We fail to recognize that we're acting out an old script, a play with alternative themes repetitively appearing depending upon the circumstances confronting us. With a growing spiritual understanding we truly have the opportunity to put away childish things. Being a spiritual adult means just that, taking responsibility for our self at the present time. In order to really do this, we must come to the right understanding that our ways of being in the world are built on assumptions and premises, deeply seated beliefs, that need to be examined. Only then can we see which parts of the old story we're living out are no longer helpful or even appropriate, and that they are indeed changeable.

Rewriting our lives is one way we can look at the dynamics of our spiritual practice because, as the Buddha described it, he simply teaches us to "see the way things are." We don't even know much of the time we're looking through story lines from the past, which obscure our true seeing of the present moment. Hence, we repeat the old stories that are played about in our head without really recognizing that they have something to do with the unsatisfactoriness we experience. We have to be willing to *stop and see.* Then we have the opportunity to change the play, change our part. This is very powerful and can be difficult to comprehend whilst caught up in the current drama. My Master referred to this as "soap opera" in which characters seem trapped in given roles that create tension, seeming resolution, followed by a new variation of tension, over and over again. We have to get an inkling of how this happens in our own lives before we can do the work of changing the script.

We resist seeing this because we're then confronted with the awesome task of trying out a new role, new speech, new action. In a sense, we need to begin experimenting. This takes considerable faith and courage because we can only change *our* part in life's drama: we don't have control over the other actors in our play. Of course, from our point of view we always have the leading role! What is our capacity to interact differently? We won't know until we're willing to try something different. This can be frightening. We risk *failing,* seeming *foolish,* even *silly.* Maybe those important figures in our play will be indignant and not understand our true need to experiment, to find new ways to stretch and grow. We shrink back and can be discouraged when appreciation doesn't greet our tentative efforts to write a new part. But once we see that we are repetitively playing out variations on the karmic theme and that it is our purpose in life to resolve these, then we can muster the determination and strength to *keep at it,* to keep going.

We can be *willing to learn* what this present moment is teaching. Right now, we can do this important work of exploring, correcting, and rediscovering who we are. All these roles we've been cast in are hiding our true Self. We are called to be brave, be innovative, and be willing to challenge the old conservative 'me' who is so limited.

The work of the heart is the vibrant journey home—it's just a little shift in understanding, a slightly different point of view through which we can view the picture. It need not be static or fixed. To live within the Flow of Immaculacy, as Reverend Master called It, is to live Eternal life. As one Zen master taught, "Eternity in the moment—this is the only important practice." Another master put it this way: "When small mind finds its proper place within Big Mind, then there is peace." And my Master would tell us the importance of cultivating a kaleidoscopic mind that can embrace change and not be stuck simply in old habitual patterns. She referred to living this way as being magnificent because we open and open to a far greater picture than the old fixed stories could ever reveal.

# Nothing Is Enough!

We are told in Buddhism *to make the Truth one with ourselves.* This Truth has many facets, and "nothing is enough" expresses one of them. This is sometimes phrased as "desire builds on desire," that it is insatiable. Shakespeare put it bluntly in one of his sonnets: "The expense of spirit in a waste of shame/ Is lust in action/ Enjoy'd no sooner but despised straight/ A bliss in proof, and proved, a very woe/ Before, a joy proposed; behind a dream." And he ends with, "All this the world well knows; yet none knows well/ To shun the heaven that leads men to this hell." Of course, he's taking the extreme position here regarding the nature of desire or craving. The Buddha lumps it all under the poison or defilement of *greed,* which when frustrated or disappointed leads to the poison of *hatred.* Both have their origin in *delusion, ignorance,* the essential poison that sets the Samsaric wheel of birth and death rolling. And, as Shakespeare noted, in the extreme of lust or addictive desire, all know this well whilst to shun this heaven that leads to hell is a repeated challenge.

For those of us embarked on a spiritual practice our desires may be more under control, and we have to use our clear-eyed training to catch the less extreme forms of desire and to see their similarity to Shakespeare's pointed description. Rabindranath Tagore, the Bengali poet who wrote about his spiritual growth in *Gitanjali,* is easier, I think, for us to relate to our own lives: "My desires are many and my cry is pitiful, but ever didst thou save me by hard refusals... saving me from perils of weak, uncertain desire." In another *Song* he expressed: "Obstinate are the trammels, but my heart aches when I try to break them." These are eloquent expressions of the Buddha's Truth that the cause of suffering is attachment, grasping and clinging to aspects of our lives that are impermanent. To make this true for ourselves requires the cultivation and refinement of our practice of awareness/ attentiveness in order to observe how the process works in our own lives. As a distant, intellectual understanding it will never *take us to the Other Shore,* to that peace and inner sense of being fulfilled, unneedy. We have to *see* increasingly into the nature of our drives, our motivations and where they are frustrated.

Human nature generally doesn't pay a lot of attention to the satisfactions that are forthcoming for very long. We often take things for granted and restlessly move on to something else. Or we become lulled into 'losing ourselves' in a book, in music, in alcohol, or whatever, the very nature of which requires repetitions that can become addictive, even though not all addictions are debilitating ones. What it all amounts to is that we're not at home, comfortable, with ourselves and so immerse ourselves in busyness and distractions to escape just be-ing. The value and challenge of our spiritual practice are that we are willing to counter this strong tendency and confront the very core of the problem: our greeds, hates, and delusions. We are willing simply to *be* with whatever arises at any given moment of time, allowing it to tell its story and then *letting it go.* We have to *see* where we are caught in sense desire, irritation, lethargy, restlessness, or doubt [the five hindrances that block our knowing the Truth] before we can simply let go and relax, just being with our fragmented self and allowing the Eternal to embrace it, right here, right now. It is *so simple* and a gigantic challenge because it confronts the basic delusion over and over again—the delusion that *we* are those movements of body-mind that simply ebb and flow.

This is indeed a chipping away at the old karmic tendencies that drive us by the implicit belief or assumption that the external world can satisfy the deepest longing of our heart. We're pulled, we yearn, and we want in an endless parade of "what's next," searching for true satisfaction. As Tagore wrote at the end of one of his Songs: "My debts are large, my failures great, my shame secret and heavy; yet when I come to ask for my good, I quake in fear lest my prayer be granted." *And* we learn to allow all of that to arise, including that naked fear of the Unknown, without flinching too much, willing to just "sit" with the heaviness of 'me.' This is our part and, on its own time, that which is a grace can fall upon us. A profound and quiet shift occurs and where *nothing* was enough, we find that nothing *is* enough. We don't 'need' anything. Adequate and secure, we're embraced within Buddha Nature. This freedom can't be bought; it comes when "all conditions ripen." We do our part by our willingness to hold fast to our faith, our knowing that these shadows or clouds will inevitably pass. The miracle of training, for me, is to keep finding true for myself that Nothing is enough. All that uneasy neediness that drove me for much of my life can rest in the fullness of the Eternal. It is not something that can be understood intellectually or figured out, but again it is a miracle that simply being with Life is truly *enough*. And for this present moment I flow with

Life, open to experience more fully and ready to move from the wonderful clarity without expectation for self-gratification. This is the freedom of Zen.

# Building a Temple

A visiting monk talked about a request he received to offer meditation in a nearby prison, which he had turned down. Explaining his decision he said, "I'm building a temple," which is literally what he and the monks at his temple were doing. He had his priorities very clear—right now he was building a temple. Another monk once commented that "You can't have it all," when he too recognized that his call was to develop a retreat center and not a city priory. We can't do everything. Coming to terms with this realistically with the intelligent eye of training can be an important reminder about what is truly meaningful for us at this point in our life. We can apply this teaching both to our long-term goals and minute by minute choices.

Each one of us also is building a temple whether we're in a monastery or not. At times this body is referred to as a temple, the Heart being the inner shrine we're protecting, nourishing, and cherishing. The Truth of our being lies beneath the surface phenomena that demand and attract our attention. Getting too caught up in the life drama each of us is playing is the karmic blindness we've inherited that brings suffering and unsatisfactoriness. We take the outer show for the whole thing, worrying about the many circumstances (inner and external) that have such impact as we move through one event and then the next. Until we learn how to slow down and step back, we're at the mercy of the karmic swing from pleasant and unpleasant experiences as they impact this body-mind, which we implicitly have taken as 'me,' my 'self.' Those of us who are dedicated to a spiritual solution to end life's unsatisfactoriness come to know more and more the folly of living simply on life's surface whether it is momentarily pleasant or not, good or not.

Then we know we must tenderly look to the inner Source beneath the play. What is it? Where is it? The longing for meaning, for security, for unconditional love is our response to Its call. We begin to see with greater and greater clarity how turning to That allows us to make more wholesome, more 'educated' choices. Clarity then throws quiet light on the consequences of our actions, and we see that creating suffering for self and others by how we think, speak, and act have sad ripple effects that can truly haunt us. This is the realm of humility and repentance for the harm we've done. It is the development of wisdom. The Heart glows with a fierce light and then a gentle softness, helping the moulding of Its outer expression. Our temple is not made from bricks and wood and concrete. It is made from the careful, yet carefree, choices that freely give to others and refuse to be limited by mere convention and fear. The Love that holds us all in a dear embrace is far bigger than we know and it is the closest, most intimate friend that never lets us down. Our privilege is to increasingly recognize It and live by It.

How do we build the temple of our heart? It is so simple: *we keep going,* dedicated and sincere in our willingness to train this body-mind, moving from the conditioned known to that vast Unknown which gives to each of us the inner light of pure awareness. As Sekito Kisen conveyed in his enlightenment poem, "As you go on, distinctions between near and far are lost. And if you lost become, there will arise obstructing mountains and great rivers. This I offer to the seeker of Great Truth: do not waste time." Dogen also assures us at the end of "Rules for Meditation" that "If you do these things for some time, you will become as herein described and the Treasure House will open naturally and you will enjoy it fully."

These teachings grow in meaning as we do the training for ourselves. And moments of delight pierce through the darkness of our delusion—"Oh, *this* is what that means." We are making the Buddha's Truth one with ourselves and increasingly bow in gratitude and wonder at Its depth and clarity. Friends, as we continue our sincere practice, right understanding blossoms into wisdom that brings light to the obscurations we are more and more willing to work with. It's all laid out for us. It is emphasized in our tradition that we are most fortunate to have been born in this human body with sufficient intelligence, energy, and zeal to appreciate the Buddha's teaching after having been exposed to it. Right now we have *everything* going for us. Right now we can take Refuge in the Buddha, Refuge in the Dharma, Refuge in the Sangha. These are riches that do not decay with time.

The Three Refuges are enduring and offer us a choice over and over again, beckoning to us to keep up our spiritual practice whatever else is happening in our lives. And we come to appreciate how suffering in our lives has lessened while a contented peace is more often present. Dogen's promise to us that our willingness to practice is "simply the lawful gateway to carefree peace." Every time we touch that exquisite peace that surpasses all understanding, gratitude, and joy are with us and we experience our Oneness with all Life. Then we truly know deep within our heart that the important thing is to *just keep going,* doing the very best we can. Through our ongoing choices, we are gradually, little by little, creating a fearless temple of the heart that becomes a shelter for both ourselves and for all those we touch.

# It Isn't Going to Go Away

"It isn't going to go away" has been going through my mind of late, an important reminder of the First Noble Truth. There is an essential *insufficiency* with respect to life when lived without a Right Understanding of its nature. The latter is expressed very clearly in the Doctrine of Dependent Origination (also referred to as *the conditional arising of a new being*), and I find it helpful to remember different links because it is a way that reveals the problem *and* the solution. The twelve steps of the doctrine are often summed up as two when describing the cause of this insufficiency—Ignorance and Craving. Ignorance refers to the inherited karmic blind spots that propel a new life, a 'you' and a 'me,' in order that they may be resolved, or perhaps better put as *dissolved*. Why "dissolved"? Because as difficult as it is for us to wrap our karmic heads around, there really isn't any insufficiency, there really isn't a problem. *That's* the ignorance we begin with! And out of this sense of separateness from the great Truth of Oneness arises a belief in our implicit *self*-sufficiency, and we go around with a seeming need to have life conform to supporting this wrong view. And the merry-go-round of Samsara is perpetuated in this very precious present life through Ignorance and Craving.

This is really important to understand if we are ever to find the true security that lies hidden beneath the phenomena of appearance. Ignorance and craving are the product of this very body-mind [*nama-rupa*] through which we function and take as self. Even to consider, beneath the words themselves, the implications of this teaching is a challenge, and I suspect that many of us have to be confronted with innumerable experiences of the insufficiency of living from the surface before we finally turn with humility to delve beneath and genuinely look at what is going on. The Buddha said clearly that whether Buddhas appear in the world or not, the Truth, the Dharma, exists. This means to me that though it may be convenient to be labeled a Buddhist for simplifying communication with others, it is also very misleading because we're *all* in the same boat. We're all playing out our own particular karmic themes of greed, hate, and delusion—or desire, anger, and confusion—over and over again experiencing their results: sometimes events of life seem to go our way—pleasant, agreeable, comforting, supporting—*and* sometimes they don't. Through ignorance and craving, we are thrown over and over again into struggling to make it all right without success, grasping and rejecting in the old way.

Those of us who are sincerely willing to go this far come to genuinely *know* that there is nothing else to do but keep up our dedicated training to *go beyond* the unsatisfactoriness, the insufficiency. Folks, we truly are like sitting ducks forgetting that we are exposed to the "slings and arrows of outrageous fortune" no matter how pleasant life may be at the moment. Why? Because as long as we *depend* upon some external set of circumstances to feel secure, the utter changeability of surface life threatens this false sense of safety. This is the big delusion: that something *out there* can really make everything all right for us. Over and over again, life after life, this major error is repeated, and by some miracle after many lessons, we understand in a profound enough way that it is only by examining our own heart that we'll ever get off this sorry round, this *saha* world. As Reverend Master would say, "It takes as long as it takes." And, hooray! We're on the Path of training that leads towards the end of this sense of futility, of vulnerability. As Reverend Master was taught, our practice is *to stand against the world of this conditioned mind in order to train in wisdom.* How could this be easy? How could anything be more worthwhile?

So here we are—*it isn't going to go away.* We're in this body-mind with all its sensitivity and reactivity. Our spiritual work is to keep chipping away at the blind spots, which prevent us from being at one with the Truth. By definition we don't see where we're blind: we don't see where we're attached and hanging onto that which may change at any moment. When impermanence hits in one of its innumerable forms that spin us around, the merit of our training allows us not to go so far off course as otherwise might be. It doesn't mean we don't experience this stuff. It is that we can more easily get back on course by deeply knowing that this very distress is offered as an opportunity to go beyond a blind spot. And we turn once again with renewed humility towards stillness and open to That which doesn't change. "Here there is no suffering..." The miracle of training reveals that there wasn't any insufficiency in the first place. Right within the heart there is an Island, as the Buddha referred to It, a place free from suffering where we don't attempt to grasp the changing turbulence which is Life. This sets us free to live more simply, more wholly, more serenely. We're better prepared for the next time we ruefully see, "Oh, it hasn't gone away" because we know more deeply that *this is what we're here for* and that it's just the way it is. "Oh Buddha, going, going, going on, and always going on beyond. Always becoming Buddha, Hail!"

# Anger is a Poison

A Sangha member noticed that she was experiencing a great deal of anger. As she had already resolved larger issues around this anger, she was now aware of how unimportant encounters could easily trigger anger within her, which then lingered, destroying her peace of mind. It's hard for the little conditioned mind/self to appreciate the gift of training represented here. We have to be willing to see how disruptive anger is to our lives before we embrace the right effort to change. Otherwise one just goes on and on falling into the same old grooves, thereby coarsening the gentle fibers of our heart. The mindfulness that sees this can then be used to investigate how these situations arise and how we truly can take charge of our lives. We must see the fall-out of the oh-so tempting expression of anger/annoyance/irritation for what it is—pain, pain, pain. The momentary satisfaction, if even that, is simply not worth the consequences that appear.

It is said that the Law of Karma is inexorable, that it is a law operating without a lawgiver, that the seed of the effect lies right within the cause. *Karma* is a Sanskrit word meaning action, particularly moral action, and *vipaka* is the fruit of the action. Loosely, in contemporary usage, *karma* includes both cause and effect. The operative principle here is that of *choice.* Through wise choices our spiritual practice blossoms. The choices we make day-by-day, moment-by-moment, are creating our future destiny, just as choices made in the past have molded who we are now. In

Buddhism the three defilements or poisons are greed, hate, and delusion—desire, anger, and confusion. All three participate in the mistakes leading to suffering and bring our attention to the unsatisfactoriness of life. When we act from the three defilements we further obscure the basic purity, our Buddha Nature. Thus we feel out of harmony and distressed, whether we recognize the connection of cause [our choice] and effect or not. The Sangha member who brought up her problem with anger *did* recognize the connection. The next step is to bring to bear our spiritual practice to convert it. Seeing clearly the karmic consequence of indulging in the anger that life conditions trigger, one has the golden opportunity to make different choices.

The steps are quite clear: first the seeing, then the slowing down, then choosing differently. Investigation, the examining of a specific situation in which anger was indulged, can help clarify where the triggers really are and can uncover some new options. Otherwise we stay in the same old groove, even while it is uncomfortable and unwanted. Such is the nature of the beast of self. Manjusri, the Bodhisattva of Wisdom, sits in stillness on the beast of self. This is a beautiful teaching of how meditation in the midst of conditions can help us make more wholesome, salutary choices. No one can do this inner work for us, and we pay the price over and over again when we let our conditioning rule us. The whole Noble Eightfold Path supports our resolve and we keep training: we practice in the midst of the conditions that come up in daily life—this *is* our training. The conditioned mind simply wants this unpleasant truth to go away and naively holds to the belief that life "should" be comfortable and predictable. We're all a little crazy here, echoing

Einstein's quote that a crazy person is one who keeps doing the same thing while expecting different results. My Master would ask how much suffering we need to endure before we're willing to change. Right Understanding of the purpose of this life gives strength to the trainee's resolve to put fire into the practice: we're here to cleanse the karmic residue not yet resolved, and we're drawn to those situations which will help us do that.

When all conditions ripen, latent tendencies are triggered. This is the consequence of past experience and expressed in terms of feelings. As it is a consequence of the past, we have no control over the arising, whether it is craving, anger, or terrible confusion in whatever their myriad forms. When we do our formal sitting practice, we have the excellent opportunity to see over and over again how we have *no control* over the thoughts, feelings, memories that appear. We can see and appreciate how we are pulled off-center by identifying with them and *choose* to let them go, returning to just sitting, just being. Bringing the cultivated light of our awareness into daily life is the key for spiritual growth. Greed, hate, and delusion transform into compassion, love, and wisdom through our spiritual practice. The consequence of not indulging in the poison *is* the transformation. We can't make that happen *and* our choice to truly live a Buddhist life sets up the conditions for change. We simply don't have to remain a victim of our past. Now is the time, and each moment brings the opportunity to grow into our very birthright of peace and harmony. Self-restraint is a necessity as we nurture and cultivate living the Three Pure Precepts. In the *Dhammapada* we're reminded that "The teaching is simple: cease from evil, do only good, purify the heart. This is the teaching of all the Buddhas." Evil refers to that which is unwholesome, that which brings suffering. Over and over again, we choose to practice our spiritual training within the challenges of life, taking the very situations which otherwise just trigger old ways as opportunities to train and grow. With this right view we can know along with Great Master Keizan that "Every day is a good day." That is the spiritual purpose of this present life.

## Resistance to Worry

During yesterday's group discussion the problem about worrying was brought up. You might say that worry comes as part of the package of being human with sufficient intelligence to remember the past and project into the future. Especially if we remember the Buddha's teaching about past lives being 'beginningless,' we can appreciate how imprinted upon this karmic body-mind are experiences which were traumatic and distressing. Whether they are recalled or not, they deeply influence our lives now and color the present with projections into the future where we want to avoid any and all of such untoward circumstances. This being for and against is the mind's dis-ease and is the nature of the conditioned body-mind that is our vehicle for training. With this right understanding firmly under our belt we can see the arising of worry as simply another aspect of mind needing to be trained.

We train with whatever conditions present themselves remembering that they are our opportunities to free ourselves from deep-seated patterns that have been triggered. The conditions that arise do not *cause* the pattern, in this case worry. It is good to remember this because it really highlights its conditioned nature. You could say that the whole teaching drops right into our lap when we recognize the present worry. Before training, ordinary mortals [as Bodhidharma called those living only on the surface of their lives] just get helplessly caught in the worry, tape-looping in imaginative projections and then the worried future becomes the present and plays itself out as feared or hoped for. It's hard to learn from these experiences without being willing to really *look* at what happened, the whole process. The purpose is to remember not to get so caught in the next worry-making episode that comes along. Even though we know that worry itself is not helpful, we can get caught in it *or* through our spiritual *discipline* we can step back from it. The latter allows us to shift out of worry mode to use our awareness to find if it is pointing to something that might be useful to deal with *in the present.* If it points us to some potentially helpful action then we can be grateful to have taken the time to notice and follow that step.

More often we'll probably just recognize two important characteristics of living: we simply don't know what the future has in store for us and we have very minimal control over it. This is simply *the way it is.* The sanity of our spiritual life allows us to live within these limitations. That is the bowing in acceptance. We're bowing to Life itself which is far bigger than anyone's ideas, wishes, beliefs, fears. Clearly by our willingness to stop resisting life we deepen our faith in ourselves and in Life itself. We learn to do this little by little by experiencing the pitfalls of carelessness and heedlessly sliding down old habitual roads, which includes the thinking cycle as well as overt behavior and speech. In other words, doing the very best we can becomes our default position and holds us on course, allowing us more often to keep coming back to the present moment. Worry arises. We use wise discernment to sense whether it is pointing to something it would be good to address now. If not appropriate, we tell ourselves 'wrong way' and firmly bring our attention back to the present. This is the important choice, based upon intelligent awareness, or wise discernment, that moves toward our freeing ourselves from suffering. This return to the present is the important choice we make based upon wise discernment. It frees us from suffering.

Then the worried-upon event happens. Because our whole practice is teaching us to be mindfully present by letting go of the past, we are more alert. No longer caught in old habit patterns, we are more able to respond appropriately. We have the opportunity to practice a bit of restraint when pulled by desire or irritation. And we quietly sense what it is good to do and can recognize that we really are doing the best we can. We can deepen our trust in the goodness of Life that extends far beyond what we want. We don't generally see the bigger picture whilst we can remember that whatever is happening didn't need to be just that way. What we can learn from this is that though we're either happy or not about the consequences, we don't have to get caught in that reactivity. And again when we have learned its lesson, then we make the helpful *choice to let go* instead of getting caught up in brooding or ruminating about it or indulging in glee about it. It was what it was, and we bring ourselves right back to the present moment and ask what is it good to do NOW.

We're learning to "live in the world as if in the sky. Just as the lotus blossom is not wetted by the water that surrounds it, the Mind is immaculate and beyond all dust. Let us bow to the Highest Lord," as it is given in the blessing verse at the very end of a Buddhist ordination ceremony. It's a promise to the new ordinee of the way training can take us gradually from the place of worry and doubt to letting our Buddha Nature shine on this little life of ours in which everything is working itself out. We're going beyond the human mind, which gets caught in the opposites and appreciating a security that can find contentment within this changing world in which this karmic life is playing itself out. This is to be found for ourselves. It's the Buddha's promise and we have everything going for us in our present situation. We don't need to stay stuck. Instead of fighting and resisting, we *choose* to enter the stream to grow the Lotus of our heart by cooperating with Life in faith and humility. In willingness we can learn from all experience whether it appears pleasant or not. Thus we keep resisting the worry that arises and it naturally weakens as we keep up our wonderful practice. Just that.

# Well, of Course!

"Well, of course" expresses a way of working with the conditioned mind when it is caught in old and distressing patterns. Over and over again, our practice of mindfulness and self-awareness reveals how, when conditions arise, they trigger certain feelings and thoughts—that is the nature of the conditioned mind. Our spiritual work is to free ourselves from taking these conditioned feelings, thoughts, and impulses as 'me' and 'mine,' which is the karmic inheritance based on confusion that naturally fuels desire and aversion. We find some feelings and thoughts pleasant, which in itself doesn't pose a problem, and some of them decidedly unpleasant, which we then want to get rid of as fast as possible. We are working to go beyond this human 'deadly duo' to find That which remains hidden as long as we are caught within the opposites of wanting and not wanting. We are warned repeatedly by the great teachers that this is the work required. Superficially considered, it doesn't seem like much because the words aren't complex or technical. Through our willingness to chip away at the unsatisfactoriness of our own lives, we ruefully discover that training the conditioned mind is the most difficult and challenging of all undertakings.

As we are willing to explore the mental habit patterns that arise, we become more acquainted with how this sense of 'me' accompanies them, which then may bring so much discomfort, dis-ease, fear, and insecurity. For a very long time we have used escape routes to short circuit their impact: favorite *habitual* ways of protecting ourselves from feeling distressed if at all possible. It is a brave and courageous act to begin to apply the antidote of meditation to these mental poisons, taking the middle path between indulging them or trying to get rid of them. This is the act of "just sitting, not trying to think (feel) and not trying not to think (feel). Just sitting with no deliberate thought." The "just sitting" outside of formal meditation becomes "just attending to the moment," just doing that which is good to do. We bring the mind back to a bare attention that is not daunted in viewing whatever has arisen. The Buddha described his teaching as just "Seeing the Way Things Are," and we develop a profound respect at its difficulty. Scaling Mount Everest is less challenging!

*Why* is it *so* difficult to see the way things are? Because it is not the way we want them to be, because immediately we bring an add-on of *self*-opinions, *self*-judgments, *self*-beliefs and get caught up in them. Hence, we don't see the way things are, but instead see through a karmic filter that colors our relationship with the world. Fear and other dis-eases of the mind arise out of this sense of separateness, and Life obliges us with the experiences that will bring them up. It's not on our time; it happens. When we stop resisting the way things are, we begin to touch our sense of helplessness. We come to gradually appreciate how we are *part* of a complexity that is effectively hidden by our maze of defense mechanisms and habitual ways of being in the world. In Tozan Ryokai's enlightenment poem, we find this line, "When all conditions ripen..." He's referring to the wondrous enlightened awareness that comes from our willingness to keep up the ongoing practice, but it is true in all situations that when conditions come together in a particular way, the conditioned mind will react. That is the nature of conditioning, isn't it?

This important right understanding gives depth to the title's teaching: *Well, OF COURSE.* We see that whatever we are experiencing is simply 'the way it is.' It isn't grandiose and far away. As the Buddha taught, his is a teaching for here and now, open to all of us with sufficient intelligence, energy, and dedication to keep exploring the great discovery of who we really are behind the fabricated self we're caught in. It's pretty obvious, but because of the basic delusion which characterizes these conditioned states, it's the most difficult of challenges to even begin not getting caught. We have to step back from the distressed feeling state, which is the *effort* of our ongoing practice whether in formal sitting or in daily life. At that point, we can remember *well, of course,* this is the very nature of the conditioned mind we're training. This allows us to pause before getting further caught up in the compelling story, allowing some breathing space to just observe the way things are before reacting.

Our willingness here can bring a salutary shift from the judgmental mind to the mind of compassion. Compassion for this fragmented tightness of anxiety or fear softens the feeling state, bringing a wholesome perspective which is the beginning of wisdom. Clarity penetrates the confusion and helps ease the tension. From this place, we ask, "What is it good to do now? What can I learn from this to take the next good step?" We ground ourselves in the right understanding that Life is not out to get us but to teach us to go beyond our current limitations. There *is* Something Greater of which we are a part and this is an opportunity to open to That. To go beyond the human mind in this way requires great faith in That, because it may not feel like we have a leg to stand on at such times. Then we grit our teeth in patient endurance to keep going, not giving up, indeed finding we can *look up* as a choice, chipping away and chipping away at those obscurations that hold us in bondage. "This is the very Truth, no falsehood here. This is *The Scripture of Great Wisdom.* Hear! O Buddha, going, going, going on, and always going on beyond. Always becoming Buddha, Hail!"

# When All Conditions Ripen

The title here is a line from Tozan Ryokai's enlightenment poem, *The Most Excellent Mirror, Samadhi:* "Avoid one-sided clinging: this is all the natural and superior Truth that does attach itself to no delusion or enlightenment. It calmly, clearly shows when all conditions ripen. When minute infinitesimally small becomes; when large it transcends all dimension, space. Even the slightest twitch will surely break the rhythm." Once again we have the most important teachings in a nutshell! Here, Tozan is referring to his enlightenment experience coming "when all conditions" were ripe. This is the earth-to-heaven kensho mentioned in Zen literature, which in an instant lets us experience the Other Shore, Nirvana, when one is not attached to either "delusion or enlightenment." This is the Great Matter for which we train, and the Buddha promises that all of us who are dedicated, energetic, and intelligent can find this Truth for ourselves. Actually, there is no other way because the Truth, Buddha Nature, is *our* truth, who we really are. It's obscured within by the conditioned mind, the judgmental mind, the karmic mind. Our efforts are to purify this mind from delusion, from the obscurations that brought each of us full tilt into this body-mind.

This is a lot to swallow at the beginning, as well as at those times when the doubting mind grabs us in its hold. Then we can ground ourselves in the basic practice itself. We use the awareness of the clouds to understand what's gotten in our way of peace, inner harmony and contentment. For me, virtually never having had much sense of inner peace, this was a tall order when I embarked on the religious life. Words like "God" or "divine" sort of repelled me, and I was really floundering in my own opinions and prejudices whilst still finally recognizing that maybe I could be wrong. That perhaps there *was something* more than this benighted 'me' thought it knew. Probably I couldn't have stated this even that clearly if asked; but then no one asked me. Happily the good karma came due that allowed me to persevere despite a thorny path of training the conditioned mind.

We come down to the nitty-gritty of our work by being willing to apply, really as a salve almost, our pure awareness to what is happening *now.* Some group members expressed discomfort with an important teaching translated as "sense of shame" and "holy fear." These don't go down well for most of us in our Western culture with the Christian emphasis on a judging God. And as was agreed, the words don't matter while it is *very* important to use the teaching they convey. What is that teaching? That when we act from a place of conditioned habits heedlessly and mindlessly, the potential for suffering follows. I say 'potential' because we all know that we can get away with a lot, without particularly noticing choice and consequence as we wend our way through a busy day. Instant karma, meaning being hit immediately by the consequence of an action, can provide instant learning! Though the latter is certainly not pleasant, it is salutary by the immediacy of the regret or remorse it brings. Our training, paradoxically perhaps, allows us more opportunities to see the truth right here.

This is where we can use Tozan's *when all conditions ripen* to understand the unsatisfactory results of an experience (rather than satisfactory, enlightening ones). For me it is a very useful way to open to Life's offerings, which stir up old karmic patterns that have gradually softened and become more subtle over the many years of training. By being willing to see these untoward events as opportunities to refine our lives, we can observe latent tendencies of desire and aversion that are no longer helpful or useful, that get in the way of our peace of mind. *This* we can see when we are willing to apply the antidote of training, of meditation in its broadest sense which is what *zazen* is referring to. And believe me, whatever we want to *call* it—holy fear is a *natural* consequence of this work. This is the heartfelt *I don't want to do that anymore, be that way anymore.* This allows the resolution of a particular episode of *sange* (repentance) which, as Dogen wrote, brings "freedom and immaculacy... purification and salvation, true conviction and *earnest endeavour...*" This is the truth we can see for ourselves by our willingness to face the karmic result of an action. Then it is important to "pick ourselves up, dust ourselves off, and *start all over again,*" as it is expressed in an old song. We have to let go of the luxury of blaming self, another, or the circumstances themselves and with firm resolve know *I can do better than that.* Strangely enough, in this lies the freedom of Zen.

# Perseverance

Last evening following meditation we listened to a recorded talk by an elder Dharma brother on the importance of persevering through difficult periods in one's life. In order to do this, he pointed out that we have to keep building on faith, meaning that an intellectual understanding alone would not carry one through episodes of grief, dismay, and anguish. Another key point was that as we do persevere by keeping up our daily training through both the pleasant and less pleasant times, we are gaining much merit like in a bank account that we conscientiously add to and thus can draw on when needed. This seemed a good talk for our Sangha because we are committed to an ongoing and dedicated spiritual practice: an important reminder not to be surprised that at times one may seem to be having more rather than less difficulty than prior to embarking on a meditative practice.

An excellent discussion followed the talk when someone almost apologetically said he respected what each monk gave but that he questioned that it had to be *this* hard, that it wasn't that way in his own experience. For others it seemed encouraging or an expression of what one had found true, and for another it was rather disheartening. I emphasized the importance of the going on and not to set ourselves up concerning the feeling tone of the experiences presented now or in the future. The point frequently made is that "You never know when old karma is going to come and hit you out of left field." We live in a world that is impermanent, which is so obvious it shouldn't need to be mentioned. However, the strong karmic tendencies that are being played repeatedly obscure this key characteristic of existence. Our training, looked at in one way, is really about learning how to embrace impermanence, which is the middle path between indulgence and rejection of whatever confronts us at the moment. In other words, we are prone to attach to the passing scene, wanting to hold onto the pleasant and to push away the unpleasant, over and over again.

Our deepening training is learning to drop beneath the passing scene and touch That which does not change. There is a stillness in the very midst of conditions, which is Buddha Nature, a true refuge—the Buddha Refuge. Because we have lost touch with our True Self, the place of oneness and harmony, we can find ourselves at the mercy of the buffeting of the karmic winds. Life is clearly set up to bring both comfortable times and less comfortable ones. These can be of the mildest sort or great hurricanes that could blow us over. From the point of view of right understanding, which we can fall back on again and again, it doesn't matter. Why? Because the true purpose of this life is to return to the Source we've lost touch with and, therefore, we need to see where we are shaken and out of harmony with ourselves. If these times don't come up, we're either living out super-fortunate karma from the past or simply cruising along a dangerous course of heedlessness. *Wherever we are attaching to that which is unreliable and unstable, the potential for suffering is looming*. This is, of course, a statement of the Second Noble Truth that *the* cause of suffering is attachment. More and more as we are willing to keep up our inner work of the heart, this Truth is penetrated—it is just the way it is.

For a Buddhist, this is not a 'downer' because we are perfecting the Buddhist tools of mindfulness and investigation, the first and second *factors of enlightenment.* We keep bringing to bear our willingness not to succumb to the karmic waves, which are experienced as feelings that can seem so real and can obscure a bigger picture. We learn how to release our identification with them by remembering that they are to be respected as valuable teachers showing us where our spiritual work needs to be addressed. Caught in the whirlwind of feelings, we find our practice truly can take hold: we step back and observe our feelings. We don't have to indulge them or reject them. We can ask in humility, what can I learn from all of this? Anyone who is sincere in practice knows how very challenging it is to find that firmer ground. The discipline of faith takes us there, when we are patient and willing. Dropping beneath the surge of emotions and thoughts, we simply persevere because we have the deeper knowing from past experience that this too will pass, that there is—to quote the Buddha—"Nothing we need hold onto and nothing we need push away." Life is a flow, a movement, in which the light and dark dance together.

This certainly doesn't mean that being in the dark, feeling puzzled, perhaps scared and desolate is in any way fun. We're not trying to fool ourselves, which is simply another aspect of the confusion that is stirred up in such times. But again, as the main point of the evening's talk, the important thing is that we persevere, we continue our training, and we keep up our willingness to be still within whatever has arisen. We open to it and ask, "what can I learn from this which is so troubling?" Besides whatever the specific situation can teach, we learn two more general things: how to relax our resistance to simply feeling whatever has arisen and thereby see directly for ourselves how transient feelings/thoughts are. One way or another they aren't going to last. We are confronted directly with the fact of impermanence. And, again as was mentioned in the talk, there is a tremendous sense of gratitude with the freedom that letting go naturally brings. It is all a process, dear friends. Reverend Master talked about the Flow of Immaculacy and, when we are at one with That, we just know with Julian of Norwich that "All is well; all manner of things are well." We'd never appreciate this solid ground if it weren't for the floundering and shakiness that are part of our karmic inheritance. And, although it wasn't mentioned in the talk, it is fitting that just before hearing it, we chanted *The Scripture of Great Wisdom* which ends with, "O Buddha, going, going, going on, and always going on beyond, always becoming Buddha, Hail! Hail! Hail!"

# Searching for Meaning

Last evening's talk centered around man's concern for finding meaning in life. In the following discussion, someone began by pointing to the enigmatic statements found in *The Scripture of Great Wisdom:* "that the skandhas five were—as they are—in their self-nature—void, unstained and pure... Form is only pure; pure is all form. There is then nothing more than this... The same is also true of all sensation, thought, activity and consciousness." What can seem more palpable and 'real' than these five ways of experiencing this body-mind that accompanies us? These bodies, though in themselves lifeless, accompanied by the four aspects of mind—sensations, thoughts, actions, and our self-awareness of these experiences—have dominated our lives. Without reflection or examination they are taken to be real. We come to see, just as Socrates pointed out, that the "unexamined life is not worth living." The Buddha invites us to look beneath the surface, beyond the appearances that these five skandhas provide, so that our lives will have meaning and worth. In other words, there is *more* than appearances reveal and we must delve beneath the external to find true stability—a safe and secure refuge. We don't start out in life doing this but instead are propelled by past karmic patterns. Without consideration we trustingly place our refuge in this very insecure place, unthinkingly and repeatedly operating from old habits. As Einstein noted in his definition of a crazy person, we keep doing the same thing while expecting different results. A willingness to just pause a little and look beneath the surface will expose this pattern in our own lives.

Can we really accept that life on the level of its form or observable shape is not a good refuge because of its utter unreliability? For many of us, it's the hard knocks life hits us with that can bring us up short so that we at least *begin* to question some of the basic premises we've been living by. Heaven is said to be the most dangerous place because it is one of seemingly unending gratification, providing what the heavenly being desires over a long period of time. Yet it is insidiously dangerous because no matter how long it lasts, there is the inevitability of impermanence: the good karma, as with a saving account, becomes exhausted because these beings forget. What do they forget? That they're not immortal, that their very indulgence in pleasure weakens them. They are losing their spiritual muscle through lack of use, and they will be ill prepared for the shock of changing conditions when these are no longer what they want. In some depictions of the Wheel of Life, the demon realm comes after heaven showing the demons attempting to climb a ladder back into heaven. They're attempting to 'storm heaven' whilst being fended off by the devas [heavenly beings] so that they can't climb back in by force.

One way to view the six realms of existence is how we experience life right now as well as destinations for a future life. While the asuras or demons are said to be delusional as their predominant defilement, devas or heavenly beings focus on greed. When we demand that life be a certain way, insist on that (attempt to storm heaven), we are caught in a painful course of taking the unreal as real. Why? Because we are using our energies to refuse to see things as they are. We're fighting the seemingly good fight against a more powerful 'opponent'—the Truth or Reality which must be accepted and will not bend to fit our limited views of how it 'should' be. So the First Law of the Universe points out that "The universe is not answerable to our wishes." This is so obvious and yet a challenge to remember as we are living immersed in this *saha* world of impermanence.

So what can we do? Where can we go? If we have followed the above carefully, it's pretty clear we have to give up the delusion that has been ruling us. This right understanding must become the very ground on which we firmly stand, and then we must have the patience and fortitude to maintain the direction that will deliver us. The Buddha's last words as given in the earliest tradition were "All that arises passes away. Work out your salvation with diligence." Our 'salvation' lies beneath the surface show that arises and then passes. As Dogen wrote, we must "Look within and advance directly along the road that leads to the Mind." When life throws up its challenges, which it will inevitably do, over and over again, we have a big choice to make: will we believe in the impermanent show our senses reveal or will we hold to a deepening faith and knowing that beneath this surface play lies the Truth for us to uncover? In the Katha Upanishads it's put this way: There are two paths, the path of pleasure and the path of joy. The path of pleasure appears so inviting and alluring that the unsuspecting traveler wanders along until coming to hidden pitfalls, thorns, and glaciers that catch them. Now the other path, that of joy, doesn't look inviting at the beginning, being rather austere and without frills, but further along there are delightful pastures and beautiful rivers, flowers and birds. The first path is that of indulgence in pleasure and ambition; the second is that of self-restraint that looks for something more enduring and sustaining than momentary gratification.

When we *really* see these choices clearly, then we simply know that whatever the obstacles, "There is only one thing, to train hard for this is true enlightenment." We are willing more and more to "train for training's sake," to "train in Buddhism for the sake of Buddhism," or as it used to be said at the Abbey, "Once you've seen a ghost you can't pretend you haven't." What is it that we have seen? What is the 'ghost'? It is that the surface appearance—the outer show we get caught up in with both its pleasant and unpleasant aspects—is simply not the true Refuge. The true Refuge lies beneath, above, beyond all of that. Over and over again, Life will keep reminding us of the imperative to go beyond the show, captivating as it is, and keep the good faith to burrow deeper into That which is calling us. This is the big karmic gift we've all been given in this life—to have heard and to keep hearing that Call of the heart. As the last lines of *The Scripture of Great Wisdom* remind us: "O Buddha, going, going, going on, and always going on beyond. Always becoming Buddha. Hail!" We must just keep going, taking one step at a time, listening beneath the surface noise as best we can, learning whatever we can from life's offerings, and always being willing in good faith to let go and go on. And as we go on, our lives are just naturally meaningful and significant—that's just the way it is!

# Self-Esteem

In the discussion following a Dharma talk, one of the participants asked about the Buddha's teaching around self-esteem, mentioning that in Tibetan society there seems to be no such issue. This question led to a fruitful discussion coming out of the excellence of spiritual effort shown in our wonderful Dharma-Sangha. It is important to mention that in a Western society of competitiveness with its encouragement to 'get ahead' and be productive, the ground is fertile for the growing of a self that gets its worth in comparison to others. Then we're dependent upon conditions to feel 'good' about ourselves. As with other personality traits this too is on a continuum reliant upon conditions. A useful observation was made about how being in a nurturing environment where one is loved and valued helps enormously to have confidence in our own lovableness. This kind of background, whether received as a child, in a fortunate marriage or whatever, certainly gives support to living a more satisfactory life within the challenges that every one of us will face. And still, I can't imagine *anyone* when confronted with the 'right' conditions whose self-esteem wouldn't be shaken.

Looking at life in this way can help us not to be so enamored by another's seeming impregnability or position. This is a right understanding—we all have conditioned patterns with both superficial and hidden aspects, which our life experiences will reveal thus allowing us an opportunity to change in wholesome ways. If we don't see them, aren't aware, then we stay stuck. This is the status quo that has its costs and benefits. So when the issue of self-esteem comes up for us, our habitual reactions to certain situations can help us see how perhaps the benefit of being this way in these situations no longer is really satisfactory. We come to recognize that the cost of feeling inadequate, frightened, awkward is sufficiently great to motivate us to look to ways of changing ourselves. It can take a very long while to reach this right understanding. Many, certainly this was true for me, look to outward solutions to feel better. Mine was changing jobs in a compulsive sort of way every two or three years in my professional life. That seems so sadly delusional now. In school, as an achiever, I would work hard to receive good grades and go for the next degree, all the way through a post-doctorate in clinical psychology and outwardly successful positions that followed. It just didn't work in the long run because I couldn't run away from my 'self'!

One influential teacher commented that "the same old person comes telling the same old lies and we believe them." This is a down-to-earth observation of the problem we face with 'self'-esteem—we're looking outwardly to assure ourselves of our worth, whilst never fully believing in ourselves. So how can any external manifestation of regard and praise, whatever its form, effectively challenge this deeply held conviction? It's a poignant problem, really, because it's very difficult to penetrate or soften this false belief and see it for what it is. This is one perspective on why at some point we look to a spiritual solution in our search for feeling better about ourselves. Somehow we come to sense that the 'problem' is not *out there* and that without looking more deeply into our lives, we'll keep missing how to move out of the sense of inadequacy.

Not everybody will be drawn to meditating and that very word may put many off. However, until someone is willing to see how important it is to develop and sustain an awareness of how they are living their lives and be challenged to explore that, not much can change. And, of course, this *never* means that no external change be made: rather, it's that we can see more clearly where it is important to make changes and gain the courage to do this. In other words, we are willing to shake up the status quo, but from the point of view of a larger, deeper perspective. Then we are into truly solving the problem of self-esteem, the feeling of inadequacy, the attendant fear and clinging to the known. In other words, we have to be *willing* to see what's going on and recognize that making changes can be done, as well as developing the fortitude to do it.

During the discussion someone pointed out that he now recognizes that not *everyone* is always going to think he's so wonderful. Everybody laughed because we all recognize how much we do look for just that, for the indiscriminate reassurance that we *really* are all right, whatever that would mean. This we can explore and investigate. In other words, we look our insecurity right in the face by maintaining awareness when it arises. This allows a clarity that is otherwise clouded when we get caught in old reactive patterns. Relationships, as we all know, are the most challenging in triggering old habits of defensiveness, hurt, etc. So from the point of view of our spiritual growth into wholeness (holiness), we can use these very challenges as teachers that are helping us to overcome inner obstacles that otherwise remain obscure. This is an exceedingly helpful shift in our point of view that over time changes everything because *we* change. It is so simple—and also so threatening. That is just the way it is!

My Master would say that she didn't make the rules, she just told us about them. The Buddha described his teaching as *seeing the way things are.* Our human condition allows us the opportunity to learn and grow from the very experiences that make up our daily lives, whether pleasant or not. It's really not so difficult in the sense that we all have the 'equipment' to do this: the ability to use our awareness to focus on the 'way things are' both externally and internally *and* to make different choices from our habitual ones when that comes up as good to do. Thus, we are challenging old deeply engrained habits of body, speech, and mind. Self-esteem is expressed in the latter three ways and, of course, the most subtle is that of mind—our thoughts, perceptions, feelings, desires, and so forth. These are the activities we take as a 'me' that color *everything.* As the Buddha taught: "With our thoughts we create our world." The cultivated awareness that is meditation, mindfulness, heedfulness, attentiveness allows us to *see* this, to see the power of the mind to pull us down roads of suffering. Our job is to find the courage and strength to *pause* before going down old unsatisfactory roads. This allows us to learn what the whole experience (outer conditions and inner automatic reactivity) is teaching. Then we can use our human birthright to *choose* not to act in ways that we know don't work.

When the Buddha was asked about his teaching he said, "I teach just two things: about suffering and its *end.*" This a statement about the Four Noble Truths: the first insight being the first two Truths about suffering and its cause, and the second insight being the last two Truths concerning its end. We have been offered a great promise by the Awakened One along with an Ancient Path leading to the end of suffering. And he invites us to 'come and see' because this is an inner journey that each of us must make for ourselves. The very unsatisfactoriness of looking for our self-esteem within the unreliability and changeableness of the circumstances that come to us all of the time will, at some point, nudge or perhaps even force us to *look inward and advance directly along the road that leads to the Mind*. Then we see that what we've taken as 'me' and 'mine,' so easily threatened when not supported in ways that bring comfort and a sense of security, is *not who we are*.

The Journey to the heart reveals how much greater comfort and security come when we move beyond shadows, beyond these delusions, to touch and be embraced by That which is, by Buddha Nature/Mind. The wonder we realize is that we've always been supported and guided, that we always are and have been adequate in ways that the conditioned mind could *never* comprehend. Through our willingness to keep stepping into the unknown beyond our conditioned sense of adequacy or inadequacy, and stop grasping at conditions that will invariably change, we find true comfort in just be-ing, really knowing That. This is the miracle of training. We *can* go beyond the opposites, scary and unfathomable as that may sound. But it can only be done *now*, in this moment and then the next.

# An Indomitable Spirit

Yesterday I read about Wilma Rudolph's inspiring indomitable spirit. She was born into a very poor family in the South, the 20th of 22 children. A premature birth and subsequent frailty made it doubtful she'd even live. Then at age four she had two illnesses that left her left leg paralyzed and useless. She wore a heavy brace and was told by doctors that she wouldn't be able to walk. However, her mother told her that all she needed to do was to have faith, persistence, courage and an indomitable spirit. She said, "I believed my mother," which set her on her inspiring journey, starting about five years later when she chose to remove the heavy brace and learn to walk well without it. Then she had the astonishing notion that she could be the world's greatest runner. The account given doesn't give the time frame on all of what subsequently happened, but by high school she was entering every race and losing them as well. This must have been painful for others to see and they encouraged her to give up. After many failures, she didn't come in last anymore and finally she won a race. This remarkable fortitude was rewarded when she found a coach at her university who trained her and she was winning every race she entered. This culminated in her going to the Olympic Games held in Rome in 1960 where she won three gold medals, thus setting a record for a woman runner.

This magnificent woman displayed a quality of being that stirs in all of us. Her mother had told her that 'all you need to do is to have faith, persistence, and courage.' These are the ingredients of an indomitable spirit and, I believe, are abundantly available to all of us whether in dramatic ways or just in simple daily life. Although the short account of Wilma didn't talk about fear, desolation, doubt, and discouragement, I'll bet these very human traits popped up. That's when an *indomitable spirit* really manifests itself, not when one is simply breezing along in the successes. Until she won, she couldn't *know* that she would win despite her dedication, natural ability, and training. Hence, as her mother told her, she needed to have 'faith' and the determination to continue with courage. We aren't told what happened next for her after this Olympic victory, but life goes on. It goes on when one achieves one's long-cherished goal and it goes on when the journey isn't so clear. The qualities of deep faith, persistence, and courage that she cultivated are the truly precious victory, which has nothing to do with winning or losing. Whatever the rest of her life holds or held, these characteristics were there to support her and help her just go on. This is the real message of her life, which would only come to be elevated because she had the astonishing victory under great odds.

We, too, in all situations can cultivate the same qualities Wilma did. The indomitable spirit is right within the core of our being, *is* our being. It manifests out of our willingness to keep going in the face of both obstacles and successes. When the inevitable doubts and fears arise in our lives, that's the very time we need to bring to bear upon our life courage, faith, and commitment. This is the spiritual life and the true victory that surpasses winning any Olympic medal. When we dedicate our life to our spiritual growth, we over and over again must call upon the reserves we may not know we have of faith and courage simply to continue the journey. The goal becomes immediate—it is our training this day, this moment. There isn't someone we're competing against so there's no measure of how we're doing in the ordinary way. *That's* why faith, persistence, and courage are essential. No matter how much it may seem we flounder, we *can* return to the simple choice to keep going, keep training daily, hourly, by the minute. Our success is really more certain than Wilma's was when she faced the then-greatest, never before beaten runner of her day. Why? Because the indomitable spirit which is the will and willingness to train truly is far superior to little self's sense of inadequacy and insecurity. We are told "One calls, one answers." That's it—it's just up to us to *answer* the call of our True Self, the Eternal, our enlightened nature, over and over again, patiently, quietly, with that same remarkable persistence that this great runner displayed. That is really the *only* game worth playing and it is open to us all.

## The Importance of Bowing

"Buddhism will last as long as bowing lasts" expresses the "deepest wisdom of the Heart," and this morning it was with renewed appreciation that its profundity hit me. It seems to me that I first heard this spoken in my early days as a junior monk at Shasta Abbey—and I was anything but impressed! My own training was sorely tested, and I encountered much resistance to *bowing*. The body-mind inwardly protested to the insistence that we bow at the entrance of all public buildings in the monastery and even more to *all those bows* which accompanied services and ceremonies. "I" didn't want to do it, but something stronger, which I now recognize was the working out of karmic jangles, did bow because it was required to stay in the monastery. At least that much I never questioned, never tested; I complied. I bowed to the necessity of following the monastic structure at least to this extent.

Now my understanding has grown, both about my resistance and about the truth of the importance of bowing if Buddhism is to last. The fundamental Buddhist teaching is that of *sunyata* (emptiness) or *anatta* (not-self). The ramifications of this teaching were expressed in a multitude of ways by the Buddha in his 45-year ministry and through various teachers who followed in his footsteps. The brilliance of the Buddha's awakening as well as its wisdom can be appreciated more and more as we ourselves follow in his footsteps. Through our spiritual practice we can make the truth one with our selves. There is so much readily available information that it is easy to become side-tracked into believing that being exposed to all this is sufficient to knowing the truth. It's much harder and yet, paradoxically, simpler than that. As the Buddha taught, we must make the effort, and that effort is precisely bowing to our own ignorance, our need to go beyond all that we think we know.

This important point is conveyed in many different metaphors and similes. One is of a professor at an important university going to visit an acclaimed Zen master. The professor decides to show off his greater understanding by probing the master's. As is the custom, the master offers tea and the visitor holds out his cup. The master begins pouring but doesn't stop when the cup has been filled. The professor protests, spluttering that the tea is falling on the floor. The master replies, "Just so, when you come already full of your knowledge and opinions, there is no room for anything more." Hopefully, though I don't remember what followed, the arrogant professor 'got it' and was able to bow. This bow would be the offering up of what *he* knew in order to be a fit vessel for absorbing something different, something new.

*Buddhism will last as long as bowing lasts.* Physical bowing shows an inner attitude of mind that is willing to acknowledge deeply and sincerely an unknowing. "The Cloud of Unknowing" is a work by an unknown Christian mystic that expresses the very same teaching within the framework of Christianity. We get so caught up in words, such as 'Buddhist' and 'Christian,' that it is easy to get stuck in the idea that there is a fundamental difference. Tozan Ryokai wrote in his enlightenment poem, "... finally we grasp nothing for words inaccurate will be." The Truth is beyond language, beyond our conditioning, beyond our conventions and our culture. Our arrogance is hidden under a false security that we 'know' so much. I remember after I received my doctorate and had my first teaching position at a university. This went to my head, so to speak, filling me with a sense of knowing so much, feeling—for a very little while—so well equipped to move into the world 'out there.' In other words, it was kind of a cover for my insecurity, a perhaps necessary or at least useful persona in the transition from student to teacher. The flip side of the coin was that of a young colleague at the University of Manitoba who had just received his doctorate. Frequently he'd express his dismay by commenting, "it's unreal." Transitions can be like that.

By deepening our spiritual understanding we can follow a middle path between these two opposites when facing a new situation, beginning a career, embarking upon a different course: *we bow.* Our humility naturally comes up in a beneficial way if we let it, if we aren't led by a sad arrogance to 'muscle our way in.' In our tradition it is said, "It is hard to keep the initial humility to the end." We forget just how precarious an established situation really is; we take too much for granted when things seem to be going well. Rather than being an obstacle to advancement, our recognition of the necessity to bow in acceptance helps ground us in learning whatever life now presents us. Each day it is our job to hold up an empty begging bowl and let it be filled with whatever life offers for our nourishment. This is the emptiness of *sunyata,* of *anatta.* Through this important choice we become a partner with the Unborn, which opens us to a bigger picture. We're not alone, and we don't need to hold on to fear of what is coming next. This inward bowing is the living expression of Buddhist understanding that can be expressed in many ways. When it becomes our blood and bones, as Reverend Master would urge, we leave all those ideas behind and are, for that magical and mysterious time, part of the Flow of Immaculacy that goes beyond—period. This is "The merit of the Three Treasures [that] bears fruit whenever a trainee and the Buddha are one," as Dogen wrote in the *Shushogi.* Here is the fulfillment of our longing and we truly know *There is then nothing more than this,* as it is put in the *Scripture of Great Wisdom.* This conveys the sufficiency that depends on naught when we are willing to bow with all our heart.

# Eclipse

A frequent metaphor found in the literature uses the Sun and Moon to provide an understanding of the relationship between the Eternal, That which is, and Buddha Nature. Here, Buddha Nature refers to our Birthright of awareness that reflects the Totality, That which is shared with all life; It is the very Life essence shining on us all. Knowing this Truth removes all sorrow because it penetrates the appearance level in which we are living out our karmic inheritance. The very Source of life is within. Buddha Mind goes beyond the body-mind we take as who we are. This right understanding will move us toward looking for a spiritual solution to the unsatisfactoriness we experience. Without uncertainty, unreliability and insecurity, which everyone experiences at times, there would be no sense of anything lacking, needing to be corrected. And without some recognition that there must be Something *more* than all of us, we'd simply be stuck and helpless. So we need both: recognition of *dukkha* or unsatisfactoriness and, even if only vaguely, Something greater, which various traditions label differently: God, the Unmanifest, the Unborn, the Eternal, the Unconditioned, the Beloved, the Tao, and so on.

In the metaphor of Sun and Moon for the Eternal and Buddha Nature, the Earth that has no light of itself is this body-mind that has a birth and death. In an eclipse, the Earth to some degree comes between Sun and Moon, and to that degree it is darkened.

Likewise, the more this body-mind dominates us, the more hidden is the reflected light of Buddha Nature. When we see this clearly we then have the beginning of an earnest search to move beyond those shadows of unhappiness. In an obscure work attributed to Bodhidharma, we find this lovely teaching: "The Light of the Lord is everywhere. The palace of Buddha Nature is within ourselves. The deep true heart wants to go quickly so that their happy meeting can soon occur." "Wanting to go quickly" propels our spiritual *practice* to return to the Source. We have to truly see that this body-mind, this 'me,' is the source of our problems before we can address its solution. It can certainly seem like we're attempting to pull ourselves up by our own bootstraps. As one of my teachers put it, "We're using a thorn to remove a thorn." In other words, the instrument with which we train is what needs training! At the beginning of training this paradox arises AND we learn through practice how to move out of it. The 'Earth' *learns* how to get itself out of the way. This cannot be grasped by the conditioned mind.

As always, we have to come back to uncovering and deepening a faith that doesn't depend upon what we *think* we know or feel. Faith is there for all of us and is expressed in the Fifth Law of the Universe as, "Everyone has an innate knowledge of Buddha Nature." How could it be otherwise when It is the very Truth of who we are, our True Self? The yearning to be free of suffering arises out of this deep knowing, even though most of us flounder a lot before we can truly turn to It. Then we really are determined to get 'self' out of the way so that the "happy meeting can occur soon." Yes and Yes. This is the affirmative position of looking up and is a choice always open to us. Victor Frankl expressed it in *Man's Search for Meaning,* in which he reflected upon his experiences while in a Nazi concentration camp. Those who survived were those who could find meaning within the midst of intolerable and devastating suffering. They were those who believed in *something* more than what their prolonged immediate experiences revealed. The human spirit is celebrated not only by Frankl but in the lives of all of us.

The Buddha's third discourse is titled "The Fire Sermon" to convey the human predicament. Great Master Dogen wrote, "Train as if your hair were on fire." Right effort is the sixth factor of the Noble Eightfold Path to the end of suffering, and these teachings spur us to use the opportunity of *this* birth to move away from complacency and resistance to change. The great promise of Buddha is that we truly are the creators of our destiny, that our choices right now are vital and important, that "going on beyond the human mind" *is* Nirvana, our awakened Buddha Nature, the Truth that is beyond. Let's get moving, folks. I think all of us have a sense of how we *could* be doing better. Now is the time; there is no other. That is why one of the great Zen masters of the last century taught that, "Eternity in the moment is the only important *practice.*" Everyone knows this and most of us are very adept at letting it slip away more frequently than we want. The secret of the movement of the eclipse which is 'me' is meditation which allows more Light to be known. That is the 'medicine' the Buddha as physician prescribed for the suffering world. Over and over again, we can return to *this* moment, bringing our attention to right here, right now. Over and over again, we can let go of our preoccupations with past and future, choosing to "live now without evil," as Reverend Master wrote. And little by little this lump of earth, this conditioned self, moves out of the way.

"Forgoing self, the Universe grows I" is how this is expressed in "The Light of Asia." St. Francis put it this way: "And it is in dying [to self] that we are born into Eternal Life." Dogen refers to this letting go of 'me' in "Rules for Meditation" when he writes, "I myself have seen that the ability to die whilst sitting and standing, which transcends both peasant and sage, is obtained through the *power* of Serene Reflection Meditation." Thus the 'eclipse' may dissolve at that very moment. Again, as Dogen wrote, "When body-mind drop away naturally, the Buddha Mind will immediately manifest Itself," to which he adds, "If you want to find it quickly, you must start at once." That Light, dear friends, is *always here.* In confusion and pain this was eclipsed. The great, true, wonderful purpose of *this* birth, this 'you' and 'me,' is to be willing to use this instrument of body-mind to move beyond it. Then in the wonderful reflection of Buddha Nature we will see that there was nothing *wrong:* we were simply mistaken, caught in shadows and confusion. We truly can turn and turn "until by turning and turning we come around right," to quote an old Shaker song. It's just up to us!

# I Am Willing

Although I wasn't yet at the Abbey when Reverend Master had her third kensho in 1976, I've heard that following her retreat the main shift she made in her teaching was just what the title expresses. To find oneself truly willing to face whatever life now presents gives a kind of reassurance for simply taking the next step. Obviously, this step has to be built upon a deep faith in the Goodness of Life, which has been challenged by what has been asked of one. The conditioned mind we are training is one of serious limitation, and it simply wants to deny this, protecting an unwarranted sense of superiority, an arrogance so ingrained that it often goes unnoticed. When we are caught in it, whether we recognize it or not, we are moving from a self-will which rests in the cozy little land of mental constructions called the opposites. This is the delusion that prior to spiritual training fuels this life. In Tozan's enlightenment poem, his first teaching is: "Preserve well for you now have. This is all." A bit later he reminds us that "Supreme Mind in words can never be expressed and yet to all the trainee's needs It does respond."

In Soto Zen monasteries this Scripture is recited or chanted as part of what Reverend Master called Morning Office, which follows the first meditation of a new day. So someone like myself who trained there as a layperson and then also as a monk has chanted this many times. And there is something quite wonderful that simply *happens* with such repetition: it keeps sinking in deeper and deeper. In other words, it sinks beneath the judgmental mind—the mind we're training. "*Preserve well for you now have. This is all.*" And my great teacher's not infrequent comment echoes: "So simple it is, so simple." Isn't it indeed simple? We have *everything* we need to get on with our training. Somehow in some recess of the little mind this is known and is expressed in the Fifth Law of the Universe as "*Everyone has an innate knowledge of Buddha Nature,*" the Truth. That we've lost touch with the Truth of our being is why we train. An eighth century Indian monk observed that without this knowing, we humans would not recognize the inherent unsatisfactoriness of life. When we don't want to see that truth—the First Noble Truth—we live karmically driven lives searching here and there in externals, seeking in externals a place of security and refuge they simply cannot provide whether we have sufficient awareness to acknowledge this or not.

Gradually, no matter how long it takes, the Buddha's teaching is that we must all eventually come to this very place of recognition. Depending upon our particular karmic package, some don't need much of a nudge to quite naturally make this key turning to "look within and advance directly along the road that leads to the Mind" (Dogen). For others of us, it can take a very long time. But when one considers the Buddha's teaching regarding the *beginninglessness* of these rounds of existence, we can all have the humility to simply accept Reverend Master's observation that "It takes as long as it takes." What I'm getting at is that *it doesn't matter* because we can be very glad to have found a *Path* of training that promises to lead us away from our karmically driven blindness to Nirvana. Nirvana is the 'place' beyond suffering and *happens* as we let go of attachments that bind us on the Wheel of Life, Samsara, birth and death spinning beginninglessly around and around. This is sobering and worth pondering, I assure you. The mind we're training finds this exceedingly uncomfortable. It's out of its league, poor little thing, desperately wanting to make sense out of the insufficiency it experiences whilst holding onto what it thinks it knows. Perhaps it is only with a certain amount of spiritual training that this can be somewhat clear. That it is an important clarity we all truly *can* get and it's an aspect of right understanding, the first factor on the Noble Eightfold Path.

Perhaps the presence of clarity being so utterly valuable to me results from my having been so terribly confused and mixed-up for most of my life this time around. Delusion can be understood as resulting when the trauma of past lives in our karmic stream reached such a critical mass that in a sense one turns off, reeling within whilst struggling to not drown as events come tumbling down. For those with less heavy-duty karma, delusion is still the basis for the sprouting up of greed and aversion, the other two defilements that prevent our experiencing and knowing our Oneness with That which is. We have to keep honing away at the desire and anger that arise, bringing to bear the weight of our ongoing training and not getting stuck in their seeming 'rightness.' Again, right understanding is the ground on which we can stand firm when greed and aversion arise to pull us down old karmic roads. We strengthen our stance to hold fast and pause before sliding along in ways that seem so natural, which before training have remained hidden under a simple heedlessness that doesn't want to see a larger picture. It really is *so simple:* through our conditioning, we automatically evaluate life as it is happening by how it affects *me:* I like this and hence desire it; I don't like this and thus try to push it away from 'my' awareness, out of my life. Since most all of us receive both aspects, we swing like a monkey back and forth on our chosen limb of a sturdy tree. No wonder 'monkey mind' is a traditional way the conditioned mind is characterized. Whilst on the pendulum swing, we sadly miss and don't appreciate the place of stillness, the still point that rests in the center of our being.

So what can we do? Obviously, we bring the mind of training to our human predicament. We remember sufficiently when the greed-hate continuum seems to have grabbed us that we have a *choice* whether or not to fall into the old belief pattern being triggered. We're saved, so to speak, by our awareness of this predicament that allows us to *pause* and get a firmer bearing on what is truly happening at this moment. We really have to be able to slow it all down. This is the meaning of *restraint* that figures so prominently in the actual practice. We don't want to do that—it's uncomfortable because we're not indulging in the old karmic patterns thus presented. Then, dear friends, we start coming face to face, so to speak, with the delusion concerning who we are. We can *see* how much we identify with this feeling and this thought and this way of viewing ourselves in the world. All of us who have been willing to keep up our spiritual work know just how stressful this *sitting still* can be and how it may reach an intensity that is frightening. Here it's extremely important to remember that we do the best we can to follow the Middle Path of training and ease off from that intensity when that is good to do.

In other words, we've turned to Buddha Nature and asked for help, whether we recognize it or not. Little self-mind does not like feeling helpless, of course, feeling the vulnerability that springs right out of the delusion that led to this new life, this 'you' and 'me.' And we learn for ourselves how what we're doing by our willingness to keep up our practice is heroic, the hardest thing in the world we could be doing—and the most worthwhile. Well, its value may not be that apparent when the onslaught is bombarding us, but on the other side we experience a relief and appreciation that is kind of unique: We've gone beyond the opposites for this time and know at a deeper level that there *is* Something More. We don't have to label it or place it into a religious/philosophical tradition. As masters assure us: The Eternal *IS*. And as Tozan so emphatically stated at the beginning of his enlightenment poem: "Preserve well for you now have; this is all." There is a 'place' of simplicity and wholeness that lies beyond the myriad things of ordinary life. The latter are not a problem in any way: they are here to help us train. When we don't get caught in our karmic predilections, when we go beyond our comfort zone of likes and dislikes, we *open* to That which is greater and holds them and all of us together. It's just up to us, dear friends, over and over again to come back to that place of childlike willingness and ask in all simplicity, *What is it good to do now at this moment?* And, as Reverend Master wrote in her Commentary on the Precepts, with a heartfelt *I am willing,* we can jump up joyfully to answer, Yes!

# Just for You

"Just for you" comes from a teaching story about Tozan as a young monk. He and his master were walking and came to a large pool where a crane had just caught and gobbled down a large fish. Tozan turned to the teacher and asked in an anguished voice, "Why?" The teacher gently answered, "Just for you, just for you," and we're given an exquisite teaching about our life experiences which include a bigger or smaller serving of suffering. At certain times it can seem a paradox of spiritual life that as we are willing to go deeper into dropping beneath the surface karmic play, the more open and sensitive we become to the pain that accompanies being alive. As our willingness to get to know the barriers of self without automatically acting upon them drops away, we gradually open to the bigger picture which reveals to us its secret: we're all interconnected, interrelated, part of a Wholeness that as 'little self' we simply cannot grasp. It's in *forgoing self that the Universe grows I.* This, of course, is from the point of view of the 'self' let go of. From the Universe's point of view, we've never been separate from It. As my Master would say, "The Eternal longed for us far before we ever longed for It." *One calls, one answers.* When the noise of our conditioned body-mind quietens we can better hear that Call, but it's beckoning to us always, whether we pay attention to it or not.

Tozan and his teacher 'happen' to come to the pond just as the crane 'happens' to spy and grab a big fish that just 'happens' to be swimming by. The surface mind sweeps it all under the convenient rubric of coincidence or chance, caught in the surface play and unwilling to delve any deeper. Tozan's been sincerely practicing in a monastery, which in itself peels away coarser layers of our karmic denseness. He's ready to take another step so he can learn through the circumstances that appear. It's perfect from the point of view of training: he's pretty raw and sensitive, his master is right there with him, and he is exposed to 'nature tooth and claw' in one of its many forms, not subtle, not brutal—it's just the way it is.

In his enlightenment poem, Tozan later wrote: "The night encloses brightness, and at dawn no light shines. This truth holds for beings all, through this we free ourselves from suffering." He's telling us the same thing—our experiences, whether 'light' or 'dark,' are 'just for us' to teach us the absolute necessity to go beyond them as they appear at this moment and then the next. *This frees us from suffering,* he adds. Why? Because we're not holding onto the limitation of the conditioned self which automatically categorizes things in terms of its preference, its likes and dislikes. His way of putting it makes it so clear—*we free ourselves from suffering* through understanding this truth and letting it inform our daily life. Life's experiences themselves are the teacher—they are "just for us." Yours differ from mine. We're all in the same boat and all in our own little boats navigating the waves and dips, the calm and the stormy, all trying to steer a safe course through the big ocean. Sometimes it is easy, sometimes it is not. Sometimes it's so dark and dangerous that we feel lost. This teaching reminds us that this is "just for us" and propels us to turn within, in a good faith that deepens and grows as we keep up our practice and bravely go on.

We are given everything we need for our particular journey.

Nothing is wasted, nothing is hidden. We flounder and find secure ground and flounder again. As Tozan did, we can open to this play of light and dark or blindly continue our old karmic habit patterns. Eventually, all of us will reach the other shore because the light and the dark won't go away. "This truth holds for beings all." That is the nature of Life, and it is here to teach us, nudge us, urge us to go *beyond* this surface show. And as we gropingly learn how to do that, we gradually *free ourselves from suffering*. As in this teaching story, the teacher can point the way but can't take our journey for us. It is up to each of us to look directly and learn from our own life experiences. Then we cultivate wise discernment in choosing what it is good to do right now. We simply don't have much, arguably any, control over what happens, whereas we can learn not to suffer from it; that *does* lie within our control. So, dear reader, as circumstances come into our daily lives, let us choose the clear-hearted way and remember that Life is saying to each of us that this is "just for you."

# A Heart of Gratitude

Thanksgiving brings various thoughts about cultivating gratitude in our hearts. This special day reminds us to look at all the things in our lives we are thankful for. As with other aspects of training, it would be good to let this day then move us into a *life* of gratitude—an overwhelming sense of the wonder that Life truly is. We then live in the Bigger Picture, the Oneness that embraces and includes us all. When we commit to our Buddhist practice, we give ourselves the opportunity to live within the security of Buddha Nature, because "to live in this way is the same as to live an ordinary daily life" (Great Master Dogen).

In his explanation of the First Noble Truth, the Buddha noted that not getting what we want and having what we do not want are two aspects of the unsatisfactoriness of living. What he called the gratification of desire occurs when these aspects are reversed: we are gratified when we get what we want, and we are relieved and gratified when that which we do not want is removed. Much of our life is spent on this level of gratification. We are caught in this web of opposites, wanting and rejecting.

On this day, many take the opportunity to look at their lives differently. We can turn it around and view all that we are given in a more seamless way—without dividing it in the old way into "this I like, this I want," and "this I don't like, this I don't want." Because we are committed to the spiritual life, we can give this day a sharper focus than perhaps is the habit of many. Our practice directs us to being alert to this activity of the conditioned me and of letting go of it.

With this shift away from viewing everything from the stance of self, a true sweetness naturally arises. With appreciation we can *remember* that everything that happens—both that which comforts us and that which brings distress—helps free us from suffering. This view, this right understanding, is built on the universal fact of changeableness. By *letting go* of this and that, we come to see how we can bring our self into harmony with the way things are. While this is very freeing, it is not something we can mandate or insist upon. But gradually, as we remember this simple truth, we can bring ourselves to each present moment *with appreciation.* And in that fullness we learn to see more clearly and serenely how to proceed, what it is good to do right now. As we learn how to cooperate with this flowing life, a sense of harmony with it all naturally arises and wraps us in its certainty. This may sound mystical, but it is simply living more and more within the very Truth. As put in *The Scripture of Great Wisdom,* "It is the very Truth, no falsehood here. This is the Scripture of Great Wisdom, hear!" We are abandoning the unreal "real," which is our karmic conditioning, just little by little so that it is often unnoticed. As we are willing to keep up our wonderful practice, the Real reveals Itself. It had never gone anywhere.

This revelation—the consequence of our choice to do our spiritual inner work of the heart—enables us to clarify some puzzling paradoxes of training: "Forgoing self, the Universe grows I." Of course, how could it be otherwise? "All we are asked is to give up our suffering." "Nirvana and samsara are one." "This very life is the

Bodhisattva's playground." Yes, indeed! And deeply bowing we take this basic principle of training to heart: "*Everything* that happens is for my good." And gratitude embraces all of life. We find a vision that goes beyond division, as my great teacher put it.

When we live the Eightfold Path and follow the Precepts naturally and freely, we are empowered in a wholly different way from 'little self' power. Our knowing faith holds us firmly as life offers its many challenges. Sometimes we know and touch that 'Place,' and sometimes we do not. As Reverend Master put it, we go in and out. There's a mixing and a melding as we play out this life in an ever-growing freedom from the old conditioning that propelled its birth. And we truly come to see that all those sad and challenging experiences actually were assisting us. They were our friends in showing us the way. We have learned from the good times and the bad ones. Now in mindful vigilance we come to see the whole show more clearly for what it is. We can let this special day of thanksgiving become "nothing special" as we choose to begin *every* day with heartfelt gratitude to all.

# Returning to Stillness

## Zen Training in Everyday Life

Reverend Meiten McGuire

# Contents

# An Invitation

A while ago a friend who is a performer sang for me a 1960's song 'Welcome to My World' popularized by Jim Reeves. Not having ever been interested in country western music, I'd never heard it before, though as it turned out many of our Sangha were familiar with it. At this point in my life of training, the song struck me as an astonishingly pure Dharma teaching found, it seemed to me, in a most unlikely place. Here is a somewhat modified version:

Welcome to my world,
Won't you come on in.
Miracles, I guess
Still happen now and then.
Step into my heart,
Leave your cares behind.
Welcome to my world,
Built with you in mind.
Knock and the door will open,
Seek and you will find,
Ask and you'll be given
The key to this world of mine.
I'll be waiting here,
Waiting just for you.
Enter into my heart
Welcome to my world.

This is the Eternal, That which is always here for all of us, kindly welcoming us into Its vast world which is beyond the conditioned body-mind we take as 'me.' We're invited to 'come on in,' allowing us to recognize that 'miracles still happen now and then.' And it truly can seem a 'miracle' that our willing determination to practice by *standing against the world of this conditioned mind in order to train in wisdom* allows us to hear the invitation to enter into That which embraces and tenderly holds us all. It is That which goes beyond the opposites.

We're invited to 'step into my heart' of goodness and are encouraged to 'leave our cares behind.' This world, we're told, was 'built with you in mind.' The encouragement continues with the familiar Christian teaching: *Knock and the door will open. Seek and you will find. Ask and you will be given the key to this world of mine.* And it is so true that 'I'll be waiting here, waiting just for you. *Welcome* to my world.' The basic causal condition that perpetuates the sad karma of our not knowing this is, of course, ignorance, which leads to our wandering within a conditioned seemingly real world where we feel separate. This is referred to as samsara, as perpetually wandering. That is the basic problem, as we are looking *outside* for security, acceptance, and love. We are seeking security within impermanence. Since all appearances are subject to change, the potential for being disappointed is ever-present. As we are willing to sustain our awareness-practice of the karmic play of the mind, this becomes increasingly clear.

We need all the reminders we can get, it seems to me, to repeatedly hear that generous *Welcome to my world* and learn to trust in its benevolence. This is our repeated choice to go beyond the human mind and discover the Great Wisdom, Nirvana, which is right here, right within. We've *never* been alone; we just have it wrong. And all the pains and stresses this life brings to each living being are signals for us to look more deeply into this limited world of 'me' and learn little by little to open its squeaky door to a grandeur existing quietly and patiently, always welcoming us to Its World.

# At the Crossroads

When we're at a crossroads at twilight, unfamiliar with the terrain, it can be difficult to see which way to go. If a storm is signaling its arrival there may be dark clouds hovering about which further obscure our view. And yet we have to go on because we're on a journey and there is no stopping place, no wayside inn where we can take shelter for the night. Life has handed us this predicament over and over again—we have to get on with our life by making countless choices. We really can't be sure of the outcome because we can only see a bit of the distance down the two roads. As Robert Frost wrote, 'Two roads diverged in the wood and I—I took the one less traveled by, and that has made all the difference.' He took the one 'less traveled by.' To me that means he was willing to try something different, something seemingly less sure.

Until we come to some kind of spiritual practice, we take the road *more* traveled by. This is the road of our old conditioned programs. As habits solidify they become less and less noticed. I won't say less and less 'noticeable' because they can be quite obvious *once we develop a* <u>*new*</u> *habit of paying attention.* These old habits are like the darkening clouds before a storm at twilight: they make it more difficult to see where different choices might be appropriate. Maybe we don't even see that there *is* a choice, that we may be at numerous crossroads, even during a single day. It's too unnerving and unsettling to really recognize what we're doing right now, at this moment of this day. We like to deal in generalities, which is another obscuration we add to the pot. Life is both more complicated and simpler than we have learned. We've been taught such a large amount by life—by our parents, our schooling, our friends, our activities—that there could be no way that this huge register were instantly available to our beck and call. We aren't aware of how our seeming choices have been influenced. Our very way of being in the world is built on a premise, an assumption that isn't examined. Our conditioning has made what we perceive and how we perceive so 'obvious' that we don't notice there may be other ways. It may seem as impossible to examine all of this as the centipede found when asked how it was able to maneuver its many feet so as to move. We can act, but *how* we're acting and what we're doing at any given moment may seem impossible to examine—we'd just have to stop.

Now, of course, this is just what we're advised to do when we're on this spiritual journey. We already may recognize to some extent that there is something potentially unsatisfactory about life, which may have more to do with 'us' than with what's 'out there,' that *we* are the common denominator to all our experiences. This is sobering, and many of us are unwilling to see this truth without many, many disappointments. Finally, this recognition propels us to look more deeply. This is the requirement for finding a more satisfying solution to life's unsatisfactoriness. We are taught, and find more and more true for ourselves, that we must *train in awareness*. We have to be willing to stop and examine life instead of going on in the semi-darkness of old habits of body, speech, and mind. There is a strong resistance we can feel to doing this. But Life repeatedly teaches us that if we want to be more balanced and harmonious in our everyday living, then we must stop and take a look at how *we* influence and in a very real sense *are* creating our world. We have to go beneath the surface level of old habitual responses which are so ingrained we often don't even recognize their powerful influence at this moment. We tend to gloss over the particular event because we may be required to see the unskillful means of our behavior, much preferring to generalize about what's wrong. This is a way that 'little self' tries to wriggle out from under the uncomfortable scrutiny otherwise required. *We don't want to do it.*

This 'I don't want to do it' is an expression of a third hindrance to our spiritual journey. A hindrance obscures our making more wholesome choices. The third hindrance is usually translated as 'sloth and torpor.' The Buddha is using strong language to make his point, giving the most extreme aspect of the condition pointed to. One translator gave the translation as 'physical and mental laziness,' which for me is more easily identified in my own unwillingness at times to simply get up and move, i.e. to make a choice to change direction. A humdrum example: I'm sitting in my comfortable chair and have had my cup of green tea. It's time to move on to something else but I'm not exactly sure *what* to do next, so there I sit. Sitting there is not that comfortable anymore, and there is this nudge to get on with the day. When we're 'listening' to our inner state, which is the practice of our awareness in whatever situation we find ourselves, we don't have to perpetuate such an unrewarding way of being: we don't have to be ruled by our physical and mental laziness. Physically, it may seem more comfortable to prolong sitting and, mentally, it's not easy to choose what to do next. The hindrance here is obvious. At some point, earlier better than later, we can confront the hindrance and move on to the next step that is good to do.

When we are working to free ourselves from simply going down old grooves, we can feel stumped on what it *is* good to do. We're at a crossroads now and we're willing to see that we don't have to respond from old conditioned habits. The twilight is lifting, though it may not feel that way initially. We have to be willing to try the Unknown. That is what is happening when we make a non-habitual choice. This allows us to come in touch with our own humanity in a rather raw way—we experience how vulnerable we can feel. We can experience the sense of *helplessness* that has been hidden under a false assurance of knowing just what to do. If this sounds vague, we can find out for ourselves simply by doing it.

There are wonderful, exciting discoveries waiting for us when we take 'the road less traveled by.' It does make all the difference because we see more and more how very binding and blinding the old programming was and how freeing it is to find other options to life's challenges. So, let's get down to work and stop being ruled by the physical and mental resistance to examining our lives to see where going down a different road would serve us best. The Buddha taught that we have to *reject laziness*, and we find that we can do this. As is said, *We must make the effort, Buddhas can only point the Way*. Truly just taking that one next step willingly into the Unknown by exploring the hidden recesses within our own minds is possible, moment after moment. An ancient Chinese proverb goes, A journey of a thousand miles begins with but a single step.' Let's not be daunted by little mind's ideas about how difficult or impossible this could be. Let's just get on with it right now because each step does lead us to our Goal. It's a process that is unlocked by our *willingness* to just keep going, doing our dedicated practice faithfully and with sincerity. Making wiser choices in this way is our little part and the process itself carries us. That's just the way it is.

# Beyond Forgiveness

The last written reflection to be included in *Reminders on the Way** was titled 'Beyond Hope.' This seemed rather startling to all of us when I rather playfully said that about myself in response to something a Sangha member had said. For the last little while the comparably startling 'Beyond Forgiveness' has been coming to my mind. This is of course not to imply that forgiving 'shouldn't' arise for us—it does and it will, just as hope arises in this conditioned mind of ours. The wonder of our own ongoing training is that we give ourselves the opportunity through the strengthening of awareness to delve a bit more deeply into our karmic inheritance, rather than simply being trapped in it, which will make sense to those who are *doing* this demanding practice of 'looking before you leap.'

The Buddha formulated Dependent Origination, Conditional Arising, as a basic right understanding of the human or existential predicament. Its twelve links are summarized in the literature as Ignorance and Craving, the first and eighth links. In one of the Connected Discourses he teaches that as long as beings are *hindered by ignorance and fettered by craving* there will be no end to suffering. He gives sobering examples on how long this wandering has been taking place. 'Samsara' is the Sanskrit word for *perpetual wandering* and is depicted as a graphic wheel fueled by greed, hate, and delusion. These summarize the varying experiences we humans

---

* *Reminders on the Way* – Reverend Meiten's second book

are caught in, helplessly conditioned through the basic unknowing, the first link of ignorance of what is the True, what is Real beyond the appearances level of seeming reality. Over and over again, this basic truth must be confronted because it just won't compute to the conditioned mind that is deluded and ignorant of it.

You may wonder what in the heck this has to do with going beyond forgiveness, but without this basic understanding the former won't make sense. We all know, sometimes with terrible recognition, how at times we've hurt others and been also terribly hurt. The conditioned blind spots are here for all of us, and it is the training in awareness that lets light shine on them. Little by little we clear away the debris so that we really do make the Buddha's teaching true for ourselves. And, of course, that is the point of the practice. The 'making it true for myself' has let me view the interconnectedness of Life as a vast karmic play, where each of us has our 'entrances and exits.' This is difficult to convey, and my great teacher many years ago took a blackboard and drew many, many seemingly random lines, each obviously separate. Then he drew some that linked, saying 'shall we dance?' And that's it, that's it. Though we often won't be aware of this process, we on some level choose to 'dance' with some and not with others.

When we're not aware, the karmic patterns are played out rather mindlessly: we react out of old conditioned patterns based upon a vast interplay of causes and conditions which formed our experiences, including how these were interpreted. At those times we acted out of ignorance, not really knowing better. As one teacher put it, 'We do terrible things out of pain and confusion.' This is another way of referring to ignorance and craving that keep the wheel turning in the wrong way, which at some point will bring unsatisfactoriness. This, of course, is the teaching formulated as the First Noble Truth. As we penetrate this Truth and the Second Noble Truth, which gives the cause of the basic unsatisfactoriness of existence as attachment, slowly we'll recognize there is no one really to forgive, either self or another. Why? Because without the precious work of the heart we really don't know any better. We react out of this ignorance with wanting, even demanding life be a certain way or rejecting, denying aspects of what is happening—out of pain and confusion. It's so clear.

The above understanding lets us truly see more and more that all of us are doing the best we can at a given time. In retrospect we go into blame, self-judgment, or recriminations of others. This is the very nature of the conditioned mind; this is why we train. In the Scripture of Great Wisdom this is expressed in many ways: *Going on beyond the human mind is Nirvana* conveys just that. Gradually, we come to see that *all-acceptance* is the *gateless gate*. This is how we free ourselves from suffering, from blaming, from criticizing—i.e., judging. Through the strengthening of our birthright of awareness we give ourselves the opportunity to see this conditioned movement or activity of the conditioned mind. We are accepting the Buddha's invitation to *stop and see*. It can seem as if we're pulling ourselves up by our own bootstraps! And anyone who is sincere in practice will know this for themselves. It's as Reverend Master Jiyu was taught: *We're standing against the world [of the conditioned mind] in order to train in wisdom.*

The wisdom is that which does not blame anyone or anything for the daily life happenings. It's a vast karmic play in which we've chosen to 'dance' particular steps with particular partners. *Now* we have the opportunity to do better. We truly *can* stop and see—is this helpful, is this appropriate, will this bring a good result—and then *choose* to do something different. Repeatedly, this we do, and this is training. We move beyond forgiveness to the true heart, which is naturally compassionate, understanding, and loving. We learn for ourselves that yes, we truly can *live in the world as if in the sky*, which is the promise of living a Buddhist life.

# Changing Conditions Challenge our Choices

This alliterative title came up this morning as I sat with the unwelcome recognition that a bunch more snow had fallen overnight instead of continuing to clear as it promised yesterday! This was oppressive: thoughts arose about how I'd not been outside for over a week, how I'd planned to drive the car today to get out as well, to be sure that its battery wouldn't die again, and how unpleasant snow is! As it says in one of our Scriptures, *when all conditions ripen* a teaching opens in the form of stimulating old habitual patterns of feeling/thinking. Perfect for training; unpleasant to one's comfort level. Surely the gift of our spiritual practice is that it allows us to move beyond conditions that formerly were so impelling that we were caught up in unwanted mental states. The Buddha promised that his teaching brought freedom and peace, *Nirvana*, which was here for us 'here and now.' So what to do when all conditions ripen that invite our sliding down old roads of fear, anxiety, discontent, and dis-ease? *We keep looking, we keep being mindful and attentive of the inner mental states aroused. That* is the work no one else can do for us. We learn that so long as we try escaping, avoiding, or distracting ourselves from these states of mind, they will come back to plague us in another form. More and more, we are convinced by doing our training that true peace won't be found through manipulating our world because the problem isn't 'out there,' no matter how enticingly old programs want us to believe that. One teacher of the last century put it this way: 'The same old person comes telling the same old lies and we keep on believing them.'

The challenge of our training is to stop doing this. Before we are able to stop, to *not* do, we must have the above Right Understanding or, as it is also called, Right View. For most of us, before we are willing to shift to this change, we have had to experiment with plenty of attempted solutions to find that they didn't work. Then we are willing, as Dogen urged, to *turn inward and advance directly along the road that leads to the Mind.* Right Understanding is placed at the beginning of the Noble Eightfold Path to help us find a promising direction in which to proceed. There are a number of different ways Right Understanding is described in the literature, which can be confusing in itself. When it comes down to establishing a *practice*, the important understanding is to *turn inward.* This is essential. Again, Dogen wrote that *the means of training are thousandfold but pure meditation must be done.* 'Pure meditation' refers to our willingness to *look within* and learn to step back from what we see, what we observe. Changing conditions offer the fuel for this training because they show us where we get caught in or trapped by the mental states triggered. Over and over again, we find 'I *have* choices, I don't *have* to go that way again.' In Buddhism our choices are expressed in actions of body, speech, and thought. The important thing is to keep remembering that every action has consequences, that what we sow, we *will* reap. This is the law of karma that is said to be inexorable. By being willing to look with unflinching courage, we give ourselves the opportunity to see this truth for ourselves, which is what the Buddha invited his followers to do.

So this morning as I sat with some tea looking out at the snow-lined trees and noting with a sinking heart how much more snow had fallen, something shifted: I turned and looked at the beautiful altar, at the Earth-witness Buddha, at the Avalokiteshwara statues, at the lovely plants and the hanging calligraphy. An inner quiet gradually seeped into my being with a reassuring knowing that I had everything I need, at this moment, right now. The teaching again showed how I'd jumped to the future: would the morning appointment be cancelled, would the group want to meet this evening, when would I ever be able to take a walk? The inner quiet let me know that it simply didn't matter, that this day would unfold as it would, and a marvelous contentment replaced the interior restlessness. I was shown again the power of training by being willing to confront the states of mind, the feelings, thoughts, and desires that arose. I didn't have any control over what arose when I first looked out of the window and saw the snow—that is the old conditioning: being raised in a warm climate where it never snowed, slipping and falling down repeatedly in graduate school, when first introduced to snow, remembering the places my jobs took me to where it snowed as not pleasant, and so on. In *turning* around in trust that all is working itself out as is good, I returned to this present moment with gratitude because truly *I do have everything I need*. Reverend Master Jiyu taught, *It is enough for me to know the Lord of the House. It is enough for me to follow the Lord of the House*. I am following in her footsteps, I am following in the Buddha's footsteps, and what on earth more could a sincere trainee, a child of Buddha, possibly ask for?

# Feelings

In the Buddha's formulation of the conditional arising of a new being, karmic tendencies (*samskharas*) come second, following the basic delusion or ignorance of the previous being who at the time of death experienced itself as separated from the Unborn. These tendencies influence the new being to act in certain ways which are the expressions of the intentions of the previous being. They are called 'karmic' because they lead to consequences that may be classified as good, bad, or indifferent. One of the *effects* of these consequences is how we feel (*vedana*). Both tendencies and feelings make up aspects of our experience as human beings. They are two of the five aggregates (*skandhas*). The other three are corporeality or form (*rupa*), perception (*samjna*), and consciousness (*vijnana*). When the Buddha went into the deep stillness of meditation, he found nothing else and taught that what we take as a 'self' or 'I' or 'ego' is nothing but these five 'heaps,' as they are sometimes referred to. He also found that they arise, remain, and pass away—the arising and falling of all conditioned things (*dharmas*). When we identify with these passing aspects of our experience, we are bound to suffer at some point or another. Why? Simply because they don't last. In the Buddhist literature, the aggregates have been likened to clouds floating by, just clouds passing and temporarily obscuring the vast, blue sky that is always there.

This may seem like theory without any application to our own spiritual practice. That is not so. When we sit 'like a Buddha' in meditation, we give ourselves the opportunity to blow away the screen of our mistaken notion of who we are. That is why the Buddha told his followers not to believe anything because he said it, but to make it true for themselves. It is a teaching for 'here and now,' as he put it. Because we have a strong sense of connectedness to these conditions, the training in letting go of the passing aggregates is extremely challenging—we are challenging our old beliefs, opinions, emotions, and inevitable sense of pride that support our basic ignorance (*avidya*) of who we are.

This can be seen very clearly when we consider our feelings. One classification given for feelings is that they can be pleasant, unpleasant, or neutral. Again, we can experience this for ourselves when we are willing to sit still beneath them, that is, not get caught up in them. When we remember that feelings are *consequences* of previous actions, we can see that we really cannot choose which ones we'll have and which ones we won't have. And yet we all fall for believing that somehow we are responsible for the feelings! We say to ourselves or out loud, 'I should or shouldn't feel this way' and are distressed. If an angry feeling arises, it has arisen because we, and beings in our karmic stream, have indulged in expressing anger in past situations. A *groove* has been dug, so to speak, so that when we are confronted with certain situations, to be angry is our habitual response. The *feeling* arises because it has been acted upon previously. This would refer to any feeling, whether we would consider it desirable or not, exalted or depraved, altruistic or totally selfish.

At a group meeting someone brought up that in his meditation he'd get in touch with, or experience, *gratitude* and *contentment*.

Could these be classified as the feeling aggregate in the same way as other more mundane feelings? Feeling states are feeling states, so yes. Also, they too are karmic consequences of choices he has made; in this instance, the choice to meditate, the choice to train himself, the choice to let go of coarser feelings, etc. Karmic consequence is not all 'bad' by any means. Indeed, the experiences of gratitude, joy, and deep contentment are the *fruit* of our practicing. They are our natural way of being when little self is not in dominance. We don't create gratitude and joy anymore than we create anger and resentment. Our training allows us the *wise discernment* to choose actions that support the former and weaken the latter. When we find skillful ways to handle feelings of anger and resentment, they lessen, and this leads over time to their not arising with the earlier intensity and gradually to their not arising at all. This is our work: we shine our Birthright of awareness on whatever experience comes up and choose to act in ways to strengthen our spiritual growth instead of falling back into old patterns.

It is said that our training is the gradual conversion of greed, hate, and delusion into compassion, love, and wisdom. Our Buddha Nature, our True Essence, *is* compassion, love, and wisdom. It is similar to water and its wetness, using two words to convey one thing. There is no water without its being wet. Words can confuse us at times. As our training matures and we live more and more with our Buddha Nature in charge, it seems to me now that compassion and love become more than simple feeling states. They become our very nature. This, I believe, is what Reverend Master Jiyu meant by *making the Precepts our blood and bones*. This is indeed the fruition of our training that helps us to keep going. It isn't an 'all or nothing' kind of a thing. It isn't that enlightenment is an end. There is enlightenment on enlightenment on enlightenment, and we just keep going. We learn more and more not to cling to any condition because they all are passing *and* we learn to hug more closely to That which *is*, which isn't changing and dying: the Unborn. As the Buddha taught, *There is an Unborn, Undying, Unchanging, Uncreated. If it were not so, there would be no escape from this here, which is born, dying, changing, and created.*

We can use everything in our training. Our questions and doubts lead to fruitful understanding that enable us more and more to let go. We return to the Place of stillness that is always here. It is the Ground, the Reality, the Truth of our being. That we do not *know* That is the cause of our suffering in samsara, this wheel of birth and death. As our practice matures, as we mature as spiritual adults, more and more we see our life as the 'Bodhisattvas' playground'. We see a 'bigger picture' in which nothing is 'out there' to hurt or destroy us. We know more and more that we are given the lessons we now need to move further along our spiritual journey. Truly, the principle that *everything that happens is for my good* seems less perplexing and more sustaining. We don't need to chop up our world into what is good and what is bad from our limited karmic-self perspective. This is truly freeing. We are on the road to that freedom when we are *willing* more and more to put our 'selves' on the line and give our spiritual training the highest priority so that it can pervade every aspect of our lives. Nothing need be excluded; everything teaches. And truly life lightens up. The defilements of greed and hate are weakened, occurring less and less frequently. We can't make them go away, while the moment-to-moment choices we make are the process by which they transform into compassion and love.

My Master was taught in the East that *we stand against the world in order to train in wisdom*. The Scripture of Great Wisdom expresses the core teaching of the Buddha: *anatta*, no separate self. All things are *void, unstained, and pure*. These are different expressions for *anatta*: 'unstained' by the false notion of self and 'pure' when we know that this 'self' is a fabrication and not real. Then we *flow* with Life. By remembering that we are always at some point on this journey, we can more easily simply 'go on' when karma again obscures the Great Wisdom. The obscurations come up as feelings and thoughts and impulses taken to be 'real' and identified with, thus creating a 'self' to suffer or to enjoy. Our training is to keep letting go of all that passes in order to live more and more in 'eternity's sunrise,' as William Blake put it. At some point, our commitment is so deep that, however difficult our lives may be right now, we will simply keep training within it. This is...*training for training's sake; training in Buddhism for the sake of Buddhism*. It is endless training in our willingness to continually put down the burden of the non-existent 'self' being expressed as a feeling state happening in the present moment.

# Five Qualities of Training

For the last few months I have found five spiritual qualities we can cultivate coming up for me, both in my own practice and when talking with others about their practice. It was during the summer renewal when I was working through on a deeper level my sister's death earlier in the year that they presented themselves, as I was willing, thanks always to training, to 'sit' with the distress that had arisen. As we know, this sitting is an inner quality that allows us, whether sitting or standing or whatever we're doing, to maintain a quality of awareness of the present moment. Its power is gradually recognized the more we are willing to do our practice. I'm the last of my family now as my father died, my mother died, my son died, my auntie died, and now my sister, only two years older than I am, has died. In a way it was like reliving these losses, now through the eyes of training, that let me see how cultivating the following five qualities is enormously helpful—*and* we can remember their importance and turn to them.

*Infinite Patience* was the one that seemed absolutely fundamental. We're training this body-mind that is the storehouse of the karma. Anyone who is sincerely doing a spiritual practice knows how strong the conditioning is. Before training we really aren't that aware of the authority it imposes upon our ways of seeing this world we're in and believing in its assessments. Our willingness to confront this 'world' is one way of describing our practice: *We're standing against the world of this conditioned mind in order to train in wisdom*. Wisdom is 'seeing the way things are,' which the Buddha said is what he taught. As we probe the sensitive areas of this conditioned body-mind, its challenges become increasingly clear. So the Buddha described patience as the potent army. Grounding ourselves in this right understanding allows the cultivation of patience. How painful is the experience of the loss of a loved one! It's tricky to just sit within the sadness, not trying to push it away and not indulging it. I saw how easy it is to revert to these old conditioned patterns when recollections about Dorothy arose. Every time the important choice is to let them go, letting go with a loving heart—patiently. Patience is rarely anyone's strong suit, even though we likely all have areas where it's less sorely tried, again depending upon our karmic load and the training we've brought to bear on it. Patience is to be recognized and cultivated. To remember this can be done—it's a *choice* we can make over and over again.

*Heroic Courage* we'll begin to see is required to stick with the myriad forms that our patience allows us to be aware of. We are told that *feelings are the reaper of the karma*. During the summer renewal without the usual activities that filled my days, a lot of feelings and memories would arise, and at times I'd be quite impatient at this. The mind would be kind of indignant that after all these years of training there they were. When we see this, we understand better the teaching that our training is *endless*. The *willingness* to keep going is the key, willingness to penetrate another deep wound that reveals our karmic inheritance. It likely won't 'feel' like courage, and yet the strength to not just fold and let old band-aid solutions ease the pain does take courage—it is the willingness *to see the way things are*. What do we see? That we are really quite helpless to make things be different from the way they are at this moment. This includes the whole ball of wax—my sister's death, her sad depression of her last year of life after her husband died, my wish that somehow I could have helped her more, my regret that I hadn't been more 'there' for her as she turned toward me in her helplessness, and my kind of frustration that she negated all my little efforts to help her—fantasies of how it could have been different. Letting this karmic play unfold itself whilst doing the meditation of not being caught within the drama does take both patience and courage.

*Profound Humility* arises as we have the strength of our practice to see how little control we have over what happens to us or over our conditioned reactivity. It's hard to bear because we're so caught in the delusion of a 'me' that thinks, feels, perceives, remembers. So right in the *first* noble truth that suffering or unsatisfactoriness is part of the nature of ordinary existence, the Buddha sums up this *first* truth by saying that the suffering comes from clinging to the five aggregates, five aspects of experience that we attach to as a separate self. So the teaching points us to look at them: at this bodily form so palpable and seemingly real, at our sensations/feelings that bring either pleasure or pain, at our perceptions/memories in interpreting what they mean, at our thought formations that prompt action, and the consciousness of these experiences that form around a sense of me and mine. What we get to see as our practice deepens is that we don't have control over what comes up in our conditioned body-mind—they are not a 'me' or a 'mine' in the way we have implicitly taken them to be. This is where we are confronted with not having a leg to stand on, no firm ground beyond our conditioned body-mind knowing.

*Stalwart Faith* is here for us, whether we 'feel' we have this quality or not. This faith is a deeper knowing that there simply has to be Something More than this trap of how we experience ourselves in this world. The suffering itself, in other words, can condition faith—this is the beginning of turning the wheel another way. The Wheel of Life shows how the karma works: the suffering that leads to more suffering. This is ordinary life before training, described as *perpetual wandering*, when we are caught in the karmic beliefs that there is surely something *external* to us that will relieve the inner unsatisfactoriness, insecurity, distress that we experience. It does take a stalwart faith not to yield to this belief that there is a true cure for the unsatisfactoriness to be found in external things whatever they are. When we succumb to the karmic veils, we're truly trapped in a futile attempt to find our peace and security within the very conditions over which we have no control. This we must see before we turn with a childlike innocence to open to the deep Unknown obscured through the old ways.

*Boundless Compassion* is here for us, dear friends. It is the *very truth, no falsehood here.* Faith opens us to an inner world that is connected with everything, not as an idea or concept. *It is.* This we don't create and really can't cultivate: as we *open* out of our limited sense of self, simultaneously we *see the way things are*, not from the limited eyes of a separate 'me' but Buddha eyes, our True Self, that has been calling to us for a very long time. Reverend Master Jiyu would say that the Eternal can wait, It's eternal. And then ask how long do we want to wait in the throes of samsara, the perpetual wandering, as we search for our True Home, the very Source of our being. We simply see more and more that Compassion, Love, and Wisdom are here for us, right within the heart and naturally flowing out as we strengthen the qualities of patience, courage, humility, and faith to keep going even though we experience sometimes the light and sometimes the dark. This we can't 'make' happen. It is the gift of our willingness to keep up our training AND this is do-able as we are willing to cultivate these qualities of a spiritual life.

# Fully Present

There are many ways of describing our Buddhist practice, one of which is conveyed by the title, Fully Present. When we sit in serene reflection, as Great Master Dogen put it, *We're not trying to think and we're not trying not to think. We're just sitting with no deliberate thought*. Earlier in Rules for Meditation he flatly pointed out that we are not trying to control *mind function, will, consciousness, memory, perception, or understanding*. This is not the way to become Buddha. Well, then, what in the heck *are* we doing? We're *just sitting, not trying to think and not trying not to think,* not trying to feel *and* not trying not to feel, which extends to all the mental activity that is typically present.

Clearly, then, we are employing right effort to repeatedly *let go* of our wonted way of being. That's what dismays many of us when we have come to this practice, looking for an inner solution to the unsatisfactoriness of this life. The question arises, *'What am I to do?'* followed often by another one, *'How do I know that I'm doing it right?'* These questions arise all too frequently because the nature of this conditioned mind, as one of the senior monks put it, wants to know and then wants to know it knows. Foreign to its habitual function is stillness, silence. When inwardly we writhe with a desire of peace from the current of dis-ease, which is the conditioned mind's nature, as you've heard me say, the *hardest* thing in the world is to 'just sit' with the keen and willing awareness to 'just be.'

So the basic meditation practice is to be aware. What do we see? How the mind shoots off from this utter simplicity of being, over and over again. Infinite patience we come to see is definitely needed. The Buddha called patience 'the potent army.' In those statues showing the Buddha's right hand pointing downward to the ground, the patience of 'just sitting' is conveyed: *As the earth is my witness, I shall not move from my sitting place.* This firm resolve of the Buddha's on the night of his enlightenment is our implicit resolve when we're willing to keep having the discipline to *just sit, not trying to think and not trying not to think.* Its utter simplicity dismays. Where's the meat? Where's the substance?

That's just it! We're moving out of the familiar fare the conditioned mind feeds on. Dear friends of training, we get to see that it often isn't subtle in the least: our thoughts/feelings center around a 'me' that churns habitually—*this* is the karmic residue of this life as well as the accruing of present karmic fruits from our current choices. As my great teacher would say, 'So simple it is, so simple.' No genius in mathematics or language or anything else is required. We have everything we need for the important inner journey back to our True Home, Buddha Nature, Awakened Nature. What do we wake up to? It's put in so many different ways as fingers pointing toward the moon. The Buddha pointed out that *there is nothing to hold onto and there is nothing that need be pushed away.* By golly, we don't have a leg to stand on!

What can we do? We can *let go*, over and over again, of whatever has pulled us away from our own sitting place of just being fully present, right at this moment. It really is 'so simple' that the complex mind conditioned by innumerable experiences of the past can't 'get it.' A wholesome dollop of humility arises—*I don't know*. That's it! The 'I' that has seemed the center hasn't a clue though it struggles mightily against this recognition. The title of Suzuki Roshi's first influential book was *Zen Mind, Beginner's Mind*. Great Master Keizan expressed it this way: *If you want to become one with the Truth, as one flame combines with another, throw away cherished opinions, old emotions, arrogance, and obstinacy, and learn the True Mind of the Lord with the naïve mind of a child.*

Every time we choose to keep up our meditation practice, we express the willingness to go beyond the human mind, which in The Scripture of Great Wisdom is put as necessary for Nirvana to appear. We get to know more and more clearly that truly there *is* Something More than meets the habit-eye, or habit-I. We explore our inner world through our childlike willingness to keep going within 'not knowing.' This requires always returning to a faith that is bigger than wherever we are. Always we can return to being simply present in this special moment. It can't be held onto and it can't be pushed away—it just *is*. We return to a Oneness that is ineffable, always present, always cherishing everything. It informs us moment-by-moment, fully present. That's it!

## Hidden Joys... Hidden Sorrows

When we are willing to face the wall and *just sit, not trying to think and not trying not to think*...we are giving ourselves over to a process which initially can bring up for many practitioners an uneasy uncertainty. Something ill-defined and strange, of course, may seem threatening. It is important to recognize that this is a phase of practice many of us go through (and, again for some of us, come back to and go through at various points in our practice). Nothing is wrong; indeed, the very uneasiness is an indicator that we have begun our practice of *looking inwards to advance directly along the road that leads to the [Awakened] Mind*. Obviously, at these times we are leaning on faith that the uneasy self is not all there is to life and that the Buddhadharma, the Buddha's teaching, can assist us to live a more satisfactory, complete life. We've had to have a glimmer of recognition that *something* isn't working for us, which isn't fixable in the usual (i.e. conditioned) ways. This is the beginning of a spiritual practice: we are willing to move into unknown territory in which we really can't know (in the usual way) what we're getting ourselves into. That willingness to so move is based in faith, whether we understand or even consider what that means or not. What we're moving toward is the Buddha's promise that we truly can live in peace and contentment *within the very midst of life*. We begin the process of renouncing our comfort zone to explore that which is hidden and vaguely beckoning. We worry what 'Pandora's box' of goblins and demons may be opened in this process.

We 'enter the stream' of *practice* in not knowing: we don't know what we'll find while we carry our old deeply entrenched tendency to want the pleasant and reject the unpleasant. These opposites in myriad themes are what we are tentatively willing to go on beyond. Training evolves as we open to more and more aspects of our experience, whether they bring joy or sorrow. We want the former and push away the latter, so it follows that the same tendencies will be operative when we meditate. In so longing we experience over and over again, whether we recognize it or not, the same ancient defilements that keep us on the wheel of suffering, the repeated round of birth and death which fuels it. How can this be easy? That is why the person who embarks and continues on this inner journey is described as *heroic*, a *Lord of Lords*. The curtain arises on hidden sorrows that have shadowed our quiet times and even our busy days. 'People don't realize the ocean of grief they carry,' one of my teachers observed after a private retreat in which he was in touch with successive past lives. This teaching refers to the karmic consequence of beings in our karmic stream who, at the time of their death, had not resolved the conundrum of living. This basic confusion or ignorance is what is eroded through our willingness to open 'Pandora's box.' When we're willing to see, we will see—this is the gift we give to ourselves by being willing to keep going in our practice.

What we'll also see—the very wonder of practice—are the hidden joys embedded right here within the box of sorrows. 'Surprised by Joy' is the way C.S. Lewis described his experience. It's not 'Catholic,' 'Buddhist,' 'Muslim,' etc. *It is*. The true peace, contentment, equanimity come out of our very willingness to face the dark side we've been running away from. As Sir Edward Thompson described his experience in 'The Hound of Heaven,' we 'flee him' through valleys and dales, up mountains, in experiences of laughter, etc. and yet steadily he follows. He tells us that we'll never find Peace except within the Heart. Similarly, the Sufis point out that *What you are looking for is That which is looking*. This Truth we can touch and truly experience, no matter how bewildering the words sound to the conditioned mind. The Scripture of Great Wisdom promises that *going on beyond the human mind is Nirvana*, bliss, peace, joy. If we want to find It we *must start at once*, as Dogen pointed out. And Sekito Kisen in Sandokai ended his enlightenment poem with *This I offer to the seeker of Great Truth: do not waste time*. Every time we are willing to simply sit, to be within that quiet beyond or beneath all the mental activity we're generally caught up in, we risk being 'grabbed by the Cosmic Buddha' as Reverend Master Jiyu's Master Koho Zenji warned. This is a reference to That which can truly appease the deepest recesses of our heart, the ache for a fulfillment that isn't transitory and passing, that goes beyond the basic unsatisfactoriness of the unexamined, vulnerable life. We find that *both* pass: the hidden sorrows were never 'real' in the way we implicitly believed and bought into, while those magical times of hidden joys truly light up the Way. We come to *know* Something 'really real' which can't be rationalized or figured out by the conditioned mind of convention and karma. This we can find for ourselves and It changes/transforms everything. As dutiful children of Buddha we can grow into our very Birthright. It is simply up to us.

# I Never Promised You a Rose Garden

This title is taken from a true account by a psychotic patient about her psychotherapy. The climax of the book, as I recall, came after the writer was free of the mental illness and commenced to live a more normal life. She reproached her therapist because she was facing problems of a new sort now that she was well. Her wonderful therapist told her, 'Well, I never promised you a rose garden.' How much have *we* bought into the delusion that *if this or that would just happen* my life would be problem free, a 'rose garden'?

That core delusion is what propels a new birth, you and me, into this life. It is essentially clinging to a belief that *something* external can satisfy this persistent longing to be whole, in harmony, secure. We either cling to something from the past that has provided a sense of fulfillment for a while, or put out feelers for something different from that which in the past was disappointing. We are on a teeter-totter of searching and rejecting, highs and lows, expectation and disappointment. This is one way to view samsara, the wheel of birth and death, which is perpetuated until we finally come to recognize that this basic search must be an *inward* one. We consider 'maybe I could be wrong' and thus allow the key turning to the spiritual life.

Our fundamental 'problem' is that we hold tightly to our delusions that are acceptable in our particular society and hence, they go unnoticed. But they don't go away. As long as we continue to be motivated by these false expectations, we strengthen the tendency itself that keeps them going. We hug our beliefs to us so implicitly that they become our unexamined assumptions about how things 'should' be. When we find disappointment, we cry in dismay for the 'rose garden' we somehow bought into. When we don't really look at this fallacy, we find fault and blame something, either ourselves, other people, or circumstances. We can *look* at this pattern. The heart of our training can be triggered right here—look at the blaming itself, which then allows us to look beyond it. Then we can see for ourselves, it was just a mistaken point of view—life isn't a rose garden that fulfills all our expectations, desires, and wishes. We're here to grow out of our limited ways of viewing ourselves in the world so that we can appreciate a 'bigger picture' with more opportunities, more freedom, more joy. Instead of a little rose garden, which has its thorns, we live in the 'Bodhisattva's playground,' helping and being helped by others as we walk along the path of training.

# It's a Mixed Bag

The title is one way that sums up the existential predicament the Buddha addressed in his teachings. From that point of view it really is so simple. Likely its very simplicity defies the complexity of the conditioned mind, which is caught and confused, so much wanting to figure things out to make them better. The Buddha addressed this unsatisfactoriness in terms of three defilements or poisons—greed, hate, and delusion—ways of relating to the world involving a basic confusion of reality so that a fragmented self, a 'me' and a 'mine,' grasps after or pushes away passing experiences. That's the mixed bag we experience as living beings in the seemingly separate world around us. The whole thrust of the Buddha's teachings is about how to get off this spinning wheel to live in peace and inner harmony with all life. He assures us that this is possible here and now within this very life.

The Buddhadharma can seem formidable with the voluminous teachings given over the Buddha's 45 years of ministry and that of followers after his death, as it spread from India to other countries. Habits of the mind strongly hold us along a course that is reactive to arising conditions so that it is a challenge to recognize when we're simply trapped in that. Then life can seem complex and bewildering. The reminder that life truly is a mixed bag can bring a firmer groundedness for the wavering, unsteady self. That allows the wisdom of the Four Noble Truths to begin percolating so that something can become unstuck. You see, we may not have even recognized that we are stuck because the condition itself arises out of a constricted and limited awareness. Hence, the First Noble Truth that life is suffering, when brought to mind as a *noble* truth, is the beginning of the loosening of the knot that binds.

And here come marching in those five spiritual qualities (patience, courage, faith, humility, compassion) to be cultivated, ready to assist the sorely tried 'me' that feels uneasy, dissatisfied, restless and disturbed. One can *begin* with any one of them, and the strength of the meditation itself allows this to happen. This morning *faith* was my foothold, or handhold, as old feelings colored an otherwise peaceful morning. Reverend Master wrote in her Commentary on the Precepts: *Whether well or sick, brightly alive or dying, hold fast to the Lord of the House*. That's what we've lost touch with. The conditioned self obscures the 'bigger picture' of which it is a part; it is never separate or alone. Then *humility* emerged as the grab bar that gradually allowed a movement out of despair. Then the 'potent army,' as the Buddha put it, of *patience* allowed a sustaining of the slow easement out of the tension.

When we see our own helplessness (*humility*) to shift out of the unsettled mood, this allows an opening to the deeper knowing (*faith*) that can't really be conceptualized because it's beyond the human mind. This allows an easing into the present moment (*patience*) and that brings a willingness to bear whatever the seeming burden is (*courage*). All four qualities work together supporting each other, which allows the turning to happen: *boundless compassion* appears and embraces the tension of self. *All is well, and all is well.* There was nothing wrong in the first place; just another episode of the karma or conditioning that was brought forth by the causes and conditions of this present moment. This marvelous cleansing *happens* because of our willingness to keep up our daily training as the mixed bag of existence plays itself out in our daily lives. We are given useful reminders to be alert and mindful over and over again. This is the fortunate karmic gift of being born in the human realm and having found a teaching that truly enhances this precious life of ours.

# Karmic Streams Intermingle

In the *teaching that is unique to Buddhas,* the cause of suffering is flatly stated to be attachment, without any qualifications: *Anything* that is held on to has the potential to bring unsatisfactoriness in its wake. And we attach all the time: *Here born we clutch at things and then compound delusion later on by following ideals [more fixed attachment].* The metaphor expressed in the title can be a helpful antidote to free us from our grip on aspects of our lives. On the first watch of the night of his enlightenment the Buddha got in touch with his 'myriad past lives' in great detail: born in this environment with this name and these characteristics, seeing what he did and how at death another life followed, over and over again. *Beginninglessly*—he could not trace these myriad lives back to a source. This is worth pondering upon, as is the teaching that came to him in the second watch of the night: beings pass away and are reborn *according to their deeds.* This of course is a statement of the law of karma: Our actions have consequences which may appear in the present life or the next or in some future life. This is the karmic stream that we've each inherited: we are the inheritors of the karmic tendencies of beings in our particular stream, given this opportunity once again to clarify the Great Matter for which we train.

The view that emerges from this teaching is dynamic and positive, bringing fire to the training for those of us who have been touched by it. It rests on the Right Understanding expressed in the Four Noble Truths: we simply do not need to perpetuate the churning desires, anger, and confusion which sully the karmic stream that is who we take ourselves to be, this 'me' and this 'you.' The beginning of our spiritual practice is built on this understanding: there is Something more than clinging to the old habits and beliefs that have propelled us into this existence. The deep spiritual *purpose* of this life for each of is to alter the course of our own karmic stream in order to return to the inner Knowing of our awakened nature. Opportunity after opportunity is presented for this process in daily life with the appearance of other karmic streams. This little karmic stream runs side by side with another and another and another. Sometimes they intermingle in exchanges that are agreeable—in relationships, in jobs, in recreation. This only becomes a problem in our habitual tendency to grasp at the pleasant and push away that which is unpleasant, forgetting to our detriment that streams must also flow apart, however satisfying or unsatisfying their time together has been—every meeting ends in parting.

When we embrace all Life as a magnificent movement of myriad steams, we free ourselves from suffering because we *know* beneath the surface level of convention that everything is changing, that the present is a shifting scene. It's just passing through. *We* are just passing through. As this knowing deepens, more and more it can become the guiding principle for living. *Karmic streams come together, move side by side, intermingle, and then separate*. Then our *hold* on life lightens. In the Buddhist Discourses followers drawn to the Buddha say to him, '*Your face is clear, your countenance serene.*' This serenity arises out of the dispassion of knowing that *All that arises also passes away*, inevitably. This is the truth we can keep bringing ourselves back to in our interactions with others. The process of our training then allows an appreciation of *each* moment—our karmic stream touching momentarily this one and now that—and each in all of its fullness because we are *open*. Our face can be clear and our countenance serene because we're not hanging on to the past or fearing the future: we live *now* in the purity of our intentions as expressed in the three Pure Precepts: Do as little harm as possible; Do as much good as possible; and Do good for others by our willingness to keep up the inner work of the heart.

We begin to catch the moment, so to speak, when the presence of an attachment flickers up. This is the best time, it is said in the literature, to train—when the hindrance has arisen. This gives a dynamic fire to our training: when we are willing to look, we *will* see these inner movements. And we can release their tension by remembering that we can't hold onto anything. This allows us to learn from the experience. Our karmic stream has 'met' another within a flowing space of time. This is Dogen's *'Uji'* which Reverend Master Jiyu translated as *Existence, Time, Flow*. The vast flowing that is Life becomes *our* life as we cease to resist or grab at whatever is momentarily arising. It is a Flow of Immaculacy, Reverend Master taught us, and we all partake of It. Our sincere and ongoing spiritual life of meditation gives us the opportunity of *knowing* It ourselves. And then we bow and bow and bow in this wonderful freedom, in our Birthright to participate in the Life of the Eternal, the Unborn, the true Source of our being.

We 'enter the stream' of Buddhism as we are willing to let go of our clinging to this phantom 'me' and 'mine' to move to the Other Shore. To have the courage to embark on and continue the Journey back Home, we shift our faith in this little self to faith in the buddhadharma, not fanatically, just willingly to 'come and see,' to find the Truth of the teaching for ourselves. As we continue to train we recognize increasingly what a radical shift we've made in the inner direction. We truly find we can more easily move away from our usual course of me-centeredness to be a willing partner within the vast Flow that includes us all. Through this process we give ourselves the opportunity to learn from each intermingling of our karmic stream with another, letting go when they move apart. As one influential master of the last century taught: 'Let go a little, a little bit of peace. Let go a lot, a lot of peace. Let go completely, complete peace.' This is the Buddha's promise—the Third Noble Truth that there is an end to suffering, *Nirvana*. Our entire training is learning how to release attachments that hold us back from fully participating in the dynamic Flow, which is Life.

# Layered Karma

At various times since 2003 when I came to Vancouver Island after over 20 years of living in a monastic setting, there's been a clear sense about this aspect of training—how our karmic conditioning seems layered. Part of this layering is what I've referred to as a cutting edge: the koan of everyday life. As Great Master Dogen reminds in Rules for Meditation: *The koan appears naturally in daily life*. Some aspect or aspects of life keep arising that challenge our ordinary stance. The 'koan' is as a red-hot ball in one's mouth which can't be swallowed or spit out, and that's uncomfortable. Typically, we conditioned humans tend to become either just immersed in what has arisen (swallow it) or attempt to push it away (spit it out). The tendencies are habitual ways of being in the world, triggered by the circumstances that have arisen at the time.

At some point, when this palliative approach is recognized as not working, for some of us there is an inner turning to look with new eyes. Again, as Dogen wrote, *All you have to do is cease from erudition, look within, and reflect upon yourself.* Then we're in a new ball game, so to speak. 'Erudition' here refers to the very nature of the conditioned mind itself, busily, nervously trying to be comfortable and secure within. Meditation is the art and act of stepping back from this persistent involvement with the mind itself. As I've observed ruefully, this can seem like trying to pick oneself up by one's own bootstraps because we've been trapped, caught, in this karmic tangle for so long that it seems 'natural.'

Of course, it is natural to the conditioned mind itself, and that effectively obscures a greater knowing, a greater awareness.

The willingness to be still within the discomfort involved here allows little by little a recognition of how karma works. There are patterns of cause and effect that to varying degrees had escaped our notice through the automatic conditioning coming out of past experiences. When the teaching about karmic consequence has been overlooked and forgotten, Life generously provides repeated situations to get our attention. When we finally 'get it,' we appreciate Dogen's rather stark observation: *There is only one thing, to train hard for this is true enlightenment.* The training hard is working with the koan that appears in daily life. The true enlightenment is the illumination coming from really seeing how the choices we make have consequences and how we truly can make different choices through seeing those that bring distress to ourselves and/ or others. It's as simple as that, from the side of practice, and as difficult as that, when we are more or less sleepwalkers moving through life in old habit patterns that are automatic.

Enter the title of this reflection—'Layered Karma'. What one begins to recognize—and this can bring a profound humility right up front—is that buried in the storehouse of this body-mind we take as 'self' are old patterns that surface when the 'right' conditions come together at a particular time. With the cultivation of awareness itself there is a better chance to see the connection. It's surprising how blurred this can be. In one scripture the problem here is likened to how a cataract affects what can be seen which then will be taken as the reality. In this analogy, our practice is as removing the cataract, the obstruction of old conditioned ways of being in the world. Then we are taking charge of our lives, taking the responsibility in a way not available before. This 'surgery' can be painful and stressful. As a particular layer of karma is seen with new eyes, dismay and inner turmoil are the signal that this is to be looked at. We're less slaves to the habit tendencies that automatically blind our awareness.

The healing balm of training may not be immediately experienced—it may burn first as we're willing to question the conditioned reactivity itself. This is the important pausing; it's a restraint. In one of the verses of The Dhammapada, we're told that restraint in everything is good. We give ourselves the opportunity to implicitly ask '*what is it good to do?*', which allows a wise discernment to guide us. This brings the challenge of actually following through and risking doing something different. This is the ongoing training because with the cultivation of this quality of awareness, the 'cataract' that's distorted our vision is being removed—on its own time. We cannot make it happen, so the particular karmic layer may again surface when all conditions ripen. That is not a problem when we truly understand that this is why we train. Faith grows, confusion lessens, and in our hearts we're comforted by Great Wisdom: *O Buddha, going, going, going on beyond, and always going on beyond—Always becoming Buddha. Hail!*

# Letting Go With Love

A theme with two parts has been recurring for me for several months. We can look at our valuable practice as expressed in the title, a right understanding to alert us when confronted with the conditions needing to be let go of. Let me start with the first part of the theme so relevant to my practice: *Loving is letting go*. The fruit of the practice simply appears when self is out of the way, when it is at any given moment dissolved, as it is put in the Scripture of Great Wisdom. It truly is all about loving. Our work of the heart/mind allows the wondrous transformation from defiled mind into Buddha Mind.

Bodhidharma pointed out that there are these two aspects of mind: the mind immaculate and the mind stained. The former is none other than the awakened mind, Buddha Mind, whilst the latter is this self-mind which is the problem. So the transformation brought about through our dedicated and sincere practice is characterized by the defilements of greed (selfish desire), hate (anger and frustration), and delusion (confusion) transforming into the compassion, love, and wisdom of our True Self, our Awakened Self, Buddha Mind.

The miracle of training is that it is truly possible for this conversion to happen. We can't 'make' it happen. It's when we give up the delusion of being in charge, which comes from the basic sense of being a separate 'me' or self, that the obstacles dissolve. This conditioned mind when unexamined is the problem, and we're repeatedly challenged to *look within and advance directly along the road that leads to the [Buddha] Mind,* the mind immaculate. Our precious birthright of awareness has been obscured in the complexity of causes and conditions that have brought forth a rebirth, a 'you' and a 'me.' At times, the barriers drop away and.... There's really no way to describe what follows because it's beyond the human mind which exists within ideas, beliefs, and concepts that are then expressed in a particular conventional language. Dogen put it this way: *When body-mind drops away naturally, the Buddha Mind immediately manifests itself ... When the opposites arise, the Buddha Mind is lost.*

The consequence of our being willing to keep up our spiritual practice is that the Buddha Mind is found. Of course, it actually has not gone anywhere; it's just in our ignorance, our confusion, we lost touch with It. When we're out of the way, for a little while we appreciate a flowing Love. Reverend Master Jiyu called it the Flow of Immaculacy. This immaculacy is the absence of the conditioned coloring that brought the obscuration. This is the Love that surpasses all understanding. This is the Love that enfolds us all. This is the Love that is free of the discriminative bias of the limited conditioned mind that naturally dwells in opposites. It is so freeing and expansive, this heart of Love, an abundant flow that is neither obstructed by nor holds onto anything. Touching this wondrous 'place' happens when self is out of the way. It is here that letting go just naturally happens. Loving is letting go. The Buddha taught: *There is no-thing you need hold onto. There is no-thing to push away.* Here is the freedom of Zen.

The title, 'Letting Go with Love,' is the other side of the coin: this is when we're stuck once again in the defiled or conditioned me that hasn't yet been converted. The more we train with the stillness and clarity of the choice to observe, rather than be caught in the 'soap opera' of the conditioned self, the more alert we become to the causes and conditions that trigger its activity. It is the limited constriction of 'me' that wants this and doesn't want that. In the First Noble Truth, the Buddha taught that this swing of the opposites is based upon clinging to the five aggregates, ways we experience ourselves and the world. When we observe the clinging then we have our work cut out for us: to let go with love. This is the basic effort in our serene reflection meditation: we're not holding onto any of the feelings and thoughts that arise and we're not trying to push them away. We're just willing to be within that tension of 'me' that identifies with the passing scene. This identification is the mistake and that is what we can choose to let go of, over and over again. And at special moments we recognize we are warmly embraced by the Love that doesn't separate, doesn't divide, doesn't grab. We have moved from the work of letting go with love to the wonder of *being* the loving, which is letting go. With this right understanding, we can truly appreciate how daily life presents us with countless opportunities to effect this change. That is the miracle of training.

# Loneliness

One of our Sangha was recently talking about loneliness. She lives alone, which she likes, but has become aware that coming home from work sporadically triggers a sense of loneliness. Her awareness has also allowed her to see that at those times she will turn on the TV as soon as she gets home as an attempt to assuage the loneliness. She recognizes that this pattern is not helpful in that often on television there isn't anything that she finds worthwhile or interesting or even entertaining. This is fruitful ground for training, which her awareness allows her to get in touch with.

First of all, there is nothing wrong, nothing to be disgusted about or ashamed of. This provides the acceptance of the way things are that allows us to change. When we feel annoyed at ourselves, we want to close off looking because it is too painful. So we begin with where we are, and our growing faith in our spiritual practice lets us know we don't have to be stuck this way any longer. This defuses the whole issue, whatever the thinking/feeling pattern is. It is understandable that after a day of intense and conscientious interacting with others, we *may* feel some kind of vacuum in the evening when unstructured time presents itself. One monk of our Order put it this way: 'How quickly delusion solidifies.' What he meant was that all the hustle-bustle of our busy lives of mixing with others, earning a living, volunteering, playing bridge, for examples, has a seeming reality that 'solidifies' around these people and events. We lose touch with that inner Place which is the True Reality, meaning that it is unchanging and undying—the Unborn. This underlies *everything,* and within ourselves we have the opportunity to touch It. We recognize That is the purpose of our whole life and our practice is the way to find It.

When we can just remember this basic truth, then we truly have the means to not fold under, whatever the feeling may be. As the person here did—she saw an inner pattern that led to an action no longer helpful to her. This is the first step in the process of transformation. This is done little by little as our awareness allows us to see the particular pattern; in my own experience, generalizations don't solve anything. We don't have to 'fix' the loneliness and we don't have to buy into it. This is important to remember. Instead, we are *willing to pause* for a moment and simply see what's going on in our inner life. *That* which is seeing the loneliness is not the loneliness: we've stepped back from the feeling we earlier invested in. A weakening of its hold on us is simply part of this process—we can't make the loneliness go away and it *does* fade. Why? Because it wasn't fixed, it wasn't real; it was simply a conditioned form that in the past elicited certain reactions. This pausing and maintaining the awareness is the second step. The fading happens of itself, so in that sense it isn't a step. Still it is part of the process that we have begun by our willingness not to act upon the discomfort of an unwelcome feeling.

As this fading happens, it is replaced by a sense of the 'all rightness' of simply being. It takes awhile to recognize that this all rightness puts us in touch with our Buddha Nature. In my experience a great relief often follows, accompanied by a natural gratitude for the training and for That arising. Within this, the teaching signaled by the uncomfortable feeling may appear. We may ask ourselves why the sense of loneliness came up this time, and not yesterday. It is all learning when we are open to the learning. The doorway within is our *willingness* to stay with the awareness of whatever mental state is passing through. My Master was taught that *all-acceptance is the key that unlocks the Gateless Gate.* To put this another way, it is our resistance that blocks our Birthright of peaceful, settled be-ing: we get a glimmer that we don't have to be anything special. We are all right just as we are. Out of this secure Place, we can more easily view where it might be good to do this or that. It may be that we or someone else did something during the day that hit a raw nerve and we didn't address it at the time—there was no time or we fell into old reactions that once done we regretted. Regardless, we have to get on living through that moment and leave it behind: If we're teaching, we get on with the teaching, if we're programming a computer, we get on with that. When we get home, we have the wonderful opportunity to recollect or reflect on this incident, if we don't try to get away from the niggle by turning on the TV or picking up a book. The power of our choices cannot be overestimated. We can be more and more in charge of our lives, and it happens one step at a time by our willingness to do our spiritual practice.

# Looking for Something that Isn't There

In his enlightenment poem Sekito Kisen wrote, *Here born we clutch at things and then compound delusion by following ideals.* The first part of this compound sentence seemed quite clear to me in my early years of training while the second perplexed me. Now there is an 'of course they go together,' the initial delusion of clutching that is then perpetuated in following ideals. *Here born*, we're always looking for something, clutching at this or that to satisfy a sense that *something* is missing. This is the consequence of birth, as it is taught in the basic doctrine of Dependent Origination. A *rebirth*, the teaching's eleventh step, is a consequence of what is called *becoming*, in the usual formulation. The *becoming* itself is a result of *clinging* or grasping at experiences that in this life seem desirable, as necessary for one's well-being. Going back one step further, to the eighth step, the *clinging* depends upon the *craving* for some things and rejection of others. Thus, the opposites are conceived and acted upon, repeatedly, many times, life after life. *What* is desired and rejected varies, but the very stance of dividing up our world in this way remains. And that stance directly relates to the first false step, *ignorance* of the Truth, which is what keeps the beginningless wheel rolling. Thus, a misunderstanding or mistaken view is at the very core of the problem of this life. Until we are willing to examine our assumptions, beliefs, premises, ideas, and opinions regarding our being in this world, we're on this samsaric wheel in which both what we consider desirable and undesirable keep presenting themselves. Yes, *here born we clutch at things,* and as much as we try to make our life all right by *following ideals,* we'll be disappointed and frustrated if we continue to search for something that isn't there.

With this Right Understanding of the nature of the human predicament, we have the opportunity to *get off the Wheel.* Long before I was on a spiritual path, the quip 'Stop the world, I want to get off' was sporadically very appealing, although it may have been only subliminal most of the time. The unwanted sense that *something was wrong* would keep coming up as the good and bad intertwined through this sadly flawed life. 'Getting off' would have been a way of not experiencing the insecurity and inadequacy which seemed to underlie whatever momentary joy or satisfaction was present. So, of course, obviously, the thing to do was to move on in the false belief that in another environment the fundamental unsatisfactoriness and unreliability of life as lived on the surface apparent level could be escaped. It was a long while before I began to learn spiritual truths and practices that helped me to get a handle on the basic understanding that what I was looking for simply could not be found in externals. No matter how appealing a new place and new position would seem, they simply could not appease the heart's aching void. Why? Because the real problem wasn't being addressed. Everything changes and what can look so good at one point may shift to not so good. Again, why? Because the self experiencing all of this also changes. Looking so desperately for gratification and security, it grabs at illusion after illusion in hopes of what they may bring.

Life after life we play out the drama in the form of karmic tendencies or beliefs of what may or may not fulfill the deepest longing of the heart, until seemingly by trial and error we finally 'get it' and turn toward a spiritual solution to the end of suffering. We begin to *Look within and advance directly along the road that leads to the Mind [Buddha Nature, That which doesn't change]*. What a blessing it is—no matter how long it takes—to have made this fundamental *turning*. Through this mundane Right Understanding we embark upon our spiritual journey back to the Source of who we are, the Truth. Everyday we can renew our commitment to this path of Truth to help us in the face of the grave challenge it is to live *standing against the world [of our conditioned mind] in order to train in Wisdom*. We keep letting go of the unreal as Life shows us in this and then that experience the three basic characteristics of existence: impermanence, unsatisfactoriness (in the long run) and insubstantiality of whatever particular experience we're attempting to hold onto. This is the learning of a lifetime! When we become complacent because life is conforming to our seeming needs and expectations, we'll be rudely awakened once again to these three characteristics of existence (impermanence, unsatisfactoriness, not-self). We can't afford to lapse from mindfulness once we truly have recognized how easily conditions and old conditioning fool us, however deceptive they are.

As this understanding deepens, we have the opportunity to see how driven we are in our habitual search for experience. We see why the Buddha placed as the ninth of ten fetters *restlessness*, the seeming need to move, the tendency to resist settling into simple be-ingness. We're driven and uneasy until we begin giving ourselves the opportunity to see the endlessness of this pattern through keeping up our spiritual practice that brings the beautiful awareness into increasing spheres of our lives. Nothing need be excluded at the outset of the journey. As we keep going, we change and we learn that true contentment will never be found in depending on any experience. Restlessness comes up and we develop the strength to *sit with it,* to not act upon it.

In that stillness, which doesn't stand against movement, our Buddha Nature manifests Itself. It's always been here, in each moment of our lives, and we've simply missed it most of the time by not paying attention, by being pulled toward some activity, by our *restlessness*. For that instant, *wrong view,* the tenth fetter, drops away and we *know* deeper than words can express That which is *Unborn, Undying, Uncreated, and Unchanging*. This is making the Buddha's Truth true for ourselves and we each become 'a dutiful child of Buddha'. Born out of ignorance life after life, searching repeatedly everywhere but within our own heart for Love and All-rightness, *We* for a little while *live in the world as if in the sky. Just as the lotus blossom is not wetted by the water that surrounds it. The Mind is immaculate and beyond the dust. Let us bow to the Highest Lord*. This is the blessing verse at the very end of an ordination in our tradition. Its promise can be fulfilled by all of us by our willingness *to turn within,* our willingness to stop our compulsive search for changing experiences, our willingness to begin *seeing things the way they are.*

# Mindfulness is All

After the talk last evening a Sangha member brought up for discussion a teaching of Reverend Master Jiyu's that I quote from time to time: *Nothing matters; mindfulness is all*. This was part of her summing up of the teaching she received from her third kensho retreat of 1976. It catches one's attention as one deepens one's training because, as many aspects of a spiritual understanding, it runs quite counter to our ordinary way of viewing life. 'What do you mean that nothing matters?' asks the 'me' we're training. 'I shouldn't care about my child, my friends, my health, my position?' Our reply is a clear, 'No, that's just falling into the opposites, and the important aspect of our practice is learning how to free ourselves from them.' A number of the Sangha members offered their understanding of this important teaching, forming a lovely kaleidoscope that revealed some of its multi-dimensions.

This morning it seems good to tie some of the important pieces together. As I mentioned, another way of expressing this was taught by an important Zen master of the last century: 'Our practice takes us to the place where there is nothing special.' We're trying to cut through the conditioned mind's wonted way of discrimination or judging whatever is happening in terms of its conditioning, which is so implicit that without training in mindfulness and clear comprehension it goes unnoticed. What is it calling our attention to? Our karmic tendency to fall into liking or disliking (or not paying attention to) the phenomena that arise, that we come into contact with. It's hard to remember that this is simply *our* point of view and that someone else might with equal validity see it differently. Our practice is to erode this tendency to judge in this way. Another Zen Master wrote in his enlightenment poem: *Avoid one-sided clinging. This is all the natural and superior Truth that does attach itself to no delusion or enlightenment,* and goes on with *It calmly, clearly shows when all conditions ripen: when minute infinitesimally small becomes, when large It transcends all dimension space. Even the slightest twitch will surely break the rhythm.*

Our judgmental mind brings on 'the twitch' and we're out of sync, out of harmony with That which transcends all dimension space. The conditioned mind boggles at the inconsistency that It can be both infinitesimally small and also large enough to transcend all space. What does that mean? As it is repeatedly emphasized, Buddhism is a practice—we must make the teaching true for ourselves. It's got to become our 'blood-and-bones' understanding toward life, as Reverend Master Jiyu would put it. Our discussions are a way to highlight where to go, shining light on the Path of training, and then we have to have the faith and courage to take each next step for ourselves. We're carried along in a hidden stream taking us to the Other Shore, which we enter by our willingness to stop and see, as the Buddha invites us to do. And what do we see when we're willing to pause in the midst of our assumptions, emotions, fears? We see that, oh so often, *Nothing Matters* in the way we have habitually related to what's happening in our lives. So *Mindfulness*, the wonder of our precious birthright of awareness, *IS All*. It allows us to see *when all conditions ripen*, which then triggers some specific karmic reactivity. This reactivity results from past experiences stored in this body-mind, which may or may not be helpful or appropriate right now.

Being able to look in this way depends upon our ability to stay right here, right now, in the present moment. Our intention to do this, which is built upon our formal meditation practice of 'just sitting,' allows us repeatedly to see how our untrained mind slips off into the past or the future. As the Buddha pointed out in one of the Middle Length Discourses: *Let a man not dwell upon the past or upon the future place his hopes, for the past has been left behind and the future has not yet come. Instead with insight let him see each presently arisen state. Let him know that and be sure of that invincibly, unshakably.* This he calls *one fortunate attachment*. Why? Because it is the way to sanity, to clearing up the inherent confusions of this conditioned self. This is the Middle Way the Buddha taught as his very first discourse following his enlightenment. It's alien to our habitual ways of being in the world as we filter most everything through our judgmental mind of how it affects ME. This can be pretty raw at times, rather primitive really, so who in the heck wants to observe it in oneself?

The wonder of training, of our spiritual practice, is that we find true for ourselves the tremendous value of doing just that. *When we study Buddhism, we study ourselves. When we study ourselves, we [then can safely] forget ourselves. When we forget ourselves, we're enlightened by everything, and this breaks our clinging to [this] body-mind.* Here we have the freedom of Zen. It isn't in living carelessly with disregard of others because one is liberated from all of that. It's living with a growing, glowing awareness of how to be in harmony with *every thing*. In Sir Edwin Arnold's 'The Light of Asia' the Buddha's enlightenment is described poetically this way: *Forgoing self, the Universe grows 'I'*. So we can turn the Nothing Matters around and recognize that *every thing* matters in its own special and unique way that doesn't have to be answerable to how *we* want, expect, or insist it 'should' be. We find the Buddha everywhere. As Reverend Master Jiyu wrote in her Commentary on the last great Precept, *Look with the eyes of a Buddha and you will see the heart of a Buddha*. This does indeed go far beyond the discriminatory mind that chops up our wonderful world into opposites where some things are clung to and others pushed away. We truly can do better than that.

We're cultivating a wise discernment that *sees things as they are,* instead of as colored by our conditioned self-view. Over and over again, our practice allows us to do just this because that is our choice, painful though it can be at times, as we all know. Giving up our illusions of who we are, our self-images, can shake us up, put us in a spin. The *freedom* of Zen naturally follows as we increasingly are alert to illusions' automatic strength to color what we see, thus allowing us the choice to *stop and see* before acting on those illusions. Life really does lighten up. It's the karmic consequence of our willingness to keep making the choice to train. We find we are training in Buddhism for the sake of Buddhism because as we keep 'forgoing self' in this situation and in that, the *Universe does indeed grow 'I'*. Countless times, we can find encouragement to do just this. We're taking Refuge in the Buddha—our own true knowing, Refuge in the Dharma—the many-faceted teaching of the Buddha Shakyamuni, and Refuge in the Sangha—our fellow trainees. The last is what we directly experience, as we did last evening and every time we join for our meditation practice. And I thank you all from the bottom of my heart for your willingness to train here and now, together and independently, *always becoming Buddha, Hail!*

# No Expectations

When Reverend Master Jiyu went to Japan at the invitation of Koho Zenji, Abbot of Soji-ji, one of the two large Soto Zen training monasteries, early on she was told to expect little. Later on, she wrote, she was told to expect nothing. At the time, she felt dismayed by this teaching because she'd come all the way from England at mid-life to embark upon something radically different from her old life. She adds, however, that despite this initial 'Well!' this was absolutely true in spiritual training: *we must expect nothing while giving all*. Any reservation holds us back. We all have hidden expectations or reservations that stand in our way, hindering our progress, which become known to us when we do sincere practice. As soon as we recognize the hindrance, we can accept it and learn from it and let it go. Then we are again back in the purity of no expectations.

We simply have to remember that *to expect nothing* is a condition for traveling in the Way so that we don't get stuck. As this simple teaching is taken in more and more, life becomes far more simple and less disappointing. Why? Because truly we can't count on anything. Life takes us by surprise and, if we're not holding on to what we supposed would happen or should happen, we simply *let go*. This is really the whole of the practice. Obviously, this doesn't stand against events happening as we expected them to happen. It is just because so often our expectations are met that we're led to a false security that they will be met the next time. We take things for granted in so many ways—that seems to be just the way we are wired. We don't so much notice all that goes 'right' for us and are taken up short when they don't. This is worth pondering.

When we are doing our daily practice, we have a wonderful opportunity to expand our awareness to notice both, and we then more often appreciate the times things seem to be working out smoothly, seamlessly, while taking the times they don't as opportunities to learn more deeply about the pitfalls our karmic tendencies bring. This is very freeing, really a joyous way to live. We don't need to hold onto resentments and are patient with ourselves as we mull over and reflect upon the particular event that surprised us. We can even look with amusement on this little self that can get so indignant and in doing so cull the truth from that chaff.

When I left the small Temple in Washington in Spring, 2003, where I'd been training for four years, to take a leave of absence from monastic life, the Abbot said 'Have fun.' In the year and a half after leaving, I found that to my surprise life could be fun. Much of my life, including that in the monastery, was stressful and inwardly anguished, whether things were going well or not. When 'little self' is in dominance—and, indeed, so often prior to a committed religious life, there may not be even a glimmering awareness of anything else—the 'fun' experienced can be just a desperate effort to grasp at some fleeting little respite from despair. The desperation underneath rather spoils and colors everything, whether it is immediately obvious to little self or others. This is the karmic inheritance we have come into this life to cleanse. We really must see the dirt before we can effectively let our practice wash the dirt away. Daily training is our willingness to see. Then we have the golden opportunity to make other choices, letting go of whatever the obstacle seems to be. This is big, even though the situation prompting the challenge may be quite insignificant in itself. We don't have to wait for earth-shaking events to train. Indeed, though such events are intense, that very intensity can be an impediment to finding that wonderful quiet Place within which our training progresses.

Our daily training itself is the 'begging bowl' we hold up to the sky; this takes on profound significance here. We just have to remember that, as in the Mealtime Ceremony we bring our carefully cleaned begging bowls to receive the meal, so must we come—or return—to *emptiness* in order to receive unsullied whatever Life puts into our bowl. The Buddha teaches that the monk on alms rounds must be mindful, have the senses restrained, and be still. This is emptying oneself of expectations for this or that 'food,' a willingness to receive openly whatever is given. It is this attitude toward life that is the 'philosopher's stone' that changes everything into gold. *Everything* teaches. The Truth is everywhere. With this attitude we have the opportunity to experience It and dwell in an otherwise unknown equanimity regardless of our karmic-seeming needs. This is *Standing against the world in order to train in wisdom*. And it is *We live in the world as in the sky. Just as the lotus is not wetted by the water that surrounds it, the Mind is immaculate and beyond the dust. Let us bow to the highest Lord.* It is a miracle of our quiet, persistent, dedicated, faithful training that allows us to know this for ourselves more and more.

The spiritual truths we read about, the Dharma Refuge, move into our own experience. This is what my Master called 'making the teaching your blood and bones.' Again the analogy of the begging bowl and our eating therefrom is apt: What we eat becomes assimilated through processes over which we don't have much control. We have the choice of our state of mind when accepting and partaking of the nourishment given. The power of faith-belief is shown in medicine by the placebo effect. When a patient believes in the prescription given by a trusted doctor, potent help can occur even when the 'medicine' is only a sugar pill. There are many instances of this well-documented finding. Obviously, this kind of belief has to be more than a superficial response to reach the very core of our being in order to be effective. In other words, we can't just *wish* that something would help whilst remaining pervaded by doubt and skepticism. Reverend Master said that the doubting mind is in hell, and we all know how difficult it is to move away from that inner mental conditioning. That is one reason that our training must become the very foundation of our life, the fulcrum around which the rest of our life rotates. Nothing needs to be negated or denied. The spiritual practice itself when done with sincerity and determination is a process bringing forth little by little these salutary changes that become astonishing transformations over time.

Soto Zen Buddhism has been called 'farmer's zen' distinguishing it from Rinzai Zen which was practiced by Samurai, the warriors of the Japan of old. I didn't much care for that sobriquet but gradually have appreciated the beauty of being a farmer as analogy: we plant the seed of faith in the welcoming soil of our spiritual heart. The soil has been prepared by life experiences that didn't live up to our expectations in sufficient critical mass so that we can't simply slog on in old ways—that's when we dig and till the ground. Next we channel the Water of the Spirit, which is always present to this little seed in willingness to allow its growth. Then, as with the farmer, who also must build on faith, we can only do so much here. We can't *make* the plant grow. If we get impatient then we interfere with the natural process of its growth. It takes that humility built upon our faith simply to be willing to keep up our practice as best we can every day. Roshi Uchiyama would tell his disciples they needed to train with him for ten years. Already this would probably discourage some. Then those who persisted were told to train for another ten years, and then another. Now they were ripe. Of course, it wouldn't take everyone thirty years, but that would certainly be a test of the trainee's sincerity and dedication. And it works! As Dogen wrote, *If you do these things for some time, you will become as herein described and then the Treasure House will open naturally and you will enjoy it fully.* What a miracle is the food that grows in the earth and is given to us for our nourishment and life! Gratitude and joy are the bursting of the Heart in appreciation for All of Life. That is the gift we give ourselves when we do our training.

## Open Hand, Open Heart

Our practice takes us to this wonderful place of opening. One important aspect of my practice in the last few years has been being open, transparent with other people and with my 'self.' This practice itself allows one to see how tempting it is to close off when feeling vulnerable and threatened. As we become better acquainted with this 'self' we take as 'me,' we more readily see how it functions. This is a very big gift of our training because the seeing allows the choice of pausing for a moment before acting in old conditioned ways. Believe me, this is very freeing and brings an uplift to the old closed off heart. Why? Because when we don't go on automatic with these old karmic perceptions, we have the opportunity to learn how distorted they may be. This is big learning and brings an expanding humility of willingness to learn from all experience instead of simply sliding into old grooves.

This way of being in the world with openness allows the heart to open more freely. What I mean is that the Love that is an inherent part of all being flows more easily and spontaneously because there is nothing, such as fear of rejection, to hold it back. Love is love and moves everywhere when the little self is out of the way. The natural response to love is love, so that increasingly people respond to us with affection and caring. We don't love in order to make this happen—that would be a mistake and one I have made innumerable times in my life. When we move out of a sense of needing something from that other person, which is the conditioned movement of the little self we are training, then we have the opportunity to notice how potentially disappointing such love can be. Other people are not here to make me feel better about myself, more worthwhile. That is *my* job of training. When I look to them in that way, sometimes they may be there for me and sometimes not. This is a position of off-balance, depending on someone, some situation, *something* to ease the lonely pain of the heart. It's an iffy sort of a thing, as we all know from time to time. The reaction to disappointment is frustration and resentment. We have the opportunity to observe how much the first two poisons rule us. First the greed comes out of a sense of neediness. When that isn't gratified then the hate or anger comes out of the disappointment itself.

We can learn to do better than this. The greed and hate are operative because of the third defilement or poison—delusion or confusion. We've over time lost touch with who we really are and have taken this body/mind as 'me' or myself. Our spiritual discipline allows us to return to the Source of our being. We can become our own best friend and not need others to support us. This does not mean that we are aloof and withdrawn from others. To the contrary, this is the Place from which genuine compassion, love, and wisdom flow. It's our True Nature, our Buddha Nature—our enlightened Self guiding and teaching us. Then all experience is valuable learning; we have 'beginner's mind,' as Suzuki Roshi put it. This flowing openness benefits us in another way; we learn increasingly the basic importance of *letting go* because we can see more clearly how much we'd like to hang on to this person or that, this situation or that. When they move through our lives and we've opened ourselves to care about them, there is a natural sense of loss with their passing through the door of our life experiences. We can see we have the choice to prolong the pain of wanting it to be otherwise, of wanting things still to be as they were before, or we can let that sense of loss simply pass through by not clinging.

This important teaching of letting go is the price we pay for openness, and it is worth every penny of wistful sadness it may bring. Over and over again it highlights the Buddha's Second Noble Truth that the cause of our suffering is attachment, clinging to something that inevitably passes, which thereby simply cannot be clung to. What I've come to see more clearly is that the sense of missing someone is not a problem, that it is part of the human condition, part of being in this realm of existence. When we understand that the feeling is not a problem, then we can just let go more and more easily each time it arises. All conditioned things both arise *and* pass, and with training they truly can dissolve *as problems*, as unacceptable. This is living in the Flow of Immaculacy. Its rewards are worth every effort. It can only be known through our continuing practice and it definitely *can* be known as we open our hearts.

# Return to Paradise

The title is borrowed from that of a book I read while at the monastery perhaps thirty years ago. 'Paradise' refers to Bali, and the author is returning there after the devastation of perhaps the Second World War to find that it has changed. The nostalgia of the 'old days' is moved by a sad longing, a disappointment, as if one *could* return. Thomas Wolfe expressed the same nostalgia in his autobiographical novel, *You Can't Go Home Again*. That's just the way it is because of the law, the fact, of changeableness. We simply can't go back, except in delusive imagination, because life has moved on, including our life, too. This theme expresses the human condition or predicament we come into this new birth to resolve: we look outside ourselves, externally, in changing conditions for that something we believe will permanently give us comfort, security, a sense of worth, love. We all seem to require a lot of experience in being disappointed in this expectation, this belief, before we finally have a glimmering that 'It ain't necessarily so,' as one of the Gershwin songs puts it.

So, if 'paradise' and 'home' aren't to be found and returned to in the way we fantasize, what are we to do? Some simply opt out: eat, drink, and be merry for tomorrow you may die. This 'solution' takes us to indulgence and addiction because we simply can't eat 'enough' or drink 'enough' to drown out that aching sense that we're missing something and that fear of death lurking around the corner, ours and those we love. The other approach the Buddha tried, but left behind, was that of asceticism, the spiritual practice extolled by teachers of his time. That delusion is that if we starve the body and shun pleasant life experiences, somehow that will help us over the hurdle of disappointment. Both these pseudo-solutions perpetuate suffering. The Buddha's koan was his questioning the fact of rampant suffering, and his renunciation of the life of seeming safety and pleasure was based on his search for the solution to the koan. So he said to the monks that he taught only two things: suffering and its end, which is a succinct way of referring to the Four Noble Truths, the first two representing the insight concerning suffering and the last two, the insight concerning its end. The end of suffering, the Third Noble Truth, is called *Nirvana* and in the literature is at times elaborated as bliss and serene contentment—i.e., paradise.

We *can* return to 'paradise' is the Buddha's promise—there is an end to suffering which can be realized, as we let go of our common delusion that it is possible to find it in impermanence, in the changing conditions that come and go. When we begin to understand on some intuitive level this wonderful Truth—the First Noble Truth that unsatisfactoriness is inevitable when we cling to that which is impermanent, including our body-mind that we take as 'me' and 'mine'—then we sincerely will embark on a path that takes us beyond the impermanent and changing. This is the Middle Path the Buddha refers to repeatedly. There is a 'third position,' as my Master called this, beyond the realm of the opposites we get caught up in. The Buddha's invitation is for us to again and again *go beyond* the various pairs of opposites, which we know and which motivate us. In this, we are moving from the known to the Unknown, so the Path of spiritual training requires a deepening of faith in That which is not known in the usual ways of our conditioning and beliefs. *Faith* is listed as the first of the five spiritual faculties or powers that help us in our spiritual search for our True home. This is a 'returning' to the Source of our being. It's Something we've known and lost touch with. My Master referred to *reharmonization* of the body-mind, our karma, with the Eternal, our Buddha Nature. This is expressed as the Fifth Law of the Universe: *Everyone has an innate knowledge of Buddha Nature,* our True Home. This understanding, expressed in these words, needs to be pondered and reflected upon for us to know the absolute necessity to keep up our training, to keep moving from the known of body-mind to a deeper knowing that is truly calling each of us. This movement is the awakening of faith.

Our spiritual work is clear and true. Built upon the foundation of faith in 'Something' more than the turbulence of ordinary experience, we are willing more and more to scrutinize and question the inner world of thoughts, feelings, impulses to action, desires, and so forth, which propel us to be reactive to the seemingly outward conditions that confront us. This is a true liberation from being pulled by these conditions, so that increasingly our actions are based on our unconditioned Awakened nature, our True Self. This beautiful willingness to be aware and *to see* can increasingly be *chosen* as the basis for what we do. *Such action and most unpretentious work* is quietly and without much fanfare taking us to the Other Shore, to a Paradise we really can return to, which is our True Home.

# Taking Things for Granted

Great Master Dogen wrote that *When we study Buddhism, we study ourselves. When we study ourselves, we forget ourselves. When we forget ourselves, we are enlightened by everything.* The second sentence is the key one here, because before we come to a spiritual practice of really taking the time to study/examine the activities of this body-mind we take as self, we forget ourselves in a different way. Before training we tend not to pay attention to what's going on except in a superficial manner. Why? Because the habit of the mind is to get caught up in a karmic story that is based on the past and projects into the future. With training this becomes increasingly obvious. As it is put in one of the Middle Length Discourses, this is not helpful because *the past has been left behind and the future has not yet come.* So the salutary teaching is instead to focus on what is happening now, really being in the present moment. The difficulty of doing this seemingly most simple thing—just staying attentive to the way things are—is suggested by the admonishment of the Buddha: <u>Now</u> *the effort must be made; tomorrow death may come, who knows? No bargain with mortality will keep him and his hosts away.* Then the great promise to those of us willing to take heed comes: *But he who dwells thus ardently, relentlessly, by day and by night, it is he the peaceful sage hath said is one who has one fortunate attachment.*

In other words, we've shifted our focus from old karmically engrained patterns to paying attention to how the events of our life are affecting us now. You could call this an effort to shift the default position to being mindful, attentive, heedful, careful of our precious self as we walk through another round of existence: we *choose* to train within the midst of conditions so that we can be still within the daily events that come to us. This requires a lot of courage and discipline. With the sincere determination to train, one comes to recognize that the work of the heart lies within: *We study Buddhism to study ourselves*. In other words, we are willing to explore, examine, and investigate this self we have implicitly taken as 'me' and 'mine.' Right at the beginning, we're into the very basic teaching of *anatta*, no-self. We're actually addressing, whether we recognize it or not, that there is *no* self in the usual way, the way we've simply assumed and fostered by building on the unique karmic inheritance which has driven each of us. For most of us, this teaching of no-self or emptiness has a chilling quality because it is interpreted *by* the conditioned self which has so dominated this life of ours. *When we study Buddhism we study ourselves,* directly, and more and more dispassionately *we forget ourselves and are enlightened by everything*, thus finding release from worldly unsatisfactoriness.

The obstacles to training, to finding that marvelous 'place' of contentment, peace, and inner harmony that is independent of the myriad conditions that bombard us, are often explained as three defilements or energies that keep us bound to the wheel of life as we know it. Succinctly, they are called 'greed, hate, and delusion.' But these three, as Bodhidharma taught, are *as the trunk of a great tree* that has many branches and buds. The 'branches' are our own particular karmic spin that gives rise to the great diversity of beings, all conditioned by ignorance of their true being. So the 'emptiness' referred to is *not a nothing*. You could say it is the remainder, what is simply *here*, when the heart is purified of greed, hate, and delusion (or desire, anger, and confusion). To do this vital work of the heart we must be willing to 'study ourselves.' This directly points to the Right Understanding that begins the path of training, the Noble Truth to the End of Suffering—the Noble Eightfold Path. That is the basic ground that repeatedly lightens our way as we walk the inner path by really looking at the maneuvers of the mind. Then we see more and more clearly how they have just flaunted their manners for so long that they seem 'natural' and have been rather mechanically followed. This might not make much sense prior to a training that is directed toward *ceasing from erudition, turning within, and reflecting upon oneself.*

Reverend Master Jiyu told us when we are at the beginning of training to 'use greed positively'. Most of us begin training because of a sufficiently strong recognition of being weighed down by unsatisfactoriness with our lives. This is expressed by the Buddha at the beginning of his basic teaching with the statement: *There is suffering, unsatisfactoriness, unreliability that accompanies being alive*, and he enumerates a number of them. Then he concludes his statement of the First Noble Truth with a summation: *It is clinging to the mind-body processes [the five aggregates or skandhas] that brings this whole mass of suffering/unsatisfactoriness into being*. In other words, right off he's letting us know that it is not life itself, with the various conditions he's enumerated, that is suffering, but that we implicitly add onto it by taking it personally as a 'me,' as who 'I am.' This is a *wrong view* that keeps us fettered to the unsatisfactoriness of life. The immensity of its implications takes us through the other three Noble Truths that follow. In other words, we simply must stop taking things for granted, sliding down the well-grooved path of our inherited karmic tendencies. So the Buddha said, *Stop and see*, an invitation as meaningful and viable today as it has always been.

We stop (or pause) in order that we can begin to see the nature of this conditioned mind that arises out of ignorance and leads to craving. We want rather blindly and we hate rather blindly, caught in the confusion of living as reactive, highly sensitive human beings in a particular environment at a particular time. Our practice is to help us *see* this reactivity which in turn allows us to *refrain* from simply being pulled by the causes and conditions that have at this moment come together in this particular way. We open to a Bigger Picture that allows us to pause before automatically acting out the karmic pattern. This restraint is difficult, and over and over again we make the *choice* not to give up, not to get caught in old doubts, building on the patience and willingness to persevere, somehow remembering that we're on the path of using the suffering to move toward the end suffering. Otherwise we remain trapped in old patterns that potentially, you might say inevitably, lead to more suffering. We're turning toward faith, toward an intuition that there simply *has* to be 'something more' than this life as we know it.

In the midst of daily life we can choose to 'stop and see' how we get caught up in what is by its nature impermanent, which then can lead to unwise action based on that mistaken point of view. Unsatisfactoriness is always the potential outcome as things inevitably change, thus revealing their lack of reliability as something that can be really held onto or counted upon. This is very sobering, and little by little we recognize that this sense of 'me' itself is also part of that which is conditioned out of changing movements and has no solid permanence. Before it had seemed so obvious and was simply taken for granted. We are seeing into the unsatisfactoriness of life, of self, and learning through that awareness how to let go of our insistence that things be the way the self wants them to be.

This freedom allows us to appreciate aspects of life that have been simply taken for granted while we searched and searched for the 'philosopher's stone' of permanent satisfaction within a world of changeability. *Something* comes to rest and Nirvana *IS*. It's the remainder that is within the Truth of Oneness, of Wholeness. This embraces and holds together all the varied movements of life that previously had been obscurations that blinded us. When we see from this different point of view, we're less likely to simply take so much for granted. We begin to open to all the grandeur and complexity. For that little while, we see into the heart of things. And this is worth everything. It is the *living* Third Noble Truth: *There is an end to suffering*. Don't cling, see clearly, and let go. We stop taking things for granted and learn to live in peace with the way things are.

# The Judgmental Mind

We are strongly warned about the dangers of the mind that makes judgments, discriminating in terms of the opposites. Dogen writes: *When the opposites arise we have almost lost our way to salvation*, and *When the opposites arise the Buddha Mind is lost*. What's the problem here, what's so bad about these opposites? Well, we can see for ourselves as our practice in awareness strengthens. When the mental activity says, 'This is good; I want it,' implicitly, and really obviously, there is the accompanying phrase of 'This is bad; I don't want it.' The Buddha in his First Discourse, Turning the Wheel of the Law, described this process as producing suffering: we want one thing and it is not always there when we want it. He also observed that we don't want something and it may nonetheless be there. This kind of mental activity—and it is perhaps not too strong to call it 'obsessive' or endemic—robs us of our peace of mind, our knowing of intrinsic Buddha Nature. This is not difficult to see when we are willing to look at what is going on within the secret chambers of our own mind.

An interesting thing happens to many of us as we see the hazards of this judgmental mind: we get it mixed up with what is called 'wise discernment.' This is the Wisdom of *seeing things as they are*, which is one way the Buddha described what he is teaching us: simply seeing the way things are *without the embellishment and coloring of self*. This is a dicey point and illustrates how the thinking mind can so easily become confused once we begin paying attention to its activity instead of simply being caught up in it. Early in my Buddhist training in the monastery I would hear that *The All is one and the All is different.* Differences are part of the Oneness of Life. We're not all the same, and what this is saying is that there is no problem. If Life of Buddha Nature, of the Eternal, isn't a problem, then *where* is the problem? It's in this judging little mind that pretty well automatically evaluates and colors experience in terms of itself with labels of desirable/undesirable, good/bad, right/wrong, and so forth. These are the opposites that arise and cover up Buddha Nature, the Wisdom of seeing the way things are.

In the Conditional Arising of a new being (such as you and me), the Buddha clearly teaches where the judgmental mind creeps into the 'big picture'. Our very sense organs (fifth link) bring the sixth link of contact with the world, and the contact itself, according to the Buddha, always has a feeling tone (seventh link): pleasant or unpleasant or neutral. Thus far it can be said that if a rebirth has been initiated, it will experience its world with one of these three feeling tones. So in this wonderful teaching, which is also called Dependent Origination, feelings are considered a *consequence* of previous conditions, which inevitably will arise. In other words, and we find this out very clearly as we train, we don't have any control or say about the feeling tone of our experiences. We can't *make* ourselves feel something as pleasant if it doesn't appear that way. Of course, we've all learned to fool ourselves that can force us to *believe* something alien to our experience: we learn what is acceptable and what is not within our particular environment.

The next link in the series of Dependent Origination is *craving*, followed by its intensification, *clinging* (eighth and ninth links).

Here is where the judgmental mind can be addressed so that important aspects of our actual behavior can change: *We don't have to act upon the craving or clinging*. We all know this: something pleasant comes into our sensory sphere, say ice cream. We remember all the pleasure of eating a bowl of ice cream or we've perhaps had some for dessert. It *tasted* so good, it is good, 'I want more' (craving). 'NO, you'll not have more,' says Mother; 'I MUST have more, says little self, which then finds maneuvers that allow this indulgence, likely bringing a bunch of unwanted trouble down the road. Ice cream is good, spinach is bad, or whatever. Can we see how we've set ourselves up to make true for ourselves the Buddha's First Noble Truth: *there is suffering when we cling to aspects of our experience as a 'self'*? This is good, this is bad—these are opposites that appear in myriad ways so long as we live an unexamined life of assumptions that lead to actions governed by conditioned habit tendencies from the past.

The mind living mindlessly within the opposites is our usual wont, so it is not surprising that we mix this up with the wise discernment at the heart of our practice. And it is tricky because the latter must be *practiced* as we maintain an alertness to the strong tendency to color what we perceive by our own likes/dislikes, our prejudices. When we open our eyes, we see, we are aware, just as a little child does or is. The difference here comes out of our background of experience, which a small child hasn't yet accrued. So there is an innocence, a naiveté, we've lost. Now, *experience* is our teacher, so it doesn't seem to me that to return to that innocence of early childhood free of life experiences is the way to go, even assuming we could. That is 'little mind' getting it mixed up again, and those who try can be childish and inappropriate, uninhibited, and obnoxious. I don't think we really want that. What is absolutely essential is that we de-condition ourselves so that where we have colored our experience, we can appreciate how limiting and distorted our experience has become.

The Buddha taught that *We are what we think. Everything we are is created by the mind. With our thoughts we create our world.* We just want to get off automatic and start being awake to what we're doing—this is our training in a nutshell. Because when we begin to see without the distortions, we have the opportunity to *respond* instead of reacting to what we think is 'out there.' Our precious tool of choosing can be exercised through our willingness to be aware, to wake up. Then we're not ruled by the past while being able to build on the past. For example, a little child likely wouldn't know that there was danger if a person came at it with a big knife pointed to stab it. Our *wise discernment* would let us defend our self or flee from the situation, to act appropriately. The wise discernment doesn't label this person as bad. I think we can see the difference here. 'Bad' is a simplistic reaction to our fear and agitation; it is old learning that can lead to vindictiveness and contraction of our world.

Our spiritual practice can help us move away from these limiting judgments to the lucidity and openness of awareness, of Buddha Mind. As my great teacher said, our practice of appreciating the Unity of life doesn't lead to our eating the peel and throwing the banana away, *and* we don't have to judge the banana as 'good' and the peel as 'bad.' Both have their place and function; both just are part of the way it is. When we get into more complex situations this is more difficult, and probably interpersonal relationships are the most challenging of all. So here is fuel for our training, over and again to bring the light of awareness, our birthright free of conditioning, into whatever situation greets us. It is thus that the teaching is *everywhere*. Our part is to be willing pupils in this great Schoolhouse of Life and thus little by little free ourselves from the compulsivity of the judgmental mind.

# The Nature of Mind

To paraphrase Great Master Dogen: *The ways of expressing the reason why we train are thousandfold,* and the above title—'The Nature of Mind'—conveys one way that is basic. Bodhidharma gave this same teaching to his first disciple, Taiso Eka: *As the trainee goes on he recognizes two aspects of one mind: the mind immaculate and the mind stained.* The basic confusion is that these two aspects get mixed up so there's an inability to see the way things are. The first link in the conditional arising of a new being, a 'me' and a 'you,' is just this, labeled Ignorance in the doctrine of twelve links of Dependent Origination. In another teaching, that of the Ten Fetters, the Buddha noted that the tenth one is 'Wrong View.' That wrong view is the basic ignorance that conditions a rebirth: it is the egocentric view of a 'me' and a 'mine' separate from the Vastness of an All that includes and embraces everything. It is *here that there is no suffering, no-thing to be attained, no ignorance/delusion or enlightenment,* to paraphrase The Scripture of Great Wisdom.

So, our training practice is a willingness to *go beyond this human mind.* And we have to begin wherever we are within the very recognition of this ignorance—*I don't know*. This is the painful recognition that Life brings as part of this human life! Karmic tendencies still not at rest form the second link in the conditions leading to a new birth which gives them expression. However, we may view our spiritual practice of 'just sitting' as basically opening to the Unknown. As the Sixth Ancestor's key awakening was put:

*We must use the mind [our awareness] to free ourselves from attachment.* We do this because we're karmically stuck in one aspect of mind—the mind stained, the mind conditioned by past experiences, which include how they were interpreted by beings in its karmic stream. We're playing out an old story in, so to speak, a new play as a new character. As Shakespeare put it, paraphrased here, 'All the world's a stage and all the men and women merely players. They have their entrances and their exits, each playing many parts.' Perhaps as an actor and playwright, he more readily could view life in this way than many of us.

The nature of this conditioned mind is that it wants to know, wants to be secure, wants to be in charge in ways that in the long run simply can't work. Why? Because it is simply a fragment of a far 'bigger picture'—the Unborn, God, Eternal Truth, Absolute, and so on. We can put a label on It, but we'll never know It as long as we are stuck with an idea. As Great Master Sekito Kisen put it in his enlightenment poem: *Here born we clutch at things and then compound delusion by following ideals.* We get trapped by taking the world of our senses, which includes mind as the sixth, as *the* reality. It's sobering to begin to remember and see how implicitly we jump into life 'where angels might fear to tread.' In a way this was the teaching Suzuki Roshi gave to his students when he flatly said, 'Life is basically *impossible.*' That is, it *appears* impossible from the standpoint of the conditioned, rational mind that desperately holds onto a mistaken view. Our inherited karmic tendencies may be viewed as attempts to survive whilst refusing to accept the basic impossibility of living with a balanced ease while holding onto believing in the permanence of a world which constantly changes.

The Diamond Sutra repeatedly points out this entrapment and ends with: *Thus shall ye think of all this fleeting world—a star at dawn, a bubble in a stream, a flash of lightning in a summer sky, a phantasm, and a dream. This* is what our conditioning obscures. Hence, the nature of mind is to take the 'star at dawn' to be more than it is, when it is just as a flash of lightning. The ephemeral is taken as some *thing* to hold onto, to build our hopes on, something to bring succor and secure peace. And it just 'ain't necessarily so,' as put in the Gershwin song. The nature of this mind we're training is not at ease, not able to rest within the simplicity of being with the way things are.

Our great challenge over and over again is to step back from the wrong beliefs that hold us in bondage. Gropingly we move in the darkness of faith, of a deeper knowing that there *is* Something More. Our wonderful practice allows us to touch this 'Place,' Nirvana, but as soon as we want to hang onto that special sense of being held and supported, we're back in the conditioned mind being trained. This is the nature of the mind, this is why we train, *and* this understanding is strengthened and made more secure by the training itself. There is no substitute for practicing, and heartfelt we can give a strong affirmation to the end of The Scripture of Great Wisdom: *O Buddha, going, going, going on, and always going on beyond, always becoming Buddha. Hail! Hail! Hail!*

# The Squeaking Door

The title may be a useful way to view our practice that, as Great Master Dogen taught, is to reflect upon oneself, rather than to be so karmically caught in the impact that daily life presents. Our practice allows us to execute that inward turning of *looking within to advance directly along the road that leads to the Mind.* I believe most anyone who has the staying power in doing meditation will find that it greatly challenges our usual stance of being in the world. Why? Because we come to see more clearly our existential predicament, our karmic inheritance, seeing its potential to bring unsatisfactoriness to our living in this world. It is emphasized that to release ourselves from this unsatisfactoriness we *must* do the practice, and Reverend Master Jiyu noted that this practice is for spiritual adults who are willing to face and take responsibility for their actions. This extends to our not being so quick to go into blame mode, targeting who is at fault when things don't turn out the way we would have wanted or expected.

'The squeaking door' conveys how our training may be experienced: if a door hasn't been opened for a long time, it can have an unpleasant squeaky sound, resisting the effort to get it to move. Our karmic inheritance itself is as a closed door that comes out of a sense of separateness from the Whole of existence, which is vast and complete. That we've lost touch with That, the Reality which embraces a 'you' and a 'me,' is called Ignorance by the Buddha and is the first condition for a rebirth. The Buddha taught that we are 'hindered' by ignorance which then fetters us to craving, which is a way of summarizing the basic teaching of Dependent Origination—expressed as twelve links and depicted as a wheel of birth and death (*samsara*) continually moving in the direction of suffering, unsatisfactoriness (*dukkha*), that which is hard to bear. How to get off that wheel is what the Buddha taught. This wheel presents the conditioning from the past, which prior to training just rolls on and on and on. It's as a closed circuit that keeps delivering currents round and round without ceasing.

To shift analogies, this is as a closed door. It is through the good karma, which is also part of our past conditioning, that at some point we go beyond simply being caught in life's pain and sorrow. Prior to that, beings in the stress of life simply fell back on strategies that are in the long run unsuccessful. The wheel is as a door that seems relentless and fixed. We don't see the door because we're confined so much in the sense of the inevitability of a 'me,' a self that suffers and enjoys, at times desperately wanting peace and grabbing at it in wrong ways. As Patrick Henry declaimed prior to the American Revolution, 'Peace, peace—there is no peace,' encouraging the Assembly to take a courageous step for freedom even if it meant facing a formidable battle.

So when we embark upon our practice, we implicitly are willing to face the potential discomfort of freeing ourselves from being trapped within the confines of our usual way of being-in-the-world. The Buddha found that out of unsatisfactoriness, we can recognize the discomfort and choose to look at it, to open the door that's been closed over and over again for eons. So the little self acts as a squeaky door that protests as we peek into this conditioned clutter that has accumulated for a very long time. Dating myself, I am reminded of the old radio show, 'Fibber McGee and Molly.' When Fibber announces he's going to open the closet door to find something he's looking for, the familiar voice of the announcer cries 'Don't open that door!' and then there is a resounding 'clatter, clatter, clatter' as the advice is unheeded. Little self is crying *don't open this door* and disturb the clutter. This caution up until now has served us well, thank you very much. So little self protests, often squeaking away so effectively that it leads trainees to stop training, denying themselves the gift of pure awareness, the precious opportunity to see beyond the strongly conditioned mind.

So, let's remember that this work of the heart is as putting oil into the hinges that have been idle so long. Little by little they'll squeak less and less. Doing this takes some skill. I am reminded of when I was at the monastery and very sensitive to squeaky doors which didn't seem to bother other monks. I asked the monk in maintenance to show me how to de-squeak doors. It was a wonderful relief and satisfaction to know how to do this! If only it were so easy learning how to smoothly open the door to our heart! It's difficult because, when it comes right down to it, each of us must learn *how* to do this for ourselves. It is an inner work with helpful guidelines, and yet there often aren't any clear signs along the way. We are supported by faith that we don't *have* to stay trapped in the confined space of our conditioned mind. Thus we begin to work with the first of ten fetters: we begin questioning our implicit belief in how we see and react to the world. This fetter is called 'personality view.'

The second fetter is our questioning whether there even is a way out, doubting the Buddhadharma that clearly shows the way. To complete the trio, the third fetter is called the 'belief in the efficacy of rites and rituals,' which means the mistaken belief that external or surface changes are sufficient to ease the distress Life brings at times. These three fetters are delusions which we are now willing to question. To see and to question these fetters is truly good karma that we can follow. When we do so we have *entered the stream*, which carries us to the Other Shore.

The door is being oiled by our willingness to keep going, to keep chipping away at the squeaky protests of the door of 'me' and 'mine.' Where it now opens easily is the fruit of our practice, which we might not even notice since there are no more noisy protests. We truly have everything working for us as the ongoing practice itself is supporting us, carrying us to the Other Shore, whether we can notice it or not. The magnificent Dharma is not confined. Hence, from the early days of Buddhism, there were *three* Refuges. Our willingness to keep up our practice with intelligence and dedication is essentially taking refuge in all three. *We take Refuge in the Buddha, Dharma, and Sangha*, allowing the magnitude of what this involves to reveal itself as we courageously do our work of opening the door to our heart.

# Three Levels of Awareness

In the last several months I've found the following teaching regarding *levels* of awareness helpful for myself and other trainees. It popped up a while ago when a *mondō*, a teaching interchange between master and disciple, came to mind. It goes as follows: *A disciple approaches the teacher and asks for some guidance. The teacher replies, 'Awareness,' and stops. So the student bows respectfully and leaves. Some while later the student returns and asks if the teacher could give more guidance, and the teacher replies, 'Awareness, awareness,' and falls silent. Respectfully, the student bows and leaves, to return a third time asking for more guidance after again working with the teacher's reply. This time the teacher answers, 'Awareness, awareness, awareness.'* The friend who told this teaching story would then burst out laughing as it typifies what possibly has made Zen so popular in the West—its cryptic style.

What came up for me on this particular morning was that awareness itself is deepened by the determination to practice. Although this is obvious, something clicked at a new level for me in a helpful way. When we sit in serene reflection we are essentially letting go of the conditioned mind by our willingness to step back from involvement with it. Implicitly we're following the middle path between indulgence and rejection: we're not trying to think and we're not trying not to think; we're not trying to feel and we're not trying not to feel, and so on for any experience that arises. This is the first and basic level of awareness: we are *just sitting*, just being within a stillness that is open to and accepting of whatever arises. Without any intellectualizing we are seeing directly that *all that arises passes away*, which was the Buddha's last teaching to monks. He added the important caveat: *Work out your salvation with diligence.* In other words, he's pointing to Something More, which doesn't 'arise and pass away.'

This is the basic, *first* level of awareness that we nourish and strengthen as we more and more ground ourselves in the right understanding that we have a choice here. We're not slaves or victims to the powerful karmic forces that propel the ordinary mind which without reflection one takes as a self or 'me.' This is what is being studied when Great Master Dogen writes, *When we study Buddhism, we study ourselves*. It seems highly unlikely that without practice most of us could possibly appreciate how very challenging this is. From the very beginning we're 'beckoning' to enlightenment; we're exercising the 'mind that seeks the Way' which 'goes beyond the human mind.' This takes huge determination and patience plus the other qualities of training that are so basic: courage, humility, and faith that allow our opening to the great compassion that is at the heart of things, including this conditioned 'me.'

Over and over again, we cultivate these qualities to bring ourselves back to this basic first level of awareness, grounding ourselves in an aware stillness that is beyond words and ideas. However, the training doesn't stop here—this is the beginning of the Path. The *second* level of awareness is what has been called a 'double' consciousness. This is an awareness of both the conditions that have arisen at the moment as well as their impact on 'me.' This level of awareness recognizes the disturbance within the flow of mental activity as a conditioned reactivity to be looked at directly. Sitting still within this reactivity without immediately being pulled off course by it requires this heightened alertness to that potential risk. With that alertness we have the opportunity to recognize a tension here that seeks a resolution before getting trapped into acting on it. When we don't just automatically fall into a habitual reaction, there is a space or emptiness; it is like a question looking for an answer. Implicitly we are asking for help, asking *What is it good to do?* We're sitting within the *I don't know,* which allows us to detach from our conditioned mind of self to open to a deeper wisdom.

This is not easy! This second level of awareness deepens through patience, courage, and faith that build upon humility, which recognizes that 'I' am vulnerable and helpless. This occurs as we turn toward an unfamiliar 'bigger picture,' and as spiritual teachers in different traditions assure us, the sincere prayer is *always* answered. And that is true. Of course, if we *knew* ahead of time what that was we wouldn't be asking in the first place, so it takes a firm grounding in the awareness-practice itself to stay within this seemingly empty space, the place of unknowing. We will get an answer that may be clear or may just give a sense of direction. We simply can't second-guess this because we're opening to an unknown, unfamiliar, and non-habitual way of being. We can see how much we prefer that which is familiar. As Reverend Master Jiyu would point out, 'We prefer the devil we know to the devil we don't know.' It can feel bewildering, which requires we repeatedly ground ourselves in the *purity of our intention*.

The *third* level of awareness in a sense is the key one: *choosing* to carry into action that which has come up as good to do *and* following through with that. The consequence or outcome then takes us right back to being grounded in the first level of pure awareness that lets us see the whole picture, the causes and conditions that are shown at this new moment in time. It may not seem like much, but little by little we are creating our destiny. We are shaping it to be one where, just as the Buddha promised, the balance shifts to our living a life that is more satisfactory, peaceful, and at ease than our life prior to our embarking upon this wonderful path of training. We are strengthening and deepening our birthright of awareness, which little by little leads to the end of suffering. It is truly our choice.

# Trusting the Heart

The enlightenment poem of the Third Chinese Ancestor of Zen, Kanshi Sosan, is translated not only as in the title but also as 'Faith in Mind.' This is one way of describing both our efforts in training and the fruit of our practice: we train within little self's doubts and limitations, which is what we are aware of when turning our awareness within to reflect upon ourselves; *and* we learn by this practice to recognize That which we can truly trust and put our faith in—Buddha Nature or True Self/Mind. This is an ongoing process open to us when we sincerely train. It is open to us because our *intention* is to move beyond the self-limitations that are driven by greed, hate, and delusion. Within this context these three defilements are expressions of selfish desire, an attitude of 'what's in it for *me?*' Until we turn in training toward That which is more than what we know, whether we are aware of it or not, our motivation comes from that self-centeredness because we come into this life with those tendencies. Then our experiences in this life tend to strengthen and fortify this approach to life. That certainly doesn't mean we don't at times come from a place of love and generosity: it does mean that generally our reactions are colored by a big dollop of greed, hate, and delusion.

With our intention to train in awareness—in moving toward a more satisfactory approach to life through inner awareness of who we think we are—we naturally become increasingly aware of this little self. Why? Because with the intention to not act from that automatic place, we are learning to get in touch with the *still, small Voice* of our True Self, which we've lost sight of in the roar of our ordinary thinking/feeling patterns. This training at times brings the puzzlement of 'how do I really know' whether I'm listening to little selfish mind or not. The very question reveals the sincerity of our intention. As in anything we have chosen to learn and practice, we learn by doing. If I had to be a skilled guitarist before taking up the guitar, it simply wouldn't happen. That wishing doesn't make it so is apparent here. Most of us probably have murmured a number of times when someone performs well how it would be nice to be able to do that, without having the least intention to do the hard practice to develop that skill. When we see someone living a spiritual life seeming so centered and serene, this can stir something in us to seek for ways to feel less harassed, uncertain, and dissatisfied in our own lives. Wonderful. That's just a beginning that requires discipline and commitment to have it happen.

Now, we learn by doing. There is no other way. We put ourselves on the line, so to speak; we put our money where our mouth is. What this means is that we do our formal meditation practice regularly and faithfully, we do our daily recollection or reflection to bring greater clarity to where old patterns have brought some kind of unsatisfactoriness in their wake, and we make the best choices we can to *do what it is good to do*. Doing what it is good to do, wanting to move from that place, is the activity of choice to move away from acting on selfishness. *Selfishness* is not a pejorative judgment; it is simply what is deeply embedded within ourselves as our reason for doing anything. How could it be easy? *This is our training* and we learn by doing. Here are the steps, although there really is no formula for doing this inner work:

First of all, we remember that we don't want to act simply automatically out of old conditioned patterns. Even to get this far we have the Right Understanding to see how suffering comes from doing the same old thing, and how easy it is to slide down those old grooves. Second then, we have developed the discipline to *pause* before taking some habitual action. And right here comes into play the wise discernment we are developing to recognize which of the latter are potentially problematic. We don't live our lives always tortured with indecision: we've developed both wholesome ways and unwholesome ones. Our lives, thankfully, have periods of harmony and ease when living is simply not a problem, when we're doing what needs to be done in harmony with our experience. A gift of our practice is that we can appreciate these times rather than simply take them for granted, so that they go unnoticed. Learning when to pause requires our ongoing cultivation of mindfulness. This means *being in the present moment*, not spinning off into the habitual mental activity of what's coming up next or carrying around what has already occurred. As one monk put it, 'Do this about a billion times,' because the nature of 'little mind' is to do exactly that kind of veering off from the present. A great Zen master of mid last century succinctly expressed it as 'Eternity in the moment—this is the only important practice.'

That sounds good, one might think, but how do I do it? The only answer is that we do it by doing it. Just as we learn French by practicing French. French immersion grade schools are based on this principle—the children learn French by hearing it and speaking it. Because they are little children they don't object by saying, 'I don't know how to do it, teach me first and then I'll do it.' Jesus said that *to enter the Kingdom of God we must become as little children.* Suzuki Roshi called it 'Zen mind, beginner's mind.' And Keizan said that *if we are to become one with the Truth as one flame combines with another, we must throw away selfish opinions, old emotions, arrogance, and obstinacy and learn the True Mind of the Lord with the naïve mind of a child.* This is not easy to do. Over and again, we have to return to the uncomfortable recognition that this 'I' doesn't know. All our sophistication, our education, our conditioned ways of being in the world are of no help here—they are the obstacles to our clearly seeing *what it is good to do now*. When we are willing to ask that question, we have come to the place where we recognize we cannot count on what we *think* and *feel* as reliable guides in directing our choices.

Here we are at step three of the discomfort of *not knowing* and being willing to offer up our unexamined habitual modes. This is the fullness of the place of pausing when we turn and *ask for help* to That which is greater than what we know. In other words, we must be willing to face the limits of what we think we know, which leads to the new Place of Unknowing. Here is the place of the Eternal within our hearts—the Place we come to learn to trust more and more by the practice of listening in a new way. We're listening with a childlike openness and asking the question with deep sincerity, *What is it good to do now?*, knowing we want to act in a way that is for the good of all beings, not just for the 'me.' This is moving with *bodhicitta*, the Way-Seeking Mind. We are quiet within, intently willing to hear an answer that is not programmed with an old agenda. We ask and we shall receive. We do get an inkling that *yes* this is good to do or *no* this isn't. We can check it out further, raising our hearts again into that Unknown. And, my Master would say, ask three times of the Lord of the House on big matters, then get up and follow wholeheartedly.

We are making mature choices, moving from that place of awareness rather than from the dim place of half-awake. We're moving right from the very center of our being wholeheartedly. We have to leave behind the wailing of little self, 'But how do I know for sure?' Poor little one, we *never* know for sure. We simply don't bother to notice that kind of worry when we're on automatic pilot. Life is such that we have to make choices before we know the outcome. As we grow in our spiritual maturity, we learn to trust our intuition—the Place that is beyond—but this certainly does not exclude 'little mind'. Then in the future we are guided by the consequences of these choices—we pay attention to how we live our lives, which is inclusive, not exclusive. We are increasingly aware of our motivations that come from old conditioning, aware through pausing, that we don't have to go down that road again, and aware of an inner guidance that allows us the freedom to move in a way that embraces the Three Pure Precepts: *1. Do as little harm as possible, 2. Do as much good as possible, and 3. Do good for others by purifying our heart. This is the teaching of all the Buddhas* that is clearly stated in The Dhammapada. It is worth every effort. As Dogen wrote, *This is the lawful gateway to carefree peace.* Trusting the Heart is living in harmony with Who we really are. It is the work of a lifetime and each step of the Journey is taking us more and more where we truly want to go. *If we want to find It quickly, we must start at once,* Dogen wrote. Great Master Sekito Kisen put it, *This I offer to the seeker of great Truth, do not waste time.*

## Twelve Turnings

The Buddha referred to the Four Noble Truths as the teaching unique to Buddhas. They are the key right understanding that is the first of the eight factors that form the Path to the end of suffering. As part of his enlightenment experience each of these truths had three turnings, hence the title's '*Twelve* Turnings.' For me, this extended way of understanding, and hence practicing, the Four Noble Truths is incredibly helpful. It clearly reminds me of what we trainees are up against when there is a determined dedication to keep moving along a Path leading to the end of the unsatisfactoriness that arises in one's life.

The *first* turning of each Noble Truth is the basic acknowledgement of the Truth itself. So the first turning of the First Truth is just this statement that *There is suffering (dukkha) as part of this life.* This has to be recognized in all its starkness. That allows opening to the *second* turning: *this is to be penetrated.* In other words, we have to be willing to practice opening to the implications of this Truth in daily life itself. When there is unsatisfactoriness it helps me settle into the training of the moment by remembering that right here is the second turning: the penetrating into this moment of awareness that *this* is unsatisfactoriness, that here is this stately noble truth revealing itself to me—thank you very much. Well, that's a bit over the top perhaps, whilst it most definitely reflects how we move along the Path. The strong karmic tendencies, however expressed in this body-mind, propel an attitude of avoidance and denial. We desire to simply get rid of unpleasantness and land ourselves smack in the world of opposites: 'I' like this and 'I' don't like that. We swing on these opposites life after life in our attempts to avoid this basic truth, even though these 'fix-it' ready solutions are surface ones only.

The *third* turning of the First Noble Truth is the recognition or understanding that *it is being penetrated.* For the Buddha this was accomplished on the eve of his enlightenment, so for him it *had been* penetrated. However, in the Jataka Tales he remembers his many lives of unsatisfactoriness as they were being penetrated. That we are *willing* to practice the Truth within the unsatisfactory aspects of this life, as they arise, can be seen as this third turning: *it is being penetrated.* This is a reassurance to support our willingness to be firm, disciplined, and creative in taking our practice to heart instead of merely succumbing to old habit patterns. The more we train, the more we can be alert to the dangers of these karmic patterns, and this allows us to take heart and go forward resolutely. This truly we *can* do; it is the deepening of the practice itself.

Now we come to the Second Noble Truth that the cause of unsatisfactoriness is attachment. Its acknowledgement is the *first* turning. The *second* turning is *this attachment is to be let go of.* Then the *third* turning is the recognition that it *is* being let go of. This again expresses the training itself. When we are aware of how in a particular situation we are holding onto a particular 'me' point of view that is habitual and not necessarily obvious, we truly have a choice to *let go* of it. That it is the hardest thing in the world to do, we ruefully come to know by our intention to train in the midst of the seeming obstacles. The key obstacle is simply this belief in an individuality that is separate and hence alone. So little by little we are releasing this wrong belief through the practice itself. This is beyond our rationalizing or our feeling—this is going beyond the human mind.

The *first* turning of the Third Noble Truth follows quite naturally with the recognition that there is Nirvana to be found within this life itself. *Nirvana* is the Sanskrit word literally meaning 'blown out,' 'cooled.' In The Scripture of Great Wisdom it is described as *void, unstained, and pure.* It is the 'place' of non-attachment. The *second* turning is that this Nirvana is to be realized. As this is refined, there is a diminishing of the sense of an isolated 'self' because circumstances can be simply less threatening. We keep learning to recognize and then not stay caught in the conditioned reactivity triggered by these circumstances. So the *third* turning here is that *it is being realized*. Hence, enlightenment is really not so very far away as over and over again we *choose* to train within the midst of the varying conditions this life brings. The excellent practice itself encourages a bright awareness of the *way things are* at this moment, which then allows the weakening of self-perpetuating limitations, truly a wonder open to all of us who are willing to keep going on the Path.

The first turning of the Fourth Noble Truth is the proclamation of a Way to follow that yields the fruit stated in the Third Truth. This, of course, is the Noble Eightfold Path that encompasses how we learn to live a Buddhist life wherever we are and whatever the circumstances. The *second* turning then is *it is to be practiced.* And then the *third* turning is *it <u>is</u> being practiced*. We come to see more and more that truly there simply is nothing else we can do. As Great

Master Dogen pointed out: There is *only* one thing—to train hard for this is true enlightenment. Over and over again as sincere and dedicated trainees we ground ourselves in these twelve turnings by letting them illuminate what is happening in our lives right at this moment. What a dignified and uplifting way to live! The following assurance concludes a Buddhist ordination: *We live in the world as if in the sky just as the lotus blossom is not wetted by the water that surrounds it. The Mind is immaculate and beyond all dust. Let us bow to the highest Lord.*

# Walking into the Unknown

Great Master Dogen found that *when one looks back with more awakened eyes, he sees no speck of dust,* an observation that seems increasingly true the longer I train. This morning, past transitions of this life seemed to invite being looked at in just this way. At a particular time, however much clarity or lack of it, a place of choosing presented itself, inviting one a choice. Robert Frost wrote of this poignantly: 'Two roads diverged in the woods, and I, I took the one less traveled by, and this has made all the difference.' This is expressing the Buddhist teaching regarding the law of karma: a complex of causes and conditions come together to impact on this conditioned 'me.' And a conditioned reaction occurs. Each past movement of choosing opens into the next unknown—the roads diverging in the woods we're traveling.

This way of viewing one's life can be very helpful because hopefully it will release the self-judging that is so much a part of the conditioned mind. As one teacher said after past lives had appeared, *If we knew better, we would have done better.* This is just so true and so very hard to live, and we fall back into the judgmental mind of swaying, blaming either self or others. Our practice allows a more compassionate alternative where we come as students to this life of ours to learn from experience. This is the serene reflection of *looking within and advancing directly along the road that leads to the Mind.* We're willing to examine this precious life as it is being lived *now*. The doors we've walked through along the way led to other doors, though the interlude between them might seem long or short. Sometimes they open to the pleasant and at other times to as sad as can be. This movement reveals the unknown in a fraction of a second, as it in turn becomes the present known.

I hope this doesn't sound esoteric or theoretical. Nor that it leads you to an analytic frame of mind. The conditioned mind is vulnerable to memories colored in many ways. Our choice to live the examined life allows us to implicitly ask what we can learn from whatever arises. *That* is happening right now, in the present moment, and of course that is all there is. As it is put in this ancient teaching of the Vedas:

> Look to this day!
> For it is life, the very life of life.
> In its brief course
> Lie all the verities and realities of your existence ...
> For yesterday is but a dream,
> And tomorrow is only a vision;
> But today, well lived, makes every yesterday
>     a dream of happiness,
> And every tomorrow a vision of hope.
> Look well, therefore, to this day.

*How* to truly live this day well is the crux of our practice. And that can only happen in this very present moment. This right understanding brings a salutary caution to not get caught in what's spinning around in this restless mind where it so clearly dwells on a dream or nightmare from the past or a vision of hope or dread for tomorrow. We *can* do better than that, and this goes far beyond how we feel our practice is going at any given time.

As we walk into a new moment mindfully, bringing the strength of our meditation into daily life, we can appreciate that we are moving into the unknown of the next minute – we choose to open this door rather than that one, expectantly with so much good will to live the pure intention of the Three Pure Precepts: *Cease from evil; Do only good; Purify our heart so that we can truly do good for ourselves and others: This is the teaching of all the Buddhas*. When we're willing to see that the way things are is repeatedly walking into the unknown, it becomes so clear that the only secure ground remaining is this purity of our intention that allows us to *live in the world as if in the sky*. Why? Because the cultivating of mindful awareness of this changing world, whether it seems like it or not, lets us little by little open to the 'sky' in all its glory. Over and over again, let's walk into the next unknown moment with childlike willingness.

# What If?

The entire teaching can unfold from the title, the plaintive cry *'What if?'* It is the death knell for the precious peace of mind that the Buddha promises is our true nature. As we see the danger of this karmic whisper, or fragrance, as Reverend Master Jiyu at times referred to it, we *know* the great importance of our spiritual work is to weaken its influence. We have to be willing to see how we, the conditioned 'me,' have moved from reality to fantasy, from the present into the future. The future is, of course, unknown; whether we're preoccupied with it or not, it remains spreading out before us, just as the past spreads out behind us. This fear of the unknown poignantly expresses our human or existential predicament—the sense and belief in being separate individualities within a big world of others. The Buddha emphasized that this very belief, generally unquestioned and assumed, is the Ignorance of the Truth that propels this rebirth; it is the delusion that perpetuates the spinning wheel (samsara) of life and death over a very long time. This is the Right Understanding that begins the Path to the end of suffering. Even while we swim in the murky waters of Ignorance, how very difficult it is to accept that we may have simply gotten it wrong.

The above explanation likely won't convey much to someone still totally caught in the consequences of this mistaken point of view, because it challenges what we believe we know and what we've been taught as conventional beliefs. In a word, it turns upside down our usual stance in the world. The more we take it to heart, the more we have to recognize where we are stuck and bring our spiritual work right to that point. It isn't going to go away, this unsatisfactoriness of sticking fast to an erroneous belief. This is what the Buddha gave as the last of the ten fetters, a wrong *view* that keeps us in bondage and unsatisfactoriness. We're caught on a pendulum of 'me' when we fall into the opposites of what 'I' want or don't want. We're caught in the feelings that are triggered by our contact with the world, all conditioned by karmic influences playing themselves out in this life. *Feelings are the reaper of the karma* is a basic Buddhist teaching. And our actions, which include our thoughts as well as speech and behavior, are the sower of the karma. This is a law of the universe, just as much as physical and organic laws are. This law is described as operating in the moral realm, meaning that wholesome actions bring good results while unwholesome actions bring undesirable results—to the 'me' that feels separate and basically alone, whether in a benign or seemingly hostile environment.

The importance of this Right Understanding cannot be overemphasized because it informs the entire Path, showing us where our attention must be determinedly placed. If we go on believing these hauntings expressed by the *What if?*, we just bounce around in an emotional soup of fear, hope, panic, desire, doubt, using up much energy while chasing shadows. Can we see this? First, it has to make some sense theoretically. Then it must be the driving force for our emancipation, for cleansing the karmic fog when it arises—this life, right now. We're not always in such a state, which can be informative itself. We can come to see more and more how the unknown threatens increasingly in ratio to our investment in a certain outcome. And this is where we really get to see how important it is to walk a *middle path* between apathy, not wanting to embark on anything very meaningful and worthwhile because it may not succeed, and overzealousness to achieve a certain goal. Hopefully, that makes sense because it expresses in one way the heart of our predicament. There is a growth factor, so to speak, of the spirit, the psyche, just as there is one of the body. A baby at some point, if it is developing normally, *will* become a toddler before it walks with confidence and ease. If the baby were to ask 'How do I know I'll be able to walk?' as it experiences the potential of falling down, it might not ever dare to proceed. Although the baby likely doesn't 'feel' faith, it is demonstrated in the *actions themselves.*

All along the way, we humans are drawn in various ways that inevitably move us into the unknown. Then it becomes the known and ceases to be a focus. We go to school, we form friends, we choose life goals, we proceed along an unknown path one step at a time. Sometimes things work out the way we'd hoped and anticipated, sometimes they do not. Before we wake up to the unsatisfactoriness of ordinary life, we're just going along for the ride, living off the good karma of the past and reacting off the unfortunate. Please remember, for the Buddha 'good' is the wholesome, satisfying, the non-suffering, whereas 'bad' refers to the unwholesome, unsatisfying, suffering. And for me after many years of training, this understanding has helped me recognize that we *live* in a moral universe that is always teaching us by these very consequences of satisfactory and unsatisfactory.

Our dedicated spiritual practice builds on this Right Understanding so that we begin and grow in getting a handle on how to cope with the strong feelings that arise when we face the unknown future: we can see more and more clearly how we've invested in an outcome to such an extent that it is defeating and undermining our efforts of the moment. We can see that it comes out of a lack of faith in ourselves and the goodness of the world we live in. We begin to sense how much that happens depends not on ourselves, but on the many conditions that are involved in whatever happens to us. And paradoxically, this brings a radical humility that is a strength. Why? Because we're seeing the way things are: our efforts, the choices we make, are vital *and* there is always much more that goes beyond what we can do, what we have control over. We must do our part, trusting that the outcome will take care of itself. In other words, *We are not in charge.*

Friends, there *is* Something More than this little self that is gripped by thoughts and feelings, impulses and beliefs in its separateness, which then suffers or is relieved accordingly. The fearful *What ifs?* can alert us to where we need to address a decisive and powerful effort. Let them be reminders of the necessity both of doing the best we can while also turning to That within where our true Refuge is, Buddha Nature right within. This is blurred by the fears and hopes of 'me' but is still always here for us. As Reverend Master Jiyu wrote in her Commentary on the First Great Precept 'not to kill,' *Man stands in his own shadow and complains about the dark, but only he can turn round.* This takes strength of resolve and a willingness to trust in Something greater than the fears and desires that arise. The whole of our training is right here for us: we use our wonderful birthright of Awareness, which requires stepping back from being caught up in the mental turmoil. This brings into focus a shining light that illuminates the real from the unreal, informing us about *what it is good to do* at this present moment. And here we have the wonder of another birthright: the freedom to choose. We can let go of the whispers of the defilements and get on with living wholeheartedly. Or we can keep believing them, hence strengthening their bond. As I seem to be saying so often these days, *This is do-able,* allowing the shadowy *what ifs* to float by. It's just up to us, and little by little we are learning to take charge of our lives and be true to the Source. This is the freedom of Zen that the Buddha firmly declared is here for us all.

## When Fear Arises

The First Noble Truth to be trained with points to the vulnerability inherent within the body-mind, which is impermanent. The Buddha points out that birth is suffering, old age is suffering, sickness is suffering, death is suffering, not having what one wants is suffering, and having what one doesn't want is also suffering. These are aspects of life that are hard to bear, *dukkha*. But, he teaches, the changing nature of existence in itself is *not* the problem. Instead the problem arises out of the basic ignorance or wrong view that confuses this impermanent state as solid and permanent by attaching to experiences as an identity, a self. How to unravel this mistaken view of who we are is the awesome task of spiritual practice. This is the work of the heart/mind, *shin*, so that we free ourselves from the trap of our conditioned body-mind.

The practice begins with the willingness to recognize the First Noble Truth. This is the right understanding that informs and grounds our practice. One way of stating this is that *we stand against the world of the conditioned mind in order to train in wisdom*. Wisdom involves penetrating the impermanent nature of what we implicitly take as real, recognizing the unsatisfactoriness arising when we do this, and seeing that within these two characteristics of existence there is no separate substantiality we take as 'me.' The Pali for these three aspects of existence are *anicca, dukkha, anatta*. When the Buddha states he teaches *seeing the way things are*, he is referring to seeing these three characteristics of existence, which are also referred to as the 'three seals.'

In the enlightenment poem of an 8th century Chinese Zen Master, this is conveyed in these possibly puzzling lines: *If from your experience of the senses basic truth you do not know, how can you ever find the path that certain is no matter how far distant you may walk?* That is, the 'experience of the senses,' our sensory experiences, can become our teacher as we are shown the folly of believing them without examination. Hence, Socrates pointed out that the unexamined life is not worth living. The Buddha as physician for the suffering of the world prescribed meditation as the medicine. Whether tasting bitter or sweet, this living, vibrating experience we take as self must be examined, looked at, viewed with dispassion. Otherwise, we simply stay caught on the wheel of conditioned reactivity without much clue about what feels wrong, unsatisfactory. When we are willing to stay with our practice, we're finding it is possible to step back from being simply caught in the experiences and be aware of them.

This wonderful birthright of awareness must be invited, encouraged, nourished, and cultivated because it is in having lost touch with that perspective that our confusion is perpetuated. When fear arises, we're challenged to do just that. We gradually weaken its hold, which is so narrowed upon itself, through the willingness to allow the awareness to shine on the distress itself. This is most definitely not easy. Fear, uneasiness, doubt, distress are unpleasant states of feeling and the conditioning is to get rid of them. But they don't really go away, though palliative measures may veil that they've just temporarily gone under cover. It is said that *we escape through awareness*. This we find for ourselves by our willingness to sit within the distress. Why? Because, dear friends, there is *something more* than these conditioned feeling states that seem so real. Hence, the Buddha gave faith as the first of five spiritual qualities to be cultivated in our spiritual practice.

Early in The Litany of the Great Compassionate One comes this important line: *OM to the One who leaps beyond all fear!* That 'One' is Compassion. Within the stillness of being, we open to the compassion that is at the heart of all life. The challenge of training is to *turn the stream of compassion within.* As junior monks, we were encouraged to find how to do this. We might go to the Kanzeon (Bodhisattva of Compassion) shrine and ask for help without understanding anything but the sad inner cries looking for succor. Faith in action, going beyond the human mind which wants to figure it all out—that's the domain of faith. This can be cultivated. The wonder of keeping on with the practice itself, which is the willingness to be still within the midst of conditions, is that we can make the Buddha's truth true for ourselves. Little by little, just keep at it; just keep going, which allows a deeper knowing. With Julian of Norwich we can quietly know *all is well; all manner of things are well.* The gentle compassion within indeed for a time has leapt beyond all fear.

# When We Are Willing to See

The phrase *when we are willing to see, we will see* has come up for me often, and once again the challenge of doing this was presented to me through the kind offering of daily life. It came in the form of one of the Sangha who came for a brief visit before I was leaving for qigong. He gave feedback on how the people attending the public talk of yesterday had reacted: one liked it very much and one didn't. Well, 'little self' immediately began a downward spin that continued through the evening, coloring the entire situation, including the short Dharma talk I gave at evening's end. The doubting mind is so close to the surface it surprised me, returning home with me from the class and still hovering around this following morning.

Once again, the gift of the training has allowed me to be willing to look at all of this, thus going beneath the surface reactive feeling of not being approved: *there is some kind of almost horror in making a mistake, in not doing it 'right.'* This vulnerability is obviously caused by placing such a value on being approved. Feebly, I immediately 'saw' the foolishness here. I remembered someone commenting, 'So you think you should be everybody's little darling.' This was the case when I was about four, and visiting relatives in Europe with my mother and sister may have contributed to the expectation. Or perhaps scratch beneath anybody's careful persona you'd find the same fear of not being acceptable. Inadequacy and insecurity are built into the human condition, the existential predicament of feeling separated from others in a big 'out there.' No wonder the Buddha succinctly taught that attachment was the cause of suffering (the Second Noble Truth).

The irrationality of implicitly believing that I'm approved of universally doesn't stand against its potentially powerful hold, perhaps quite the contrary. An *unwillingness* to look at this just keeps it lingering and certainly is poisonous to that precious sense of 'being peace' that is our Birthright. There is no quick way to turn this around *and,* thankfully, our training allows the gradual dissolving of the tension here. The steps to this are clear. What makes it so difficult is that the timing is not up to us. As my Master said in another context, 'It takes as long as it takes.' The profundity of seemingly casual remarks she would make has been hitting me more and more as I continue my own training! It's like the little kid who reaching a certain age is surprised at how smart his parents have become. Obviously, the importance of patience, built on faith, cannot be overestimated. The Buddha called *patience* 'the potent army' and St. Theresa of Avila wrote, *Patient endurance attaineth to all things.* She added, *Whom God possesseth in nothing is wanting: God alone sufficeth*. We lose touch with our self-sufficiency, or Buddha Nature-sufficiency, which provides the impetus for and the challenge of our training in whatever form it comes to us.

We have to be willing to feel *helpless,* to recognize and appreciate our vulnerability—though it is definitely not easy to *feel* the importance of this aspect of the ongoing training. Such an opportunity is offered by a given situation, in this case, it was when my friend observed simply as a point of interest that the person he thought might *not* like the talk liked it and for this other person it was the reverse. *He* simply found it interesting, clinically almost. And, of course, the only way to grow from his observations is for me to take that *same attitude*. As long as 'little self' stays simply hurt/perplexed/vulnerable, there is a blockage to understanding. So our practice is taking in the impact and reeling from that without retreating. This allows the reeling gradually to lessen. Of course, that will happen anyway because life moves on. However, the key difference is that with the precious light of awareness on my reaction, I can *learn something about 'me,' who I take as 'me.'* What could be more precious than this learning? Of course, it may not feel good. However, with our increasing awareness, we are actually growing saner!

The next step is the *penetration* of what's going on here. This is not an intellectual process *and* it uses our intelligence in an effective way. What came up for me is that I'd lost an important point of view in Buddhism and one that I truly believe, although it wasn't helping me now: *We are always doing the very best we can at any particular moment* and, *with the salutary application of our training, we can see where we can do better.* So now is my opportunity to bring this knowing to a deeper level, make it more my 'blood and bones,' as Reverend Master Jiyu would say.

What's the big deal here? The self-image of being perfect, so out of kilter with reality, is challenged. It truly is strange to me that when I recognize just how imperfect I am that such a self-belief could be lingering around anywhere! Now that's hard, really hard to face. A little piece of 'me' has to give way. How strange that it's been held onto in the first place. The useful psychological concept called 'cognitive dissonance' is right on: *if 'I' am not one who makes mistakes, how could it be that someone was not happy with 'me,' with 'my' talk?* There's the hub of it and the rub of it: I've attached to being 'the doer' and the karmic consequence of suffering has followed. I'm penetrating, once again, right here in this homely little event, the First and Second Noble Truths of Buddhism: Suffering exists, and its cause is attachment.

We can't see all the ramifications of such a profound teaching at once *and* we can see them little by little, many times over, when we are willing to do our practice. As I've said so often, we can't train in *generalities*, such as 'I'm *always* upset by....' That slides us right off the cutting-edge of our training. The koan does appear in daily life, seemingly endlessly. We just need to be willing to see where the difficulty is right within our own skandhas, our sense of 'me' and who 'I am.' What is the benefit in doing this? There certainly is a cost—the old 'cost-benefit consideration' arises. Well, believe me, the benefit of letting go of cloudy shadows far exceeds the price of staying with the discomfort. When we are not willing to pay that price and go for distracting ourselves to feel better, that is a palliative no-cure and we'll be hit with the dis-ease once again when conditions ripen. Experience teaches when we let it teach. The teaching really is everywhere: *when the student is ready the teacher comes.* We simply open and remain open so we don't limit our learning through preconceived ideas of the 'teacher.' Now, with this training exercise, I can learn to do better in giving public talks. What's wrong with that? I'm certainly no expert in doing this, and to be able to improve and be more helpful to people—that's what I've come here to do, to make this offering of my Master's Transmission as available as possible. Now I can bow wholeheartedly and go on. This is the *letting go* process allowed through our wonderful spiritual practice. This is the freedom promised by Zen—the willingness to see the way things are!

# A Beam of Light

On the opening day of a fundraiser, one of the books donated was brought over by a Sangha member for me to look at; its title was *The Holographic Universe.* Reluctantly I agreed to take a look at it although the subject matter was not one of current interest. After reading a bit about what a 'holograph' was, without getting into the technicalities offered for the general reader, I put it aside, finding it only mildly interesting without seeing its relevance to spiritual understanding. It was 'put on the back burner,' as Reverend Master Jiyu was advised to do with puzzling teachings when she was a junior monk at the Japanese training monastery. Today it just popped off the back burner: 'A Beam of Light' is a reflection on an interesting connection between physical theory and spiritual *practice*.

A holograph—and this is certainly where 'a little learning is a dangerous thing'—is created when a laser beam of light is refracted or bent so that the image of an apple, for example, is projected in two ways that when combined give a three-dimensional view. Well, something like that. This was a big and at the time controversial way of understanding all manner of phenomena which had been unexplainable through quantum physics at the time, including both abnormal and paranormal experiences. What popped up for me this morning was that though visually the apple, in this case, could be viewed as three-dimensional, that image could not be grasped in any other way. A hand would just go through it, if that makes any sense. And into the quiet morning meditation, a beautiful Light just beamed illuminating the basic spiritual teachings in a deeper way.

When we sit in meditation not *trying to think and not trying not to think*, not trying to control the wayward conditioned mind that thinks, feels, imagines, and twirls about in so many beguiling ways, we are returning to the original wholeness of unrefracted light. In serene reflection, we are seeing, via this totality of Awareness, the seemingly three-dimensional forms that play upon the screen of the Mind. The 'bending' is the illusion of a 'self' separate from the endless play of phenomena observed: single light beams are bent or refracted through the conditioned sense of a self. So Great Master Tozan at the beginning of his enlightenment poem, The Most Excellent Mirror—Samadhi, asks us to *Preserve well for you now have. This is all.* He's pointing to the wholeness of the light of awareness which we lose touch with because of our karmic predicament conveyed in the next line of his poem: *The white snow falls upon the silver plate, The snowy heron in the bright moon hides. Resembles each the other yet these two are not the same, Combining them we can distinguish one from other.* Then he comes back to emphasize the 'basic Truth': *Supreme Mind, in words, can never be expressed and yet to all the trainees' needs It does respond.*

Tozan is pointing right at the beginning to That which is beyond words, ideas, and beliefs of a *separate* 'me.' The latter is as the single laser beam that has been split into two rays to form a seeming three-dimensional reality. Here is the comforting reassurance that we are looked after, cherished, embraced, and not alone. How very precious indeed is this birthright, which we are to *preserve well for we now have—this is all.* Later Tozan gives an important basic reminder for us spiritual seekers: *The night encloses brightness, and at dawn no light shines. This truth holds for beings all; through this we free ourselves from suffering.* How does this right understanding free us from suffering? Because the teaching again points to a Light, a Truth, that we *now have.* It is always here and It is helping us, responding to all the trainees' needs. However, this we cannot know through the seemingly real holographic images formed out of feeling separate.

We must open to a faith, a humility. With dismay, as someone in last Tuesday's group observed, we may see more clearly aspects of this refracted 'me' which has dominated in its apparent three-dimensional 'realness.' It has obscured That which we 'now have,' the very Source of Being itself. As Tozan so clearly teaches, words themselves can enslave us: words convey our ideas, our beliefs, our particular ways of construing the world of our senses, and these are conditioned—refracted. We *fall into a hole and go against the basic Truth,* and *come to a dead-end.* This is scary, dismaying: it is troubling to see more clearly, which is a paradox of the practice itself. So, as the Sangha member said, after years of training she feels less settled inwardly than she can ever remember. Of course, this is the coloring of the conditioned mind itself, which by its very nature cannot see clearly. To *see* this troubled 'me' surely is wondrous, requiring the full merit of our practice of willingness to stay with the Awareness itself rather than remain caught in the seeming reality of the objects observed.

Repeatedly we can and must choose to strengthen our faith that *something beneficial is happening.* Obviously, if we 'felt' that to be so, we wouldn't need any faith at all; we wouldn't even consider it. The right understanding to support us at such critical times reminds us that truly here is an opportunity to grow that comes out of our willingness to move into the seeming darkness of the Unknown. There is no other time than right now, this present moment, and truly we can learn ever more deeply to *preserve well for we now have. This is All.* We lack nothing for the great Journey of this life, and over and over again we can choose to trust that Awareness that shines as a 'bigger picture' without distortion or refraction where nothing need be excluded or grabbed. It's a point of view that is expressed in the Mahayana teaching as *Samsara and Nirvana are one:* this very life and eternal life are not different. This is a key and basic turning we can choose to make in how we live in the world. Here we find peace within the midst of the varying conditions that make up our lives, resting within the assurance that to do the very best we can and learn from the outcome itself is enough. And indeed within that we *are preserving well that which we now have,* which is our precious birthright of Awareness itself, unrefracted, whole.

# Going, Going, Going On

Hold life gently, tenderly
Willing to let it flow
Without fear or uneasy doubt
Faith appears, blossoms, and grows
Opening us increasingly
To the many gifts that all around abound.
Follow, follow, follow
Where the Path doth lead
Going, going, going
Oh so gently
Beyond the doubt, beyond the dust
Beyond what 'I' can see
Bowing, bowing, bowing
For Eternity.

# Coming Home

Coming Home

## Taking Refuge Within

Reverend Master Meiten McGuire

# Contents

# A Gift of Gratitude

We are told by the Buddha that training is its own reward. It is also put as "We train in Buddhism for the sake of Buddhism" and as "Buddhism will last as long as bowing lasts." Sekitō Kisen elaborated on his cryptic answer to what is the buddhadharma ["No gaining, no knowing"] with this beautiful description of where our sincere practice takes us: "The vast, blue sky does not obstruct the clouds." All of the above convey a sense of how it is possible to "Live in the world as if in the sky," as the Blessing verse begins after a Buddhist ordination ceremony. I don't know if you, dear reader, can sense this freedom to live in harmony with That Which Is. This is conveyed by these ways of pointing to That which is beyond the ordinary mind, the conditioned mind that so dominates and colors our usual way of living in the world. However, something nudges and prods us to go beneath this superficial living off the very surface. That is what the Buddha was getting at when he began his profound teaching with the First Noble Truth, a statement of a certain unsatisfactoriness or unreliability that is simply the nature of life's surface because of the fact of changeableness.

*The Diamond Sutra* sums up its teaching in its last line: "Thus shall ye think of all this fleeting world. A star at dawn, a bubble in a stream, a flash of lightning in a summer sky, a flickering lamp, a phantasm, and a dream." Oh, how the little self of conditioning rebels at this teaching! It can seem so threatening when the 'world' has us in its grip. What is there to hang onto without this sense of a self, a 'me' relating to a real 'out there' world of others? Well, the Buddha invites us to "come and see" for ourselves, and we have to begin by recognizing the insufficiency of our ideas, words, theories, opinions, beliefs, and shared conventional views to provide more than a feeble pointing to that which lies beyond our thinking. I think on some level everyone knows this. Huston Smith in "Religions of the World" states that religions exist because people feel separate from God, from the very Source of their life and being. Religion expresses this need and its resolution in different ways, depending upon the particular culture. Still, the underlying message is the promise that *there is Something More* than that which we can know through our sensory equipment. We have to drop our arrogance and accept that there is a limitation when we experience ourselves as separate, isolated, alone. This is also described as the existential predicament when viewed philosophically.

Our Buddhist practice, which is living from the mind of meditation, promises to free us from this delusion of separateness. We are a part of Something greater than the ordinary mind can conceive from the place of separation. So it says in *The Scripture of Great Wisdom* that it is "going on beyond the human mind" that is Nirvana. 'Nirvana' is a Sanskrit word chosen by the Buddha as one way of describing this Beyond and literally means 'blown out.' Alarm and puzzlement are natural reactions of the conditioned mind since it requires giving up this limited mind, and that very mind certainly cannot figure out how to do that. Reverend Master would say that we prefer the devil we know to the devil we don't know. And I think when we really look at life, we'll recognize how often we cling to the status quo as long as we can. And of course, it is a Middle Path we always want to come back to, the place beyond the opposites. How that is done is what our Buddhist practice is all about. It's not theoretical—*that* is what we are going beyond. The words are to help us, not to bog us down. Tōzan Ryōkai wrote in his enlightenment poem that "Enslaved by words we fall into a hole. If you should go against the basic truth you'll come to a dead end" and also that "Finally we understand nothing, for words inaccurate will be." So, we must keep remembering that we are asked to go beyond the verbal teachings to make the Truth true for ourselves. This is our responsibility.

One Zen master is quoted as saying, "Hey, what are you staring at? It is all about you," and another Buddhist master reminded us that the Dharma is about us, "these two eyes, ears, nose, mouth..." Dōgen taught that it is not so very far away. We must pay attention to where we are and learn to look with fresh eyes, to look with the naïve mind of a child. This may seem daunting but is a wonderful message of hope. We just must start from where we are right now and take each precious step into the unknown. As a Lakota chief put it, "The longest walk you'll ever take this life is the sacred journey from the head to the heart." We learn how to let go of the seeming comfort of what we think we know. Over and over again, bringing our attention back to the simplicity of this moment, freeing it/us of the clutter of the scattered mind that flits restlessly from past to future, missing over and over again, all that we are simply given by virtue of being alive at this very moment. This can seem so obvious that only when we apply the teachings in a serious and dedicated way will we see how very far we are from living in this way. Dōgen points out that "to live by Zen is the same as to live an ordinary daily life." Can we see and remember this? Each time we're willing simply to pause in the busyness of our lives and quietly return to the inner sanctum of the heart/mind, we give ourselves the refreshing gift of the wholeness that only the present can bring. We're out of our heads, scary as that may seem, and simply living our lives, flowing with all that abounds.

The gift of gratitude just naturally bubbles all around because for that precious time we have made the teaching true for ourselves, and that is far beyond words. That is why Zen has been described as the transmission outside of the scriptures. To paraphrase de Chardin, "Gratitude is the first sign of the presence of God." And as Saint Francis put it, "It is in giving we receive. It is in pardoning that we are pardoned, and it is in dying [to self] that we are born into Eternal Life." As Sir Edwin Arnold expressed this wonderful exchange in *The Light of Asia*, "Forgoing self, the Universe grows 'I'." 'We' aren't the loser in any way. We are learning to put the heavy burden of 'self' down and experiencing a buoyancy that naturally results. In that place it is natural to give whatever we can because the little self clinging to a 'me' has dropped away. This is to be realized for ourselves, and we learn indeed that *gratitude is the first sign of the presence of God* because in this openness to the Oneness lies true freedom and joy. The more we recognize and remember this truth, the more zeal and fervor we give to living fully the life of training. This is the important choice we all can continue to make and it changes everything because the gratitude that flows forth so abundantly weakens that sad sense of separation which seemed so real. I promise you.

# A Heart of Goodness

Probably the biggest stumbling block in our understanding of the Buddha's teaching is the Second Noble Truth, that the cause of suffering is attachment. At our meditation group yesterday, the question again was asked if there is non-attachment how can one love? Our conditioning certainly leads to obscuring the fundamental difference between being attached and being loving. Our wonderful practice over and over again will reveal to us how our very attachment to this person or situation interferes with our true, pure love. As we are willing to train with our expectations and attachments, we penetrate this second noble truth and come to realize for ourselves the precariousness of our balance when we implicitly expect or insist that some external situation be the way we want it to be. Usually, our attachments or expectations are as hidden ground that we believe to be firm and reliable—until we take a step or are confronted with an unexpected event that doesn't hold us up. That is when we can truly come to understand the hazard of attachment and penetrate that unwelcome teaching of the second noble truth.

For me after many years of training the above is axiomatic, an 'of course' how could it be otherwise. Nonetheless, the strong-seated tendency to attach is something that comes up for me and challenges my moving to a deeper level of acceptance. We can come to see that *what* we are attaching to really is some aspect of 'me' which implicitly expects the object of attachment to conform to our wishes. If this were obvious, we'd all have been free from the confusion between attaching and loving probably many lives ago. We're in this life as another opportunity to go beyond these opposites of desire and aversion, in the present context expressed as attachment and indifference/coldness. Life offers plenty of opportunities for this work of the heart. Our job is to be willing students to its great lessons: every time I confuse caring a lot about someone with the expectation that they then conform to what I want/expect from them, the potential for unsatisfactoriness, for disappointment, is initiated. It comes back to that basic First Law of the Universe as seen in Buddhism: The universe is not answerable to my wishes.

The Buddha repeatedly emphasized that the nature of this realm of existence has three main characteristics: impermanence, unreliability or unsatisfactoriness, and thereby not-self: *anicca, dukkha, anatta*. I think that the first two are obvious while the third characteristic is puzzling. The Buddha taught that any appearance, any form, called *dharma* and often translated as 'thing,' is not substantial and real in the way it appears conventionally. This is what we are invited to "come and see" over and over again. Do we 'want' life to be this way? A big, fat NO—so over and over again we deny the truth that is right before our very eyes. We implicitly cling to unexamined beliefs about the nature of things—we're deluded. And then we begin penetrating this perplexing second noble truth regarding attachment, as the Sangha member did yesterday. We can do this because we are reflecting on these great truths, not just skimming the surface intellectual understanding of the words. It's uncomfortable; the truth is not necessarily comforting as we struggle with our own particular mix of desire, anger, and confusion that propelled this life. *And* it truly is freeing. "The Truth will set you free," as Jesus put it. Why? Because as we little by little truly see the danger of attaching, we can *let go*, let life be as it will be.

Some of the teaching given in my early days as a junior monk ring so true all these years later. Reverend Master would say, now I think rather sadly, "It takes as long as it takes." She'd also say, "I didn't make the rules, I just tell you about them." Another teaching I understand so much better now and can truly relate to is that we "help others to be a success *in their own way*," not as 'I' want them to be. Can you see that this is the very heart of being non-attached? Here is the place of a true, deep caring for the other as independent and separate from 'me,' while yet truly related within the great wholeness of which we are all a part. The key teaching of Tōzan in his enlightenment poem is "He is me. I am not Him. When we know this, we are instantaneously one with the Truth." Reverend Master translated this in the Scripture T*he Most Excellent Mirror—Samadhi* as "You are not Him; He is all of you." This is the Great Matter for which we train—to know this for ourselves. And, man, it is worth everything. Every little bit of awareness that lets us see where once again attachment has colored over our world and we believe that our well-being *depends* upon this or that.

As we touch the "deepest wisdom of the heart" that is our Birthright, we at times simply know, as Kanzeon, the Bodhisattva of Compassion did, that all is "void, unstained, and pure," as it is put in *The Scripture of Great Wisdom*. When we release from this basic confusion of needing the other to be this way or that, to do this or that, the loving heart, the heart of goodness, is naturally experienced. There is this *flowing love*, a truly unconditional love, that rests upon the firm conviction that something cannot be only good for me without including you in the picture too. Why? Because beneath all these myriad differences is a Oneness, a Truth, that is beyond our human conception. As again as it is expressed in *The Scripture of Great Wisdom*, it is "going on beyond the human mind" that *is* Nirvana. That mysterious, beckoning 'Place' within this very heart truly is always here. And the Buddha promises in the third noble truth that when we free ourselves from our clinging, from our attachments we will know it for ourselves. To live in the security of our own loving heart of goodness is truly the great gift of training. It's here for us all, waiting and calling. "This Light of Buddha is always increasing in brilliance." Our work is to do the *practice* of being willing to keep going deeper and keep penetrating how in this situation right here and now, attachment to having 'my' way has again brought in its wake disappointment. The work of the heart is to be willing to experience this pain and to learn from it. Then we learn also how to let go into the newness of the next moment, knowing that our choices are greater than we thought—from the heart of goodness we embrace self and other without the overlay of the confused mind that dwells in opposites. The Buddha has shown us the Way to the end of suffering and we have the great, good fortune to train together, giving support to each other, to courageously take that one next step that is good to do—over and over again. Yes!

# A Metaphor for Our Spiritual Journey

*Water, water every where, and all the boards did shrink;*
*Water, water every where, nor any drop to drink.*

I thought of these lines from Coleridge's *The Rime of the Ancient Mariner* this morning when I was walking. The story in this famous poem can be taken as a metaphor for our spiritual journey.

At the beginning of the story, everything is going along fine. The ship is sailing in the best kind of wind, there is a gentle sunshine, the sailors are content and happy. Everyone thanks the golden albatross for bringing all this good fortune. And then the Ancient Mariner *kills the sacred albatross*. Without seeming malice or greed, or for any reason in particular, he wantonly, carelessly kills. For a short time after the murder, everything still seems to go fine, and the sailors congratulate him. And then the karma of this act starts to come due little by little, and all this good fortune turns to ill.

After sailing at a greater speed, the ship stalls without any wind under a relentless sun, and stays and stays and stays there. Night offers no relief and scary repulsive crawling creatures show themselves on the surface of the ocean. In this utter, prolonged helplessness, all the other sailors gradually drop and die. But he in utter horror, the killer of the albatross, cannot die, and his anguish mounts and mounts. Then at some point it all starts turning around, a gentle breeze stirs, the rain begins to fall, and, miracle of miracles, the ship begins to move. And he cries and cries in utter relief and tremendous gratitude for all these gifts that are returning to him. The ship halts at some land where a hermit, a healer, lives, and the Ancient Mariner for the first time tells his story, and this confession to another person helps the spiritual conversion that is happening within the Ancient Mariner. He is beginning to find some peace. He is told—and this is an important part of the work he must do to clean up the karma of his act—to go wandering, telling his story when he is compelled or drawn to do so. Hence, the poem begins with the line "It is an Ancient Mariner and he stoppeth one of three."

Seen as a metaphor for our inner spiritual life and journey, the Mariner's killing of the albatross represents our blinding ourselves through carelessness and callousness to That which is most precious and sacred within ourselves—the Buddha Nature, the God within. Now the Buddha Nature cannot really be *killed*. But we can live our lives in a way that is heedless of It.

Wisely, Coleridge didn't write this as a story where we might expect to know *why* this person would do such a dreadful thing—we *all* make mistakes, sometimes horrible ones. We reap the consequences of our actions, one way or another, as did the Mariner. And, as in the poem, the karmic consequences of our mistakes do not always become visible immediately. If when we made a mistake, we immediately were hit with the utter pain and futility of this [or if we had the vigilance to be aware immediately of the consequences of our actions], that would be it: we would be more likely to immediately change course. But, to take one simple example, we can indulge in junk food for a long time before we get diabetes.

The poem is beautiful in describing what happens inwardly. Just as the boards on the ship shrink in the relentless sun, so we shrink in spirit as a result of selfishness. In the poem, the water is everywhere, yet there is not a drop to drink. Similarly, the Ocean of the Eternal embraces ourselves and everything else, yet we can be suffering from terrible spiritual thirst. Why don't we see the Eternal? Why don't we know It? Actually, this is the question that Great Master Dōgen had as his koan that prompted his search which led him to China where he found a master who showed him the way, and where he experienced a kenshō. His question was, "*Why* are training and enlightenment differentiated since the Truth is universal? Why study the means of attaining It since the Supreme Teaching is free?" He couldn't get his head around the seeming paradox that everything is part of the Eternal and yet we still have to seriously walk a spiritual path if we are to *know* with our 'blood and bones' that we are one with the Eternal. And he found his answer: We have to train ourselves in all-acceptance, pure meditation. We have to accept the *whole of Life.* We have to do something about the fact that we want the pleasant without the unpleasant, the light without the dark, the easy without the difficult. Our training, slowly and gradually, helps us develop the Faith to embrace the whole again, the wholeness within ourselves—the God, our Buddha Nature, that has *always* been with us, that has been leading us, through all the pain and wandering, back to Itself.

The ***other*** part of the Mariner's hell, so graphically presented in the poem, is that the sun was beating and beating down in an increasingly unbearable way. To me, the sun in the poem represents the awareness that shows us exactly what we have been running away from, hiding from, the mistakes we've been making and not wanting, not daring, to face, to look at. And the terrible heat is the anguish that comes from judging ourselves relentlessly as we no longer can hide from seeing the harm that we have done. *This is the epitome of hell.* Death will not remove this problem, for if we don't face the truth about our harmful actions in this life, we will be confronted with it at the time of death. And all the while our own Buddha Nature, the Eternal within ourselves, is saying "Look, look here, finally stop and look and you can change, you don't have to suffer like this forever."

Eventually, we become so miserable that, like the ship in the poem, we are *stopped.* The Mariner's ship was utterly stalled with no wind, nothing moving, a frightening stillness. The Eternal does not punish, but we are allowed to experience the painful consequences of our own actions so that we can *change.* It is *really* painful, hence the multitude of distractions that we cultivate, nurture, to help us avoid the uneasiness, the disharmony that lies within. Now this is a human *condition,* a part of the package we bring into this world. As one teacher put it, we have our entire enlightenment kit right here: our Buddha Nature, the innate knowing within of God, the Eternal; <u>and</u> we have our unconverted karma, those impulses, tendencies—ultimately the ignorance that we are part of the Oneness—that we bring into *this* life. It is the existential predicament of believing ourselves to be separate from the world we live in, separate from Universal Life.

So this being *stopped* helps us begin to face this mess, our own particular hell. *This* allows the *turning.* We begin slowly to turn away from externals as answers to our problems and, having tasted the bitter fruit of our mistakes, we begin the *return journey Home.* Now we start to take to heart the Teaching embodied in the precepts, we start to long to make this Teaching our 'blood and bones.' In wantonly killing the albatross, the Ancient Mariner set in motion a chain of events that led, through terrible suffering, to his conversion. He became a man who knew from his own experience the Truth taught in the first of the ten precepts: "Do not kill." He learned that all life is precious. The ordeal that he endured as this Teaching was driven home, above all, the *remembrance* of his own actions, and seeing the consequences both within himself and externally, seeing how he hurt both himself and others—*this is the real nature of hell.*

In the end, the Mariner is again *alive* spiritually and the Water of the Spirit is allowed to flow, does flow, and the light of the sun is now bearable for he knows there is more to Reality than this limited, benighted, misguided, and struggling little self that seems so isolated from everything else. So at the end of his story, the end of the poem, Coleridge writes: "He prayeth best who loveth best *all things* both great and small; For the dear God who loveth us, He made and loveth all." The Ancient Mariner had been redeemed—he *experienced God's Love,* and he found for the rest of his life what was truly *good* for him to do. You can say that his wandering of the earth telling his story is his repayment for the blessing, the astonishing blessing, he had been given. Gratitude abounded and overflowed. Hence, this inner urge to tell his story, convey this message of Love. But only to some. Again, Coleridge in his genius didn't amplify the story. *Why* did the Mariner choose *one of three,* apparently the most important of the wedding guests, delaying him from participating and joining the feast? Well, it seems clear to me, he chose the one who was ready to hear, to learn from this great Teaching he was offering. The teaching can *only* be really alive when its gift can be received upon the telling. Otherwise, it is as dead wood, no life in it. The living Dharma, the living Truth, is a sharing. So, though it is commonly said, "When the student is ready the teacher appears," it may also be said, in this context, "When the teacher is ready the student appears." It is a two-way flow, so I'm sure the Mariner was as grateful to the wedding guest, who really had to stop and hear whether he wanted to or not, as the wedding guest must have been grateful to him. This was vital guidance that he needed to hear at just this time—that's my take on it. The magic timing was just right and this wonderful poem emerged.

## Asking for Help

I recognize that right now a key aspect of my practice, developed over the years so that it's more articulated than previously, concerns asking for help and receiving guidance from That—the still, small Voice within, our own True Self. We learn to do this by practicing doing it. Here is one way:

1. Our willingness to be aware, both when doing our formal sitting [zazen] and living our daily lives, lets us get in touch with those possibly fleeting times of uncertainty about what might be good to say or do at the present moment. We have to notice when that uncertainty or question arises. That is the first step.

2. The uncertainty itself is raising the question "Should I do this?" "Is this good to do?" When we 'hear' ourselves asking that, we have the opportunity to pause before acting or speaking.

3. The pausing allows us to 'hear' Something greater than little self, perhaps a quiet 'yes' or an emphatic 'no.' I know that seems strange, but it's true, and I believe we all do follow this direction many times without being aware of it. How on earth did we all survive otherwise?

4. Since there is only one Mind, this kind of dialogue happens quickly [or not]. We don't want to program ourselves that it has to be a certain way because it doesn't. What I have found is that if 'I' really want something, then it is hard to listen/

believe/follow this other direction. So the inner practice itself, if nothing else, highlights where our 'intense desires' or 'selfish desires' exist.

5. If we're not sure of the guidance, we ask again. On important matters, Reverend Master would say "ask three times." Here is the passage from her Commentary on the Second Pure Precept, Do only good, which is part of her commentary on the Kyōjukaimon [Giving and Receiving of the Ten Precepts, the taking of which is a formal commitment to being a Buddhist]:

   > *"Always you must ask the Lord of the House; always you must be humble in His presence. 'Please teach me that which it is good to do this day'...and know, indeed that when the still, small voice within my mind and heart says 'Yes,' I must obey this teaching. When it says 'No,' I must not disobey that teaching. When the Lord speaks, spring up joyfully to answer; then, indeed, it is good to do anything whatsoever He asks; know that the Lord will never break the Precepts."*

   Because this is a big learning, little self can get mixed up. So it's tricky and we don't want to be foolish [by asking insignificant questions].

6. We choose what to do. We take the next step. We do something [choosing not to do is an action also]. The purity of our intention [i.e., to our best knowledge having gotten little self—desires and opinions—out of the way] will protect us because we know we haven't wanted to harm anyone and wanted to help as much as possible within our own limitations.

7. Every action has consequences, so we can learn from these. We can be open to what happens whilst knowing there is nothing wrong, nothing is written in stone, it is all good. We're just being stretched when little self is uneasy about what has followed.

8. We may recognize that there is another step to take now and, if it seems good to do, we do it.

I hope this doesn't sound too cumbersome. Lots of life just flows and the niggle doesn't come up. When it does, it may be a signal to slow down and give something else a try. Daily reflection can strengthen our ability to do this kind of asking at the moment; it also can help later clarify what happened.

## Attached to an Outcome

The Buddha's Second Noble Truth is that the cause of suffering is attachment, clinging. This clinging is to the 'five heaps' or 'aggregates,' those inner experiences which we take as who we are, our self. When feeling distressed and ill at ease, we have a golden opportunity to discover *what* in this specific instance, here and now, is the problem, what we are attaching to. Because distress is painful and murky, the discovery of the *cause of our immediate suffering* is a challenge. The tendency is to want to just get out from under the discomfort, wriggling this way and that as if followed by a dark cloud that kind of envelops one. This is when training can be especially fruitful, though it is hard to remember that in the initial stages of fear and dis-ease, which can seem to be protracted and unrelenting.

What we must remember, hold on to, is that everything is all right. The remembering is an act of faith, or built on our faith—this we *can do.* In other words, in the helplessness of the dis-ease, we can *look up.* This is Reverend Master's teaching from her third kenshō. When down there in the pit of darkness, *look up.* One way of describing this is that we are actually acknowledging our helplessness. Here we are, just living life, and feel stuck, distressed, uncertain, ill at ease, scared, which are feelings that none of us want. Can we see that right within this is the clinging that leads to suffering? A large part of the sense of distress is just that we *can't see* clearly. So to allow the inner faith to bubble forth requires *patience:*

we have to be willing to *wait* in the darkness for the Light of our True Self to get through. You see, we are *blocking* that inner Light, our wonderful Birthright, even though we need it so desperately. We block it by dwelling *outwardly* on this circumstance or that, of either the past [worried about what happened or what it 'means'] or the future [what might happen that we don't want to happen]. This is our attachment to a certain outcome even if it remains mostly undefined.

The *eight worldly conditions* that we are tossed around by on this wheel of samsara include success and failure, approval and disapproval. The point, of course, is that when we *want* success, that reassurance that we are all right coming from some outer condition being a certain way, we're on the relentless wheel of Life with all the uncertainty thus entailed. We live in an uncertain world. Change is at the very heart of Life. As my great teacher said, "Life is movement; life is going from here to there." Even if we choose not to move, life is going to spin around and challenge our immobility. This is just another way of expressing how *suffering is caused by attachment* because we are only one little part of a Vast Life and must play the Game of Life, participate in *this* body-mind life, with only a glimmer of what lies ahead. We really have only *this moment.* More correctly, we don't *have* any thing. The moment moves away whether we want it to or not. The challenge of living is to accept and embrace all of this uncertainty by living within the security, the certainty, that life, which includes 'me,' is unfolding as is good, just as it should, even while little self "sees through a glass darkly" and can't get it. When we rest in our Buddha Nature, we *know* we can play our part in this game of life by doing the very best we can in whatever circumstance we happen to be in now. We know we have only this moment, this precious exquisite *now,* and our Right Intention gets focused on what is the best next step. We allow ourselves once again to get grounded by looking at that which is good to do *now* without jumping ahead into the uncertainty of the future with all its unpredictability. This important shift in our way of viewing life brings us right back to the present where our choice does matter and where our sense of helplessness dims.

That is why de Caussade eulogizes the present moment so much and puts such emphasis on the duty of this moment. Doing that 'duty' is *our part.* We are given choices over and over about what to do now. We learn here how powerful old habits are, how desires can lure us off course, how the calculating mind wants to figure out self-protective ends. We get seduced into believing these old patterns and end up in a stew, over and over again. Wherever the lures of little self still pull, that is where our work is because as long as we are ruled by old patterns, we will continue to suffer somewhere along the way. This is just the way it is. Our work is to keep steady when circumstances challenge our equilibrium. It doesn't work to just try to protect ourselves because we simply don't know what is going to happen down the road, no matter how much we want to play it safe, to protect ourselves.

We simply over and over again have to give up attachment to a particular outcome while doing the very best we can at the present time. Then we are giving up while looking up. This is the ground on which a spiritual life is founded because we are *willing to see* both the uncertainty *and* the certainty. We turn within and do our own training without demanding [clinging to] a particular result over which we truly have no control. How very liberating it is to return to this Ground where we know at a level beyond feeling and thought that *we are part of Something far greater than that which we know.* When clinging to *this,* we have the One Fortunate Attachment that the Buddha taught. That attachment is to our Pure Awareness cultivated by staying firmly in the present, the steady state of not clinging to the passing phenomena. Gradually, more and more we glimpse 'the Real as real and the unreal as unreal.' This is the state of Wisdom, the end of ignorance. That ignorance is the belief that we are separate, independent 'selves.' This is the main obstacle, the root of the problem. It is the belief in the *idea* of 'I.' When we attach to an outcome, get caught up in the desire of little 'me' to have things turn out a certain way, we solidify this false belief. That we've done just this through great spans of time has made it deeply ingrained, embedded in the very stance of our being in the world. It is the premise on which this life is based, unquestioned, assumed.

So our spiritual work is to patiently chip away at our ignorance. Intellectual understanding by itself will never satisfy in the crisis-moment because it's part of the surface we tend to rely on. When it is shaken is our opportunity to move to another, deeper level of understanding, which is a *knowing* that goes beyond thoughts, feelings, and biases. That we all can move away from this grip of 'me' is the miracle of training because the 'me' can't simply free itself from the delusion of separateness: we can only do our part. As Dōgen admonished, *"Train hard for this true enlightenment." Training hard* means to bring our spiritual practice to the very heart of our life, over and over again letting the purity of our awareness shine on this shifting, changing world we've taken as so real. Then slowly we are moving out of darkness to light, out of fear to security, as little by little we can through the sincerity and dedication of our practice touch the Permanent, That which doesn't change. As the Blessing Verse at the end of the Ordination ceremony promises: *"We live in the world as in the sky. Just as the Lotus blossom is not wetted by the water that surrounds it, the Mind is immaculate and beyond the dust. Let us bow to the highest Lord."* Then this puzzling Mahayana teaching is simply understood, not intellectually, but at this deeper level: *Samsara and Nirvana are one.* There is *nothing* to look for, nothing to seek, nothing to gain.

This important teaching is expressed by Dōgen in this way: "... the Way to Buddhahood is easy. They who do not perpetrate evil, who do not grasp after life or death but instead work for the good of all beings with utter compassion, giving respect to those older than themselves and loving understanding to those younger. They who do not reject anything, or search for anything, or think on anything, or worry about anything—they have the name Buddha. You must look for nothing more." Dōgen has expressed the Three Pure Precepts in this teaching which is explaining what *our* part is to 'have the name Buddha.' By living without 'perpetrating evil' through not grasping at selfish desires [First Pure Precept] and dedicating ourselves to work for the good of all beings with utter compassion [Second Pure Precept], we are over and over again moving toward the wonderful freedom of *not rejecting, searching for, thinking on, or worrying about anything,* which is when we can truly do good for others by purifying our heart [Third Pure Precept]. Here is a teaching we can rely on and return to when we are back at 'square one,' when through the myriad challenges of life, we have once again lost our way. We simply have to have the patience to be still within the midst of our confusion and remember the Eternal. This is the gift of our training that allows us to do this.

# Being Grounded in the Present

I'm seeing more and more clearly the ceaseless activity of attention. Most of the time it is caught up in the play of the skandhas, the never-ending flow of activity in thoughts, feelings, fantasies, broodings, play-backs of the remembered past. It's all over the place, or we are all over the place as we are dragged around by all of this. It is what was meant by a Buddhist monk when he would admonish himself each morning to, *"Wake up, don't be fooled!"* He wasn't referring to being fooled by others, but to this very dominating tendency to get caught up in the skandhic activity.

I can see that the trouble I'm having with physical balance, and hence walking, is a gift urging me to be *in the present,* otherwise I am off balance and could fall. This makes me very uneasy, so you would think it would be simple to just stay grounded in the activity of standing and moving, but no, it isn't that easy. When we are "grounded in the present," we are really "functioning with awareness"—it is the same thing put in different ways. Within this precious awareness the Voice of God, the Eternal, the Lord of the House may be heard. It is *always here, right now, every moment.* The trick is to stay tuned to It instead of all the activity within our little minds. The latter is included within the Whole, but it is only a *part* of It, and the mental noise can drown out the "still, small Voice" of the Eternal just as our pointed finger can block out the sun. Then we take this little tiny bit, this 'me,' as the center of everything—and suffer, accordingly. The Buddha said that when we grasp at anything, Mara stands beside us. *Mara* is how Buddhists refer to the doubts, desires, and muddle that confound us when we mistake the part for the Whole and then place demands [grasping] on how that Whole *should* be.

The antidote for this is simply to pull ourselves back to an awareness of *this moment.* This is a place of quietness for it is just *being one with that which is. "Seeing the Way things are"* sometimes is a synonym for being enlightened. Momentarily we let the veils of our desire, hatred, and confusion drop away—or rather they just do drop away when we have grounded ourselves in the present. This is the place of peace and security. There's nothing to fall from, it's solid, it's real. The very serenity and simplicity and evenness make it hard to notice.

When I get caught up in the stream of thoughts and feelings and then wake up, so to speak, and return to just *being here,* I am bemused that something so precious is so difficult to do. Well, that is the rub of it of course—one *can't* attain it in the sense of holding on to it, for then we are once again in the land of samsara, the suffering that comes with grasping at anything. By letting go, we have what we were afraid we'd lose that led to the clinging, the attachment. And it takes a lot of trusting, a lot of faith, to just let go.

Fear of the Unknown, of what comes next, prevents our living in the Flow of Life. In that Flow come both pleasure and pain, success and failure, all the opposites that prompt our swinging, wanting the one and scurrying away, if we could, from the other. This is why *all-acceptance* is so very important to cultivate. Reverend Master called all-acceptance the Perfection of Zen, of our training. We can veer off from staying in the Simple Present, which is the Place of all-acceptance, because being in this spiritual Place not only exposes our suffering, but also threatens to expose the *causes* of the suffering. And that can be very unpleasant to endure. So we opt for the 'devil we know' instead of the 'devil we don't know,' and *do things that create more suffering so that we can avoid facing the causes of suffering within ourselves.*

Our own humanity, our own limitations, the consequences of our own actions, help us wake up from this nightmare again and again. When we are thrown back on our need for help from Something greater than ourselves, and when we are able to cry out for that help, we cut through the negative cycle. And in fact, we can't do it all ourselves, we need to rely on the Eternal to help us. This help is always available to us, but so often it is only when we come to that exquisite place of uncertainty that we really get in touch with It. When we feel all self-sufficient and on top of things, then we think we are in charge of our life, and it does not even occur to us that we need the help and guidance of the Eternal. Of course, deep-down we know this isn't so. Any moment life could be snatched from us, or some catastrophe or another could fall right on top of us totally unexpectedly. I am finding that there is nothing so salutary as the humility of knowing there is nothing that I can count on and that God is running the show. I am assured that it is all working out, that everything is being taken care of. Over and over again, I am getting proof of this in my daily life.

All-acceptance can be grounded in seeing the value of what befalls us, rather than trying to hold things to another course. It isn't a Pollyanna view that ignores life's difficulties, but it is firmly rooted in that faith that whatever happens is for the best. Now how we understand what really is *best* has to be from the point of view of our spiritual development—I think that is the only way to get out of the realm of the opposites. The recognition that we can't see the whole picture can help here. It is said in Buddhism that Buddhism will last as long as bowing lasts. And bowing is an important part of our practice in a monastery, the getting down on our knees and bending head to the floor kind of bowing. The physical act hopefully puts us in touch with the more important heart-act, giving our heart over to That which is greater. We do a lot of bowing each day in the monastery, conveying that this kind of acceptance can't only be done once. It is a constant re-dedication of our lives to what is fundamentally important and helps put into balance our daily concerns, if we let it. It is a very wonderful way to live, a way to cultivate the faith to stay grounded in the present and listen to the Voice that can guide us.

# Chasing Shadows

One way to look at our practice is to understand that the ordinary way we humans approach life is with a wrong assumption, premise, or belief. We take this body-mind complex as self, as who we are. The right understanding that is the first factor of the Noble Eightfold Path is that we've got it wrong: what we simply without consideration take as real is not the *whole* of it. In Dōgen's "Rules for Meditation" he refers to the proverbial blind men who each feel one part of the elephant and generalize it to be the whole: "O sincere trainees, do not doubt the true dragon; do not spend so much time in rubbing only part of the elephant," adding "Look inwards and advance directly along the road that leads to the Mind." When we don't know any better, which is our human predicament, we take for granted that our experiences are real and true. This is as chasing shadows because unknowingly we're playing out *past* experiences as they are stored, so to speak, in this conditioned body-mind, reacting through these filters automatically, unmindfully.

What wakes us up from the shadowy dreams is their basically unrewarding, unsatisfying nature. So the Buddha quite brilliantly begins his teaching by emphasizing this aspect of our experiences. He points out the obvious: birth is suffering, old age is suffering, illness is suffering, death is suffering, being with the undesirable is suffering and not being with the desirable is suffering. In summary, it is the clinging to the five skandhas that brings this whole mass of suffering in its wake. The five skandhas are the Buddha's enumeration of 'heaps' or aspects of experience that we take as 'me,' a separate self: form, sensation, perception, thought formations, and self-consciousness of these experiences as a 'me.'

Our practice of "looking inwards and advancing directly along the road that leads to the Mind" involves a willingness to *stop and see.* We simply have to be willing to recognize where we get stuck in this karmic play in a repetitive and compulsive manner. This is the big challenge when the energetic pursuit of shadows [reacting without examination to experiences on the basis of past impressions] is in full force. It's really hard to step back from what is at times referred to as this karmic tangle/jangle because of the huge momentum of past experiences which have been repeated and repeated and repeated. The good karma brought into this life moves some of us to "look inwards," and we're on our way to getting a handle on the unsatisfactoriness of our lives. Our spiritual work is to stop the chase of desperation that believes that these shadows are real and can bring lasting satisfaction, security, and ease. So long as we're caught up in chasing these fleeting experiences that make up our lives, we reap both the pleasant and unpleasant consequences—the karmic law of cause and effect. We have to see this for ourselves. And Life continues to teach us repeatedly the futility of being on this pendulum.

We have to cultivate the determination and energetic pursuit of our practice, by giving that a priority in our busy lives. It can be scary because implicitly in being willing to examine the known we're moving beyond the comfort of our habitual stance. Hence, faith, strong and purposeful, is the first requirement here. There is Something More. Our whole being can cry in anguish, and that can turn us to an innocence, which is sometimes referred to as nakedness or emptiness. In *The Denkōroku,* Great Master Keizan wrote, "If you want to become one with the Truth, as one flame combines with another, throw away cherished opinions, old emotions, arrogance, and obstinacy, and learn the True Mind of the Lord with the naïve mind of a child." Over and over again, we have the opportunity to let go of the opinions, emotions, and arrogance that keep us chasing shadows hovering from past experiences which includes our interpretation of their significance.

All the teaching comes down to our determination to keep *mindful* of the karmic inheritance and use our ability to make *choices* out of that awareness, rather than mindlessly. And a seeming miracle happens, not on our mandate, but whilst being the result of our willingness to stop chasing the shadows from the past: little by little our birthright of awareness, being awake, grows and we sense for ourselves within the silence that we're a part of Something that includes All. As my great teacher put it, this is a vision beyond division. Since It is beyond the human mind of accumulated knowledge, there is no usual language that can help. Within the stillness, however, little by little we learn another language—the language of the Heart of compassion, love, and wisdom. Resting in That we no longer need be victims of the shadows because the light of our Awakened Nature is as the sun appearing when the clouds pass. It's Here, dear friends, never be disheartened, never give up. That's our part—to keep letting go of the shadows and look up.

# Cleaning up the Mess

Teaching has been tumbling in thanks to the wonderful Sangha members who talk about the cutting edges of their practice. To clean up the messiness of our lives, the unsatisfactoriness, we use with increasing precision and vigor our spiritual practice. The little St. Francis Prayer adopted by AA is applicable here: "Lord, give me the serenity to accept the things I cannot change, the courage to change the things I can, and the wisdom to know the difference." The third echoes the third Pure Precept: Purify the heart so that I can truly help others. Purification of the heart/mind or Wisdom is what allows us to make the important choices implied in the acceptance and courage of the AA prayer. This can seem abstract and grandiose until we start actually bringing to bear our regular spiritual practice onto more and more aspects of the way we live. While it is the most difficult thing in the world to do, it is simplicity itself in what is required.

A useful way of finding one's way in all of this is to separate two aspects of our lives: structure and flexibility. Structure, in this context, refers to the long-term choices already made which provide a predictable framework for daily living: where we live, our job, our marital status, etc. These clearly define certain of our choices if we are responsible and mature adults. Obviously, all of this is changeable as is all of life, but from day to day they provide a useful structure for our lives: when we get up and what we do at specific times of the day. I think this is obvious. What may be less obvious it that within this very structure we have enormous flexibility of how we are actually living life. The first application of wisdom or purifying our heart is to be willing to *look clearly* at what we are doing, look at where our lives are not satisfactory, where the niggles are. In order to do this, we have to stop reacting automatically: we have to give up some old engrained habits, and we all know how tenaciously habits stick. This is the first step, and Confucius pointed out that "A journey of a thousand miles begins with but a single step."

I've heard some people upon being introduced to Buddhism exclaim that it is so difficult, so enormous an undertaking; they balk at getting started, backing off from the imagined enormity. How do any of us know? The important thing obviously is to start and keep going, which I think is what the Cheshire cat or someone advised Alice in Wonderland when she asked for directions. We are told that where we are right now is just where we need to be as the place to begin our inner journey. So the first step that we take from this perfect place is to *look* at what is unsatisfying to us. Again, it is fortunate if the overall structure provides stability at this point in our lives, that we begin this inner work before everything seems to be crumbling all around us. *Now* we can begin recognizing where there are salutary changes we can make, which means recognizing where some of our earlier patterns have led down the road to frustration, tension, unease. Often when we recognize the distress, we become so caught up in its various ramifications that we forget that it is a result, a consequence, of choices we've earlier made. My great teacher would say, "It is so simple, so simple." Bare-bones, dispassionate looking brings that simplicity because we are allowing ourselves to *see* where we've put blinders upon seeing.

This first step leads naturally to a greater dexterity in making wise choices: choices that reduce frustration and maximize satisfaction. We see more and more clearly that when coming from a position of 'me-ness' there is a meanness or littleness, a narrowness of vision, that obscures our seeing the likely outcome of our choice to do this or that. Most all of us 'want to eat our cake and have it, too,' which is just a way of describing the built-in greediness that is one of the three poisons or defilements that create suffering. One of the masters would simply comment, "You can't have it all." We can't have it both ways, or we have to have it either one way or the other, at a specific juncture of space-time, i.e., at a particular moment of choice. We'll not clean up our messes until we are willing to see how we blur our vision by the greediness of wanting it all or by the anger at being frustrated in believing in impossible solutions. The advanced training of our Sangha reveals this important point within the different structures of their lives. For one it was expressed this way: "I want to hear your talk this evening and I want to spend time with my husband. Since this is a special occasion in our lives, I'll do the latter. But one of our issues is that he can get so caught up in work he can forget about the agreed time for coming home. If he does this, I'll react with annoyance and anger." When she reviewed this, we saw there was clearly another step she had to take: somehow despite his busyness she needed to find a skillful way of talking to him about her conundrum, somehow get his attention. So she made an appointment with him and they actually talked this over together.

The satisfying outcome was that he came home even earlier than agreed upon for an exceedingly pleasant special occasion. Our Sangha member's comment when we reviewed her choices that led to this outcome was "It was WORK!" I reminded her that it was called Right Effort, the sixth step of the Eightfold Path. Indeed, it is work that *is* worth every effort.

In the scheme of things this is a very minor incident *and* these are the little aspects of living that bring its special nuances of well-being or discontent. Why? Because these small choices, and the following through on the niggles, build on themselves, just as avoiding or ignoring them create more confusion and vexations. The little things *do* count, and when we *look* at and see where we don't want to bother, we have the opportunity to *see* how important it is to pause and take a good look. We can brush things under the carpet for quite a while, as we all know, but the dirt piles up and becomes less easy to avoid or ignore. That's just the way it is. We have the opportunity right now to "take hand against a sea of troubles and by opposing end them." Now Hamlet was talking about suicide, followed by his recognition that he couldn't take this seemingly easy escape from the painful decisions he faced. Why? Because "what dreams may come when we have shuffled off this mortal coil, must give us pause." Our choices have consequences that have their own momentum and that will have to be confronted, some time or another. So let's take that first step right now, right here. First, we conform to and honor the structure our lives require and then we learn to listen to when wisdom suggests that we take in hand our courage to look at choices in how we live the rest of the day.

It is as simple as that, and as demanding as that, because when we pause we will stop seeing 'through a glass darkly,' as St. Paul put it in another context. Our vision will lead us to the freedom of Zen, to making wise choices here and now. When people call me to explain they won't be coming to a group or a talk, something in which I am involved, because they've recognized this or that is important for them to do, what is good for them to do, I applaud them: be clear about the choice you make and then go for it wholeheartedly. This is the way to move out of wishy-washiness, that half-hearted mind of wishing or wondering if one shouldn't be doing the *other* thing. We can't have it all; we can't have it both ways. With that kind of attitude of mind, either way we choose won't work because we bring to it that sad unclarity of not being willing to see the whole picture. This we must keep seeing by learning from the consequences of our actions. Our practice naturally lets the fog lift as we are willing to confront the consequences, whether satisfying or not. These are wonderful, freeing lessons we give ourselves, over and over again. And it is in just little things that we have the best opportunity to learn these lessons about who we are. Getting down on ourselves or others is just another way of obscuring the teaching—the 'if I'd just done this or someone hadn't done that...' The next time we 'pays our money and takes our choice,' we can simply have the assurance that I can do better now that I know better. And then we make the difficult choice and go for it, giving ourselves a hearty *good for you*. The messes do clear up, life clears up, living 'for self and others' naturally follows, and we know blood-and-bones how to train in Buddhism for the sake of Buddhism. So simple it is!

# Enlightenment

For many people, the word "enlightenment" has the connotation that someone has arrived at the end of a process, achieved a goal, and now there is nothing more that needs to be done. It doesn't really work that way.

I believe that everyone who sincerely follows a true spiritual path touches the Place of Oneness—calm, peace, spiritual harmony. That helps us keep going. It helps us take the next step into the unknown, into the darkness again, which is really the karma that we still need to work on, our particular mix of greed, hate, and delusion. And this karma is going to come up whether we want it to or not. That's just the way life is.

The Buddha so often pointed out that we have to see and accept the way things are. And that doesn't just mean that we need to accept that there are problems in the world. No, the Buddha emphasized that the problems that we most need to work on are the problems within our own minds and hearts. That is the focus of Buddhist teaching.

We have 'good' and 'bad' days. 'Good things' happen to us and 'bad things' happen to us. Some things we like, some things we dislike. Each of us is a psycho-physical organism that is geared this way. That is not, in itself, a problem. It's just part of the functioning of the world. And then this little 'me' comes in with "I want it *this* way, I don't want it *that* way. *I must have it this way, I won't stand for it being that way.*" This is attachment—getting stuck in the opposites.

And this colors and distorts everything in our life so that we fall out of harmony with the Source of peace and oneness.

In Buddhist practice, we are working to overcome these opposites. My Master used the word "transcend"—we are working to *transcend* the opposites. Well, this requires a lot more than a few brief experiences of Oneness. I don't believe in quick fixes. I have heard of weekend, or maybe week-long, deals where someone promises that if you come to their 'enlightenment retreat,' you will get enlightened. And maybe people come out of such events with a 'high,' and that is probably better than the high they would have got from doing drugs. But you can't do the real work within the heart in a weekend or a week. You can't clean up your own life overnight. You can't see where you need to make changes, understand your own karma, in a moment.

The spiritual journey is forever. Instead of thinking of enlightenment as a static goal to be achieved, I think in terms of *training and enlightening,* a process in which the *doing* is itself the goal. I think it is very easy to misunderstand some of the Buddhist scriptures that suggest that someone comes to train with the Buddha, and, with diligence and sincerity, becomes what is called an 'arahant.' And sometimes what it means to be an arahant is described in a way that can give the impression that the arahant has *completed* the training and has no more spiritual work to do. But it really means that the person is *doing* the training very well. So well, in fact, that he or she is continually transcending the opposites—as long as he or she keeps up with the practice!

I have had a number of spiritual teachers. And I have been very fortunate that none of my teachers encouraged people to put them on a pedestal. They all had 'feet of clay.' And they knew it and were not afraid to show their humanity. And this can be very comforting to the student or disciple. Sometimes I think with fondness of some little foible or that, some way in which a very fine teacher has shown their humanity, and often this can be more endearing than anything else. Being an ordinary human does not stand against enlightenment.

Rev. Master sometimes said, "No true master ever says that he or she is enlightened." She also said, "You never know when you are enlightened, but you sure know when you are not." There isn't just 'one grand enlightenment, and there you are and off you go.' This is a misleading way to look at training. Experiences, including the experiences of Oneness, come and go—that's the teaching of *anicca,* impermanence, change. There is much foolishness within each of us, and unkindness, jealousy, disgust, harshness, hostility. Also within each of us is kindness, generosity, goodwill, gentleness. We just need to nurture the latter, and to turn away from the former. Then we are on the true path of enlightenment.

# Feeling as Meaning

This is one of those teachings that one intuitively understands perhaps, which has meaning in the sense that the words are understood, or so one thinks. Anyway, this can become the *living* teaching at any moment that we recognize that our negative feelings are not inherent in the situation (whatever the situation is), and that as long as the real cause within ourselves continues to plague us, the feelings will find a suitable situation to arise.

We *can* realize that the situation that stirs up such feeling is *not* the problem. As we see this more clearly, it brings relief. We can start out being miserable and end up doing bows of genuine gratitude, as well as the renewed offering of *everything* and the sincere asking for help to overcome the obstacles of self.

This is where the big thanks comes in—for the whole of training is this very effort to come to the Wholeness, the Oneness, the Eternal. *That is why I became a monk, that is the training that brings Eternal life and the end of suffering.* I really see the suffering so clearly and also its cause—the suffering of desiring/expecting something to be different from what it is or may be and its cause being an attachment.

So many times we go through this sequence to really be able to let go and simply *be* in whatever situation we are in. The key is the basic teaching of simply letting the feeling arise without condemning it by being detached from it, making the knowing of it far more important than what it is. It is the shift to the Lord within, the 'fortunate attachment' of 'invincibly and unshakably' seeing the rising and the falling away of whatever arises, seeing its conditioned nature and hence its emptiness. So it's the "going, going on and always going on" over and over again. Bowing, accepting, not being daunted, watching the show/the play of life. *This is the way it is!*

It throws one back on faith to strengthen faith. The faith is that the Lord's hand is in all of this and that it is all for our good. Really, our heart yearns for that Oneness which can only come when there is *no self*, when everything is let go of, where nothing is held on to as 'me' or 'mine.' Just keep offering up everything that arises to the Lord, and go on and on and on!

# Gently Flowing Love

There is this wonderful way of being in the world that many of us often have lost touch with. One way to look at the purpose of our training is to return in this most simple way to living from a place of love. In our society love is generally taken to be very personal because our world is divided into 'me' and 'you.' This is a self-centered position and is dependent then upon the conditions that arise. You're nice to me, a pleasant person to be around, and I like you. A growing friendship follows with feelings of affection. It is a pleasure to be with you. How deep or superficial these feelings are will only be revealed when something shifts. You give your time and attention to someone else; you don't call me anymore, and are busy when I call you. My feelings get hurt and after a while I feel a bit bitter and say some unkind things about you—I don't like you anymore. This is the nature, played out in different themes, of the conditioned love—it's conditioned by many factors that usually remain more or less unnoticed. We are dependent upon those conditions and hence face the potential of disappointment, a sense of loss. This can, of course, happen with a person, a position, an activity, a place. It is an expression of the Buddha's Second Noble Truth: anything we attach to has the potential of bringing disappointment, bitterness, and resentment in its wake when things change.

It is said that through our spiritual practice this conditioned mind which is propelled by the three defilements of desire, anger, and confusion transform into compassion, love, and wisdom, the expression of the Unconditioned or Unborn Mind—the Buddha Mind. Our work primarily is on the side of chipping away at these very habitual modes of being, which are automatic reactions to conditions that arise. This happens through our willingness to use our precious birthright of awareness to make different choices when it is good to do. And all of us who are sincerely embarked on this spiritual path to lessen the unsatisfactoriness of our lives know how exceedingly challenging this practice is. Why? Because, as the Buddha would say, it requires "Seeing the Way Things Are," not as we see through our deep-seated habits' filtering. It's dismaying to find how difficult it is to do this. Over and over again, we have to bring ourselves back to simply being in the present, grounded in what is happening now. This allows us to see, over and over again, how very much the mind flits around, so infrequently being just with what is happening in the present moment.

When we begin training this can be particularly dismaying, sitting there with the intention to be still and peaceful—wham, stuff pours through like a dam that has broken loose. What's happened? We're beginning to see the way things are. When we can view the restlessness of the mind, of 'me' this way, then we can settle into training through understanding that *letting go* as a deliberate choice to return to the stillness of 'just sitting' or 'just doing' whatever it is in the present moment is the practice. We also come to understand how the judgmental mind is another 'add on' that needs to be let go of. This gradually brings a salutary humility by revealing just how little control we have over this unruly mind with its thoughts, feelings, emotions, impulses, and so forth. At the same time, we start appreciating more and more the importance of taking charge of our lives, of making choices over those aspects of our lives where we can. This is the process of the transformation referred to above. We simply have to keep being willing to see when certain habits are not helpful, not appropriate, undermining the purity of our intentions not to harm anyone, including ourselves. And this illuminates the teaching Reverend Master was given in Japan: *Our practice is to stand against the world of the conditioned mind in order to train in wisdom.*

Obviously, this requires disciplining, being firm with those mental impulses that get triggered by conditions. The prayer attributed to St. Francis gives a guiding principle here: "Lord, give me the serenity to accept the things I can't change, the courage to change the things I can, and the wisdom to know the difference." For Buddhists, the wisdom comes first. We follow the Noble Eightfold Path, the Fourth Noble Truth that leads to the end of suffering. We start with Right Understanding because it is our basic guide and ground for our entire spiritual journey—just as "a journey of a thousand miles begins with but a single step." Or paraphrasing Dōgen, when our first step is right we won't immediately stumble. Out of Right Understanding comes Right Intention, also grouped as the second Wisdom [prajna] factor, which gradually encourages the transformation process—we make *choices* just as best we can to do as little harm as possible; to do as much good as possible; and to purify our heart to maximize doing good for others, which of course must include ourselves as part of the package. In this, whether it 'feels' like it or not, we become bodhisattvas in training, beings who long to be one with the Truth, to be in harmony and wholeness within themselves. We more and more sense the interrelatedness of everything so that we come to know, 'blood and bones' as Reverend Master would say, that our inner peace of mind comes out of these choices we make. And the merit of our willingness to keep at this demanding inner task reveals itself in a gently flowing love, a love that surpasses all understanding. It doesn't ask for anything; it is simply grateful for what is. This is difficult to describe and yet as palpable as feeling the flowing water when in a boat, which is one of the ways Reverend Master described It. This is beyond self. It is the Unconditioned, Unborn Buddha Mind. It is worth everything, dear friends, and it is open to us all.

# God Writes Straight with Crooked Lines

Reverend Master often said, "God writes straight with crooked lines." I have heard this so often from Rev. Master and from other monks that I just assumed that it is a common saying. To my surprise, no one that I have quoted it to outside our monasteries seems to have heard of it at all; it's not the least bit familiar. I often think of this teaching, and I find that when I share it with people it is appreciated by most everybody. Two times recently, I have been asked to explain just what these 'crooked lines' are.

God *is* writing straight, our path is straight, what happens in our lives, both good and bad, 'makes sense' when looked at from God's point of view—the 'big picture.' Unless we do the training that helps us to look more and more frequently with "God's eyes," we won't see the goodness in all that happens to us in this life. Every time we can see the goodness, which usually seems to be in hindsight, our faith is strengthened and grows. So it is said that it is the very adversity that fuels our growth.

Reverend Master used the lotus flower as a metaphor for our training. The lotus grows in the mud of some body of water. Its root gains its nourishment from the mud and water, and at some point the stem of the lotus begins to grow, first under water, unseen, and then it pushes its way above the water. There is still no flowering until the stem has gained sufficient strength to hold a beautiful lotus flower. When the flower does blossom, and this is the reference found in the earliest Buddhist texts, it is held sufficiently above the water so that it is not wetted by the water that surrounds it. This last is likened to the Mind of enlightenment — "We live in the world as if in the sky. Just as the lotus is not wetted by the water beneath it, pure and beyond the world is the mind of the trainee." And, as Reverend Master points out, everyone wants the flower of enlightenment, but not everyone is willing to do the hard spiritual work that grows a stem that is strong enough to support the great lotus flower of enlightenment. The stem in the metaphor is our training. She named the book in which she described her own deepest spiritual experiences, and the teachings that were given to her during those experiences, *How to Grow a Lotus Blossom*. And in her first book, which is a guide to the practice and core teachings of Sōtō Zen Buddhism, the first part is entitled *The Stem of the Lotus*, because in it are described the practical ways in which we grow a strong stem of training in our Sōtō Zen tradition.

In this metaphor, always the lotus plant is rooted in the 'mud' of daily life—that is where it gets its nourishment. However, we must use our daily life as training in order for the stem to grow. This requires considerable faith, so we are growing faith when we train. We are growing the willingness to find the good in all that happens to us. The lotus flower is not 'wetted' by the water beneath it and around it. That means that the flower of enlightenment rises above (or *transcends*) the opposites that are so constant in our lives, the opposites of good and bad, happiness and unhappiness, health and illness, and so on. They are all there in the life of every single one of us, and we have learned through long years and through our conditioning and tendencies, that one part of these pairs is 'good' and another part is 'bad.' We want the 'good' one and reject the 'bad' one. In the bigger picture, however, the opposites *go together.* In this life, in the world we live in, we can't have the one without the other. Why? Because of the fact of changeableness. Everything in existence is always changing, always impermanent. And we all really know this for life constantly teaches us this Truth, this mundane truth, over and over again, but we don't want to learn it. Or we can't learn in until we are ready to do so. As Reverend Master said, "It takes as long as it takes." The stem of the lotus that wants to grow is thwarted over and over again by our unwillingness to accept this truth about the impermanence that permeates our lives.

When we sit down to meditate, we are really saying that we are willing to let go of all the opinions, judgments, ideas that hold us within the world of the opposites, the world of Samsara, the world of the suffering that inevitably comes to us when we cling to one opposite and reject the other. This is a stark truth that we can realize more and more by doing the meditation, by looking at ourselves and our lives through the eyes of meditation. In our tradition, this is called 'just sitting' without trying to *control* the flow of thoughts, feelings, memories, and so forth that will arise. We want to sit quietly, and in the beginning, we probably have some idea that we *should* not be having all of this mental activity come up, or that we should have only pious, holy thoughts and feelings appearing. It doesn't work that way. What we gradually learn is that everything that comes up also passes away, that there is a rising and falling away of all these conditioned things that we took to be so real. In order to begin seeing this, we *have to step back* from our involvement with all this activity which has been our habitual tendency for a long time. In other words, we've invested a lot in all of this. We have a self-*image* of who we are, of how we behave, of what our thoughts *should be.* We think we are rational, reasonable folks with our emotions under control unless there is something that justifiably provokes them. So we justify ourselves, argue with ourselves, condemn ourselves, distract ourselves with fantasies, and so on, and all this mental and emotional activity *will* show itself for what it is when we make the effort to meditate.

The process that is set in motion when we begin to meditate seriously is essentially value-neutral: all thoughts, feelings, and so on are aspects of one flow of experience; it is all simply passing through. We can see this as long as we can maintain a pure awareness that doesn't get caught up in the activity. Repeatedly, we get pulled away from that awareness and do get caught up since this is habitual, strong habit. The secret of the meditation is to simply return to the awareness as soon as one recognizes having been pulled off. Just return to the 'just sitting,' patiently and gladly without worrying about it. Gradually one finds that it all quietens down, at least some of the time. And in that quietness we are finding a new way of being. This new way of being, this quiet place of calm, is our *True Center,* our Buddha Nature, our Birthright. It is the Place of the Unborn—That which *preceded* all the streaming thoughts, sensations, feelings. This is a gradual and growing experience that changes our life.

You see, what we are learning is how to grow a lotus blossom, how to strengthen that stem of faith into the certainty that there is Something much vaster and greater functioning within our life, sustaining our life, than we could possibly comprehend. We learn about this through letting go repeatedly of all that arises and passes away, that which we have taken as so real. And so that we can find the *true* Reality *within ourselves. "The K of God is within."* We can't find It in any other place than in own spiritual heart, and the journey back to It is the hardest of a undertakings, much more difficult than any external challenge. That is really sobering, and it is true.

I am reminded of the Sufi story in which God made man and all created things, but God hadn't yet decided where to put the most priceless of his gifts, part of Himself, a spark of the Divine which is to be given to each. He considers placing It atop the highest mountain, or deep underground, or at the bottom of the ocean, and rejects each. He thinks that if He puts It in these places, it might not be appreciated when It is discovered. It might be discovered too easily, maybe even just by accident. So He decides to put the Jewel within our hearts. Now it is so close to us, the most intimate part of our entire being. How could we miss it? We miss it, don't see it, by looking outward, by expecting to find our satisfaction, our fulfillment, from externals, from education, from marriage, from a good job, from lots of money, and on and on. Of course, there is nothing wrong with getting an education, being married, having a job, and earning money. The problem is when we try to make these things, or anything else, take the place of our own inner spiritual Jewel. *"Seek ye first the Kingdom of God and then all things will be added unto you."* Why? Because then we have a firm foundation on which to build our life of changeableness.

All those hardships, disappointments, limitations we bump into are God's way, using the law of karma, to show us over and over again that we can't *count on external things and conditions* to tisfy the longing in our heart for safety and security, unwavering reassurance and totally unconditional Love. When we try to make externals our refuge, we're looking in the wrong place, we're going in the wrong direction. And at some point, we recognize this and make the essential turn-around. Then we are on our way Home, to our True Source, to That which doesn't change and simply cannot, and never has, let us down. It's waiting for us. It's the priceless jewel, treasure, within the heart of each of us. That is why the Fifth Law of the Universe in Buddhism is *"All beings possess an innate knowledge of Buddha Nature."* How could it be otherwise? When we are One with That, then we look back on our life and see there is not, and never has been, a single 'speck of dust.' And we see that all along God has written with *straight* lines. It was just that we couldn't see the straight lines for what they really were; we saw them as crooked because of our own ignorance.

There is a relief and gratitude and awe that overwhelms with this knowing. Suffering is being diminished because our practice is weakening the power of clinging. We are learning all-acceptance. This is the strengthening of the stem of the lotus which makes possible the budding of the lotus flower. That it takes a long time for the lotus to fully blossom doesn't matter. We are on the Journey, going in the right direction, and all else will follow in good time.

# Is the Dharma Uplifting?

After the talk last evening, we had a fruitful discussion when someone wondered about an observation a friend of his had made: "The Dharma should be uplifting." He wondered how or if this could be reconciled with what I'd quoted from one of the Middle Length Discourses of the Buddha: "A Perfect One's feelings, whether pleasant, unpleasant, or neither pleasant or unpleasant, are known to him as they arise, known to him as they are present, and known to him as they subside.... This is a wonderful and marvelous quality of a Perfect One." It was agreed as the discussion proceeded that whether a feeling is pleasant or not cannot be the criterion for the Dharma's being uplifting. That's just imposing another condition on Life that is bound to fail, not live up to its promise. As someone pointed out, there are *Four* Noble Truths. If we stop at the first two concerning suffering and its cause, likely we won't feel uplifted. That has seemed to some who have heard just that much of the Dharma like a downer, as pessimistic, and they aren't drawn to the Buddhadharma at all. Obviously this is, to say the least, a superficial glossed-over understanding that doesn't get one into the heart of the matter at all. As the Buddha said, "Let the unbelievers depart."

One Sangha member reminded us of Reverend Master's teaching that "Always we must be disturbed by the Truth." Could being *disturbed by the Truth* be uplifting? Someone else said that for her she had to struggle when first hearing this teaching with how feelings could be neither pleasant or unpleasant, as well as pleasant and unpleasant. And how this vast array where the conditioned 'me' isn't caught now seems uplifting for her. Someone else pointed out that resolving a particular lump of a current unsatisfactoriness through practice was uplifting in the sense of bringing the relief of a greater understanding. And another added that it depended upon what one meant by the word itself, which is the nub of the problem. As Tōzan Ryōkai observed in his enlightenment poem: "Finally we understand nothing for words inaccurate will be." He also found that "Enslaved by words you fall into a hole. If you should go against the basic Truth, you come to a dead end." So we can answer the title's question "Is the Dharma Uplifting?" with both a yes and a no; it depends on what is meant.

In the Oxford Dictionary, the second meaning of *uplift* is: "elevate morally or spiritually." This is it in a nutshell, isn't it? Because it is the *trainee* who needs to be uplifted by the Dharma, spiritually and morally. This is why we train. Again, from Tōzan's enlightenment poem: "The sage will tell a trainee who is feeling low and all inferior that on his head there gleams a jewelled diadem and on his body rich robes hang and at his feet there is a footrest. If the trainee hears this teaching with surprise and doubt, the sage assures him that of cats there are some kinds as also some white cows that perfect are just as they are." Tōzan is here describing how the master uses the Dharma, the Truth, to uplift and encourage the disciple who is training with him/her. As we are truly willing to see our need to do something about ourselves, the need to come to grips with the unsatisfactoriness experienced via this conditioned body-mind that we take as a self, a separate 'me,' the Dharma gives tremendous help, a boost that is always here for us. Why? Because it is pointing the Way to the end of suffering—*that* is its purpose.

The Buddha said, "I teach only two things: suffering *and its end.*" What can be more uplifting than that? The Buddha's promise is that there is an end to suffering—this is the Third Noble Truth. As we train, we get to *see* for ourselves gradually, little by little, how the *cause* of suffering comes out of our attaching to some experience that we're holding onto *and* how we have the choice to *let go*. The Third Noble Truth is that of Nirvana, That which is beyond the human mind, beyond our karmic tendencies to identify with the five aggregates of clinging—form, feelings, thought, activity, and consciousness, as they are translated in The Scripture of Great Wisdom. The Great Wisdom—the beautiful, magnificent Dharma—is That which is not caught in the karmic play. Here is the freedom of Zen, the "peace that surpasseth all understanding." It is an inspiring, yes *uplifting,* way of being and living in this *saha* world where compassion, love, and wisdom gradually replace the karmic energies of greed, hate, and delusion. As is promised at the very end of a Buddhist Ordination ceremony: "We live in the world as if in the sky. Just as the lotus blossom is not wetted by the water that surrounds it. The Mind is immaculate and beyond all dust. Let us bow to the Highest Lord."

The Dharma beckons and calls, always has and always will. The Buddha said that whether there are Buddhas in the world or not, the Dharma is *always* here. This is emphasized when he assured his followers that "They who see the Dharma, see me, and they who see me, see the Dharma." He's pointing to That which is beyond our sensory experiences, beyond form, feeling, thought, activity, or that limited 'me' consciousness — "*This* is the very Truth, no falsehood here. This is the Mantra of Great Wisdom, Hear! O Buddha, going, going, going on beyond, and always going on beyond, always becoming Buddha, Hail! Hail! Hail!" Friends, let us get on with our training. Nothing need be excluded whilst we are cultivating over and over again in this moment and then the next the skillful means to use wise discernment in *letting go and going on*. As a Buddhist master of the last century taught, "Let go a little, a little bit of peace. Let go a lot, a lot of peace. Let go completely, complete peace."

That is the challenge of our training, and to keep grounded in this wonderful Dharma is the uplifting message that *It* is *always* here to aid us in every moment of this precious life. The Three Refuges themselves from early Buddhism have been offered to uplift the sincere trainee who inwardly bows in humility and takes Refuge in the Buddha, takes Refuge in the Dharma, and takes Refuge in the Sangha. There is no problem, there is simply the *willingness* to keep going, always taking that courageous next step into the Unknown whatever the feeling state of the moment. This is the way to be uplifted by the Dharma, That which is both right here and now and also the Beyond.

## Light Goes with Darkness

In *Sandōkai* (one of the scriptures that we chant many mornings in the monastery) is the line, "Light goes with darkness as the sequence does of steps in walking." We cannot just have light times, flowing times, easy times. There are also going to be dark times, difficult times, painful times. Thus, light and dark alternate as our feet alternate positions (which one is ahead and which one is behind) when we are walking. This is *just the way it is* and it is pointless to keep resisting and fighting it. The *only* problem here is that the little self wants only one side of experience, the pleasant, enjoyable, and immediately reassuring. But we can't just have the side that we like.

Buddhism doesn't advise us to pretend to enjoy that part of the flow of life that is dark and painful. What we are asked to do, and what we *must* learn at some point or another, is to *accept* the darkness and pain along with the light and enjoyable. And what I'm finding more and more is that it is in the dark, painful times that much, much teaching is given. Now it doesn't *seem* that the teaching is being given when I'm in the midst of the darkness, for then the darkness wouldn't be the state of suffering that it is. It is on the other side, on the light and flowing side, of experience that the teaching comes pouring in. I've noticed that the more I can *stay* with the suffering, not distracting myself, not finding one thing or another to ease it, the greater seems to be the light on the other side. That reminds me of the Zen teaching, "Small doubt, small enlightenment; great doubt, great enlightenment."

Light and dark go together. Really, you can't have one without the other. And still it can be very hard to be in the dark part of it. That too is just the way it is and must be accepted. So, as Keizan wrote, we must learn to *"turn the Stream of Compassion within"* by doing true meditation, true acceptance. Rev. Master would say that the hardest thing to accept is our own humanity, our own vulnerability, our own seeming faults. Perhaps above all else that is what we need to work on. It is the learning to bow to everything, appreciating God, the Eternal, in all. How very wonderful!

*"Seek ye first the Kingdom of God and all good things shall be given unto you."* I've proven this true for myself. I gave up the Ashram, the Yogic teaching, my wonderful spiritual friendships, my pride, my certainty, the activities of reading and teaching that I loved—and it is all given back to me in such abundance that it blows my mind away. But pride had to go before the Lord, the Eternal, could shower all these blessings on me. The I had to get out of the way, not think it knew it all, not think that it could be in charge. *"The Lord is my Shepherd; I shall not want. He leadeth me..."* This is the *living Truth,* one that has been given to me many times, I now see, in the course of my training. It was given to me in my greatest need by the Lord of the House directly in words so clear that I can 'hear' them every time the same teaching wells up within me—*I am here. I am here. I am always here, loving you, guiding you, protecting you.* What a life-giving message, what reassurance.

This is what all the people in the past lives that I have remembered were seeking. This is what I have looked for in this life—this *Love,* this *Reassurance.* I looked for it from something external, but that always led to disappointment in whatever person or thing or event I had attached to. Nothing satisfied my longing. I think this is why the teaching *"nothing matters, mindfulness is all"* was given to Rev. Master during the darkest time of the kenshō that she describes in *How to Grow a Lotus Blossom. Nothing matters* because it is all illusion, deception if one tries to hold on to it, cling to it, expect too much from it. Hence the simple Wisdom of *just letting go, not holding on to anything.*

*This too may pass*—Sometimes, in the midst of life's pains, this may be all we have to hold on to. It is also something to be remembered in times of happiness and enjoyment. It's all passing. The *Diamond Sutra* gives this teaching: *"Thus shall ye think of all this fleeting world: a star a dawn, a bubble in a stream, a flash of lightning, a phantasm, a dream."* One must keep learning this and bowing to this great Truth and *keep going, keep letting go, keep trusting.* This is the teaching that most often is given me when I do my bows before the altar.

# Part of the Story

I often find comforting Reverend Master's saying that "Every morning I have breakfast with Mara, and when I do, I use a long spoon." Mara is the personification of the varying desires, anger, and confusion that arise unbidden. It is said in the literature that even after his enlightenment the Buddha was visited by Mara seven times. Also, Mara was the big challenge on the eve of his enlightenment, which is depicted in those statues of the Buddha in the earth-witness position. His resolve as he seated himself under the Bodhi tree was not to move until achieving enlightenment and he put down his right hand to touch the ground as an expression of this determination. Well, we're bodhisattvas in training, as the Buddha called himself prior to his becoming Buddha, a fully awakened one, and it may be helpful at times to recognize that we're facing the temptations of Mara often by the very nature of living in this human realm. Then figuratively we too can put down a firm hand to the earth as our witness that we won't move from our sitting place, that we'll do our faithful practice so as not so readily slide down those old habitual patterns that are karmically driven and thus perpetuate the unsatisfactoriness we experience.

This theme comes up for me right now during renewal time, which has been pretty busy until the last couple of days. So I come suddenly to a halt in the usual pattern of activity that this wonderful life of teaching the Dharma has brought. I'm tired but it's the kind of fatigue that has layers. This brings a restlessness that is looking for something to appease it. An old familiar pattern. You've heard me say, paraphrasing Reverend Master, "Every morning I wake up with Mara—yuk!" Mostly this is karmic residue since after approaching forty years of spiritual practice I've learned better the sheer woe of not using restraint when faced with the particular conditions that for me trigger the desire and anger. It's always based on that sad confusion which propelled this round of existence, so very often the important action is the seeming non-action of *pausing,* not just sliding right down those tempting patterns of grabbing at something I want in order to feel comfortable or pushing away something unpleasant, not wanted.

We just have to see over and over again how it doesn't work to live simply reacting to the surface of life's offerings. We're conditioned folks, part of the huge complex of cause and effect, just as everything else is. And we have this wonderful opportunity to get off the wheel. This is considered the very height of good karma: being born in the human realm with an intactness of body-mind and having been exposed to the buddhadharma, a path leading to the end of unsatisfactoriness, suffering. It is called the *opportune moment* and we're cautioned not to let it pass, not to treat it lightly. Every moment, regardless of what has happened, we have the precious choice to train, train within the midst of the conditions of the moment. It can only be done *now,* though in our confusion we can compound the difficulty by conveniently believing it is too difficult now and hence kind of slough along, lethargically or desperately looking for another way out. And there isn't! That's what Great Master Dōgen meant when he wrote, "There is only one thing, to train hard for this is true enlightenment." And also, in Rules for Meditation he reminds us that "To live in this way is the same as to live an ordinary daily life."

In The Dhammapada we're told how to do just this: "The training is simple: Cease from evil; Do only good; Purify the heart [so you can truly do good for all beings]. This is the teaching of all the Buddhas." These are the Three Pure Precepts which can be our sure guide. The crunch comes when Mara in its many varying guises comes whispering, urging us to go down old ways and to believe in old stories of what's good and what isn't. This is the nature of karma, of cause and effect. Repetition strengthens patterns, restraint weakens them. For a very long time we've been playing out these karmic tendencies; gradually, little by little, we truly learn from the consequences. As willing students, now we can learn faster and not have to keep repeating quite so often that which becomes increasingly clear is a wrong way, is counter-productive. The Buddha promised that we have the power to choose in vitally important ways to decrease the unsatisfactoriness in this very life of ours *and* to increase the times of peace, contentment, joy, and gratitude. And, as is said in one of the Scriptures, "The Buddha's words are true, not something empty and vain." We just must make it true for ourselves through our *willingness* to go beyond the shadows that seem so real, through our zeal, courage, and determination. What a wonderful gift to be on this path together, dear friends, what a grand way to begin another year of our precious lives!

# Pride

Pride is the first of the Seven Deadly Sins; it is the first and basic defilement. It is the basic wrong understanding that starts the wheel of Samsara rolling, this world of suffering we are in, the world of pleasure and pain, sadness and happiness, gain and loss. There is the saying in the Bible, "Pride goeth before a fall." I've often wondered about the meaning of that "goeth before." Was it in the sense of pride preceding a fall, or was it that when we have fallen our pride falls away and we sense our helplessness? And, of course, it refers to both. Pride precedes the fall, is the inherent cause of a fall, and as the major and purposeful consequence of that fall, pride also falls away. It no longer has the support, the illusion of its invulnerability. So the consequences of indulging pride will one day show us clearly the utter futility of pride. When we think that we are the one in charge of our lives, when we go around acting as if we were God, we are setting ourselves up for a 'fall.' And this very fall eventually pulls the rug out from under pride.

Somewhere along the way the lessons of countless lives sink in and someone in the stream of karma thinks, "Maybe I'm going in the wrong direction, maybe I *could* be wrong." Reverend Master writes in *The Wild, White Goose, Vol. I* about reaching this very point in her monastic training in Japan, and how the simple thought, "I could be wrong" triggered her first kenshō, the wonderful breakthrough in a flash of That which lies behind this driven sense of a separate self. In her diary she details some of the difficulties that she endured being the only woman, and a Western one to boot, in an all-male training monastery in Japan during the early 1960's. She had left her home from across the sea at the invitation of Kohō Zenji, the monastery's chief abbot. She was truly seeking the *perfection of Zen.* She realized that she had to be willing to take everything that happened as being for her good. She held on to this insight, and to her faith in her master, Kohō Zenji, for dear life. She made her share of mistakes, as we all do, but she kept going. Well, one day she reached the bottom when one seeming unfairness was just too much, and she decided to leave, packed her suitcase, and walked out. Now the ordinary mind at this point says, "*Hooray, good for her, no one should have to put up with unfairness.*" She made it to the monastery gate, put her hand up to open it, and then *stopped.* The thought that stopped her was, "*Maybe I could be wrong.*"

As she turned around, the first kenshō happened. And you see, it happened because she had *surrendered* her pride. This wonderful experience is described in her published diary, the highlight of it being that she now *saw* that *everything* is in Reality immaculate and shining. She felt gratitude for *everything.* Her heart bowed to *everything* as Buddha, both the 'fair' and the 'unfair,' both the 'clean' and the 'dirty.' She saw that all the seeming indignities were *working for her, not against her.*

Pride can be dissolved in an action that is as simple as asking someone for help: "I'm having trouble with this. Can you help me?" Yet how difficult it can be to do this sometimes! There is a ceremony in Zen monasteries in which the Head Novice answers questions from the other novices. At the beginning of the ceremony, the Head Novice offers a short quotation from Buddhist teachings that he or she has found to be helpful. This is what I chose: "If you want to become one with the Truth as one flame combines with another, throw away selfish opinions, old emotions, arrogance, and obstinacy, and learn the True Mind of the Lord with the naive mind of a child."

# Simplicity

*Basics of Practice and Life.*

A Shaker song goes something like this: "When true simplicity is gained, to bow and to bend we shan't be ashamed. To turn, turn will be our delight, 'til by turning, turning we come 'round right." This came up for me this morning as I was sitting in this growing stillness I've been talking about since our groups resumed earlier this month. Something quite palpable has taken a new depth or clarity—the Dharma is busting out all over. As it is put in the Dhammapada, "The gift of the Dharma excels all gifts." This is the gift we give ourselves by our willingness to keep going, dedicated to a spiritual practice that moves us toward the end of unsatisfactoriness. We can't mandate that anything 'happen' and gradually we see that a quiet faith in our innermost being gives comfort and support, from which the encouragement to *keep* going springs up again and again and again...

From this 'Place' there is a lucidity, a magnificent light of understanding which reveals the simplicity of the essentials of our practice and out of that our lives. And, as we all know, this is often so alien from our conditioned, habitual ways of being in the world, the existential predicament we bump into repeatedly, that the utter simplicity stands not an iota against its being the *most* challenging of anything we choose to do and learn from. That is just the way it is. As Reverend Master commented, "I don't make the rules; I just tell you of them." Or as the Buddha said, "I just teach seeing the way things are." And what, one would think, could be more simple and direct than that? Well, again that too is just the way it is. So here are some guidelines of right understanding that can help take us to the Other Shore:

1. Stay in the present: keep returning to mindfulness when you find your mind having strayed.

2. Note that when it has strayed away from the here and now, it's moved to the past or future.

3. See how dwelling either on the past or future takes the mind further and further from the stability of the present moment, into fantasy or memory, longing for or fearing something not at the moment here-now.

4. See how this new stance, the straying of the mind, is a place that is thereby off-balance, even when it is anticipating the pleasant.

5. This reveals the basic teaching of Buddhism, expressed in the beginning of the Buddha's answer to the question of what is wisdom-knowledge: "The removal of the desire for pleasant things, and the grief." Punch it into the old brain-computer that it is *desire* itself that is the disturber of this moment's peace.

6. *See* how the nature of desire can be pretty gross and exceedingly subtle. As the practice deepens, we can note that when there is nothing 'wrong' we can still feel uneasy without being able to understand why that is. Perhaps this quote from a teacher in another tradition will help here: "One of the most bitter aspects

of the unawakened mind is that when there is nothing wrong physically, the mind creates fantasies to crave and to fear."

7. *Bow* to 'the way it is,' meaning accept it: don't make too much out of it as is our wont when our expectations are so entrenched that it or 'I' shouldn't be this way. Oh, man! — *this is the way it is.*

8. Now we're back in mindfulness of the present moment and can figuratively or literally take a deep breath; then within that simplicity and humility which our practice nourishes is *ask* within this center of stillness what it is good to do now.

9. And if it indeed is 'good to do,' or in my experience at least not clearly ill-advised as old ways can take us, take that one next step.

10. This brings on its own time a wonderful momentum that allows us increasingly to live with ease in the midst of this changing world that then ceases to threaten. And this, dear friends, is the freedom of Zen.

# Surrendering

The essence of the Buddha's teaching is *anatta,* no independent separated entity 'me.' The *Heart Sutra.* or as it is referred to in our tradition *The Scripture of Great Wisdom,* elaborates on the meaning of anatta. It is chanted daily in our training temples and it is my understanding that this is so in all Sōtō Zen temples. We can't "get it" through our heads, so another meaning of 'Heart' is that we have to let the teaching sink down into a deeper level of being no matter how well it seems understood at the thought level. Obviously, this is perplexing because the very core of our beliefs is threatened here. And little self can set up a flurry of *thoughts* to try to figure out what is there if there is no 'me.'

The Buddha didn't spend very much time trying to answer that question directly. He told his questioners that this was not a question conducive to edification, that what he taught was suffering and its cessation. In a famous account, the Buddha, walking with his monks in a forested area, picked up a handful of leaves from the ground. He asked them which was more, the leaves in his hands or those on the trees. They replied, "Lord, the leaves in your hand are few and those still on the trees are many." The Buddha then pointed out that what he knew was like all those leaves on the trees and what he taught was like the few in his hand. His answer again as to why was the same as the above—he taught about suffering and its cause; in other words, he taught the Four Noble Truths. Again, the Buddha would liken himself to a physician for the suffering world, and the medicine he prescribed was meditation. Why meditation? Because through this practice we would make his teaching true for ourselves, we would find out for ourselves that there is Something more than little self and its extensions into the world it knows. He invites us to 'Come and see.'

Why can't he just *tell* us and let it go at that? Because any telling in the usual way is via language, and language is our communal device to communicate what is shared knowing. It also supports our whole belief system that is hidden under a bunch of shared assumptions about life and our being in the world. We are told that *this* is the problem that our practice over and over again must address. To move to the Beyond is the invitation the Buddha extends to us who are suffering and floundering in the sea of *Samsara,* the perpetual round of the impermanence of birth and death. Until we become really aware of our plight, we simply don't pay attention and resist seeing ourselves in the world in any other way than our conditioned one.

We find in the Vedanta tradition the beautiful refrain "Thou art That." The 'That' is left unelaborated in Buddhism because 'That' is not the problem. We can be enticed by inspired teaching, by a Mantra, by religious/spiritual songs to heighten our longing to be 'That,' free of the inevitable uneasiness that our sense of a separate 'me' entails. As long as we remember that we still have to meditate and that we must take that Journey *into* the Beyond, the Unknown, for ourselves, these means can be helpful reminders to encourage our more intensive searching. Then *we* must make the effort and go for it. "We must make the effort; Buddhas can only point the way." This is just the way it is. As my Master would say, "I don't make the rules; I just tell you about them."

Over and over again, our spiritual practice leads us to the Place of *not knowing*. Everything we think we know is conditional knowledge. The unexamined life, as Socrates said, is not worth living. We must bring to the light of awareness over and over again what we *think* and believe to expose its conditionality, its relativity. It is in this sense that it is unreal. The Buddha taught that his teaching is to know the real as real and the unreal as unreal. This is wisdom knowledge. We have to get pretty fed up with our conditioned life in order to take up this challenge. When we do it a little, we get a little peace and when we do it a lot, we get a lot of peace and when we do it totally, we find that Peace that surpasses all understanding. This is called *Nirvana* by the Buddha, which is the Third Noble Truth, the truth that there is an end of suffering. The miracle is, just as the Buddha told us, that we *can* discover this Truth more and more for ourselves.

The Buddha called the Fourth Noble Truth the *Way to the end of suffering*. This is an 'Ancient Path' which he discovered at dawn on the day of his enlightenment. It is the Noble Eightfold Path, a dynamic, all-embracing Way that can be lived every day of our lives. "Today is the first day of the rest of your life" says an old Indian proverb which resonates with what the Buddha taught. *Now* is the important, auspicious moment, now is the time to embark upon the Journey, now is the time to begin shedding old baggage of karmic conditioning. The Buddha taught: "Let there be nothing behind you. Leave the future to one side. Don't clutch at that which is left in the middle." In other words, keep letting go. This is the surrendering over and over again of whatever it is we're holding onto. We come to know that whatever we're grasping at is shifting and moving on; therefore, we're bringing suffering in some form down the road—this expresses the Second Noble Truth that the cause of our suffering is attachment.

We're simply making the Buddha's teaching true for ourselves, just as he admonished his disciples to do. He told one learned Brahmin that it was not his habit to save anyone from confusion, adding that his was a teaching for here and now which could be made true for oneself by any intelligent, dedicated, and energetic person. The purification comes *naturally* through the surrendering over and over again of the ignorance of little self. This is the ultimate Journey into the Unknown and requires on an *inner* plane the giving up of everything. This is giving up, yes. The important thing is that we remember to *look up* at the same time. What are we looking up to, asks little self? The Buddha's answer: *Come and see for yourself.* It is beyond little self. That which is asking the question will *never* be satisfied with answers it can comprehend. Does that make sense? If the little mind can understand, then it's still here on this conditioned plane of mundane truth.

We stumble and are more and more willing to fall on our face in order to come to touch for ourselves that *Something* ineffable which truly is supporting us, guiding us, loving us. And It's *right here* within our Heart, the Source of our being, who we really are. Our practice takes us here and is supported in this. We more and more can embrace and be embraced by the training itself. Then we are "training for training's sake" and understand that "Buddhism will last as long as bowing lasts." Dōgen's main teaching that "Training and enlightenment are naturally undefiled," that they are one, also is illuminated. These are simply ways of conveying the kind of surrender to be made over and over again in trust, in faith, in humility. This is the Way to the Beyond.

# The 'Not Mine'

The Buddha Nature can make use of anything—all of what we think of as our 'faults,' all our suffering, all the things in life that we don't like, that are difficult for us to endure. All our interests, all the skills that we have developed. Even our little 'I.'

If that is so, then when I give teaching, really the teachings that pour through are not *mine.* They are an aspect of the Buddha Nature making use of what I think of as 'me.' And the teachings are being *given* temporarily to me so that I can pass them on. And when the teaching flows through me, since it is not *mine* in the first place, there is no point in my becoming attached to the outcome. That is the staying focused on the work, and not attaching to its fruits.

Over and over again the great religious teachers point out that there is a *way* of working, being in the world, in which actions flow from the Eternal, from Buddha Nature. Buddha Nature is not bound up in the world of the opposites. We *have* to get self out of the way to *be*. Yes, to just *be*, to let action flow out of our True Self.

Every time I am invited to give teaching, it is possible that the teaching may not seem to come out as purely as the little 'I' would like. Here I have to cultivate faith and surrender to the utmost so that I do not give way to the tendency to blame myself. My job is to continue to be willing to *follow* even when that following is unclear. When I make my actions an *offering* to the Lord, then I am on safe ground—the *only* safe ground. I must remember, and keep returning to the Lord. This is what I'm told frequently at the end of meditation when bowing: *"Keep returning Here!"*

Surely it is worth *every* effort. As the Buddha said, the Truth can be realized through "energy, dedication, and care." The energy fuels effort; the dedication to this Noble Path, the Dharma, the Eternal, gives the direction, the focus for that effort; the care points to the actual practice of how we are living our lives, the Life of Buddha manifesting in our 'blood and bones', as Reverend Master said. It worth paying any price to soar to another level of being when, as Dōgen says, "The Buddha does all and we follow that doing effortlessly and without worrying about it." He goes on to say that this is how we "gain freedom from suffering and become ourselves Buddha." This is the way to live a life of sanity and equanimity right in the midst of *Samsara,* our human life of alternating pleasures and pains.

Oh! I bow in gratitude at being given this Teaching, this insight that isn't 'mine.'

# The Default Position

"What is your default position of the mind?" can be a useful question in our spiritual practice. For most of us until we begin a meditation practice, we wouldn't even have an inkling of the meaning of this question. When we choose to become acquainted with who this 'me' is, then for many of us there is dismay at what we begin to see—why this mind is jumping all over the place! And this is quite disturbing to the point that a confusion can arise: that it is the *meditation* causing the disturbance. Certainly it is disturbing, and it is important to recognize that our default position of mind, where it is set, is just this restless monkey mind. We think there is something wrong and that is true: it's just not in observing the scattered mind, it's the scattering mind itself. When we really begin to understand this much, we can begin to step back from our involvement with all this jumping about, to and fro, in a dither about this or lulling out into a drifting spaciness. And we are beginning to set a new default position, that of the observer, the knowing awareness of whatever is happening. This is a *radical* shift which we come to appreciate more and more *with the doing*. There is simply no substitute to practice, which means to *face* the old conditioning as it displays itself in the here and now. What we'd like to do is run away from the whole thing, escape into the seemingly comfortable position of unawareness.

Bodhidharma said that "As we advance in training, we can clearly see *two* aspects of mind: the mind immaculate and the mind stained. The mind immaculate is none other than Buddha Nature, while the mind stained is that conditioned by greed, hate, and delusion." "Here born we clutch at things," observed Sekitō Kisen in his enlightenment poem. This grasping is such a given, the very premise of our way of being in the world that it generally goes unquestioned. This is the default position that has gradually developed as we relate to the environment of our particular family, society, and culture. Reverend Master said that if a child were lucky, he wouldn't lose his 'intouchment' with Buddha Nature, the Mind that goes beyond, until about age seven when society's norms win out. In the need to conform and be accepted, a child can be pulled away from that inner knowing, which is its Birthright. This is a sad situation. Once recognized, it can fuel our spiritual quest with a deep longing to return to the Source, return to a simpler, less cluttered way of being in the world

We are told to develop a mind that clings to naught. This development is what we encourage every time we can remember to shift our default position of the mind to the simple, choiceless awareness of *this moment.* This is every-minute mindfulness: over and over again, through our *intention* to shift our mental set in this way, we come back to what we're doing now, come back to the richness of the present moment. When we do our formal meditation practice, we are cultivating a new way of being-in-the-world by "just sitting, neither trying to think nor trying not to think, just sitting with no deliberate thought." Our Right Effort is to bring ourselves back to this quiet stillness within regardless of where we are and what is going on. This is the default position we cultivate. So difficult this is that we come to really appreciate why the Buddha taught that "patience endurance is the great army" for a Bodhisattva in training. We have to be very patient with ourselves as we address this ingrained, seemingly intractable habit of slipping out of the present into thoughts about the past and future, to and fro, to and fro. It is helpful to remember that Wisdom is born of Compassion and Love and that we can be gentle with ourselves within this essential discipline—it isn't easy! Simple, yes, but *not easy.*

The great advantages of putting forth the effort to shift our default position in this way aren't particularly appreciated for quite a while. We gradually do see that we live in greater harmony with ourselves and the conditions that come to us in our life. We find that we are judging ourselves and others less as we recognize how very caught up all of us are in the blindness of old conditioning. We are opening our eyes to *seeing the way things are,* which is how the Buddha described his teaching—just *seeing* the way things are. This default position of 'stop and see' shines a clarity on all the seeming confusion of being pulled this way and that: we don't have to *like* what is happening, or dislike it, in order to see clearly and take appropriate action. Liking and disliking are movements of the conditioned mind, the old default position we weren't even really aware of. They arise, and we *have a choice* whether to be pulled into old behavioral patterns or not. This way of 'standing still' allows us to *see* a Bigger Picture. This gives us a better chance of doing what is *good* to do now, acting in ways that are not harmful to ourselves or others. Is this not worth every effort to cultivate? Gradually, a miracle more of the time we find a shift has happened and our default position is Buddha Nature, our True Wish to be in harmony with all of life. We must do our part, make the effort, and it *happens.* It's a growing habit that will take us to the Other Shore, and, as the Buddha promised, we *all* can do it. This is the life-enhancing teaching for *here and now,* so let's not put off the practice. Our part is to cultivate the *intention* to be mindful—in this situation and then this one and then the next. No matter how often we lapse into delusion, to sleep mode, we *always* have the choice to wake up and come back to right now, grounding ourselves *here.* Let's all do it NOW.

# The Eternal

Far and away the most wonderful, wonderful thing in my life is having found the Eternal. In the Christian framework it's the 'Holy Presence.' And, for me, finding It is the fruit of the 30 some years of spiritual practice and training, plus no doubt the sincere seeking that was present in the midst of all the mistakes and unhappiness in my life before I found a spiritual path.

Someone asked me recently what I mean by 'the Eternal'? The Buddha taught, "There is an Unborn, Undying, Uncreated, and Unaffected. If it were not so, there would be no escape from here: the born, the dying, the changing, and the affected."

In Buddhism, what we think of as 'me' is a psychophysical organism with a body, and with sensations, feelings, memories, thoughts, tendencies to act in certain ways, and so on. This is the package each of us comes into the world with: body and mind. But there is a Lifeforce which is our Buddha Nature, and this is part of the Eternal which is reflected within ourselves. In other words, the Eternal is not separate from the 'me.'

Here's a metaphor that I like. There is the sun that shines its light in all directions. That is a good metaphor for the Eternal. Then there is the moon which reflects the light of the sun. That is a good metaphor for our Buddha Nature. The light is one light, and it reflects off of everything: everything is part of the Eternal. So in our tradition there is a scripture that says, "You are not Him. He is *all* of you." Obviously, this little psychophysical package called

'Meiten' is not God. That is the "You are not Him." But there is more to it, for though this little 'me' is not God, there is no aspect of me that is separate from God. This is the "He is *all* of you."

Buddha Nature, the Higher Self, the True Self—that's who we really are. It's like this bright light that we have within us, within our little psychophysical package. But that bright light has veils over it. The light is there. But with all these 'obscurations' as they are sometimes called, 'defilements' is the word often used in Buddhism, we don't know that we have that bright light within us. We think that we are just our body/mind. The cleansing of the heart is about peeling off the veils. And it's endless training. No magic in it. No magic, but it does seem like a miracle when one of those veils peels away, and suddenly it is brighter! This experience is not as unique as one might think. It can happen to anyone at any time. But to recognize it for what it is and to treasure it, that's special. And to carry on through all hardships and keep peeling the veils away, that's endless training.

In doing the training, we are allowing the Buddha Nature to "get a word in edgewise," as my Master would say. We're not on 'automatic pilot.' We're opening ourselves to Something greater than, but never separate from, this little psychophysical package that we call 'me.' Why is it so important to do this? Why meditate? Why not just slip along with the stream of thoughts? Because this is the noise that drowns out the 'still, small Voice' of the Eternal. Reverend Master told a story about a Christian priest or monk who told her he wanted to have conversations with God. Her answer was that if *he* would stop making so much mental noise, he would be able to hear Something more. It's really obvious, and yet so easy to forget, that we have created habitual patterns that are detrimental to our well-being, and we've done this by repeated choices which we didn't likely even know we were making! Now we need tremendous clarity of purpose and right effort to shift out of these habitual patterns. So be it. It *can* be done. Patience, patience, and more patience is needed, as well as asking for help from that very innermost True Self that we are always at least dimly in touch with.

On and off throughout my training, I have been given glimpses of that *Something that lies beyond.* Indeed, these glimpses are a gift of Grace that comes as *It* wills, and each glimpse helps faith grow. If we keep facing the challenges of life without turning away, the *Knowing* that the Eternal *is* becomes more firm. Then, when *experience* of that Knowing isn't here, for like all experiences, it is transitory, we are more able to continue to rest within It. That is faith. My master said that the only true purpose for meditation is to find the Eternal for ourselves. To do this we need to make the Buddha's teaching our 'blood and bones' through sincere practice.

This can't be done just through reading about the great truths and being inspired. The reading is an important step for it helps us take refuge in the Dharma, but the knowledge that comes from doing this is different from the Knowing in the heart which is the result of directly taking refuge, again and again, in the Buddha within, the Eternal, the Iron Being, Buddha Nature.

How to keep living this Truth when we feel scared and overpowered by the little self? To keep going on in training in the midst of fear and suffering is the way to make the deepest Truth our blood and bones. Reverend Master said that we mustn't let in "the shadow of a shadow of doubt." We just keep going back to the basics—meditation, faith, the precepts—and stand firm there. That faith in *Something greater* must be nourished again and again. Sometimes the Eternal does not seem to be there. Don't worry about this! Just keep taking everything as being for your good. Let go of doubt. Going on, going on, always going on, always *becoming* Buddha.

# The Life Of Training Wholeheartedly

The Way of Purification of Karma and True Freedom

Take EVERYTHING that happens as good: ALL–acceptance.

Bow, accept, embrace.

See the Eternal everywhere by remembering.

Keep turning to Pure Awareness.

Let go of each passing, fleeting thought/feeling: non-attachment.

Relax gladly into the Unknown.

Trust and deepen faith.

NEVER stay disheartened.

Let it go ... careful, we're not trying to push anything away!

Look up, over and over again.

Keep slowing down mentally by offering up worry and doubt.

Do that which needs to be done, that which is good to do NOW.
KEEP GOING.

# The Problem with Hope

During last evening's discussion following meditation and Dharma talk, I had referred to being beyond hope in response to a comment made. Someone said that for him hope was very important, that it was a looking up that came out of his practice. Well, something like that. As many of you know, I generally am pretty tired by that time of night [going on to 8 pm!], but that is my recollection. It is so good when someone is willing to share their understanding, helpful to all of us, and certainly helpful to me in formulating how the Life of Dharma shows itself to me at this particular point in training. My first response was to recognize that "words inaccurate may be," as Great Master Tōzan Ryōkai wrote in his enlightenment poem, the Most Excellent Mirror—Samadhi.

For me, hope is a dangerous ally. It projects into the future, and this invariably and naturally is colored by what I want, what comforts me. The 'me' that is projecting can be decidedly wrong, and at one point in our interchange it came out so strongly how often in my long life I'd been disappointed. It was just the way it was because I wasn't seeing things, me, life, clearly, bound by the karmic past which colored everything. Trying to make something better, that in looking back really didn't need 'fixing,' I'd end up frequently right back [from the inward point of view] where I started from. As someone wrote, "Wherever you go, there you are." To which he added, "and what are you going to do about it?" Hoping for the next good thing without looking at where you are simply doesn't work. This is the problem, or so it certainly was in my life, of hope.

Now faith is another thing, and it seemed to me that the trainee who kindly brought up the topic had perhaps equated the two. Faith is the deeper knowing that everything is all right and is working out the way it should. It of course includes that we certainly have a part in this working out. Our wonderful practice helps us ground ourselves in the present moment to look at what we're doing, *how* we're participating with Life, with this grand karmic play in which we all are involved. We can get to see so clearly, by our willingness to train, that when conditions arise that trigger the defilements of self-desire, frustration, and blurring confusion we fall out of harmony with the Oneness. The potential for this to happen is a part of our karmic inheritance, by which I mean the numerous events that have happened in the past including our ways of reacting to them. This body-mind is said to be the 'storehouse of the karma,' a vast inheritance of impressions that it is our opportunity to work with and cleanse.

Wise discernment of what is happening in the present is grounded in this right understanding: when we are again hooked into the conditioned self-reactivity, we give ourselves the opportunity *not* to go down old deeply grooved patterns. These may or may not be appropriate to the current situation. Recognizing the confusion allows us to pause instead of being trigger-happy. This may not be comfortable whilst it is certainly salutary. In that 'wait a minute' we ground ourselves in a trust of our willingness to change, to grow, to be in harmony with life, and, though it may not seem so at the time, this makes possible the magical moment to turn, change directions, try something different. We're in the unknown that our trusting whilst not foolish heart opens us to. We're willing. For me this truly is 'beyond hope' because it isn't resting on some future outcome. It's here and now, doable and worthy of all the energy, dedication, intelligence, and zeal we can muster to our aid. Here is the freedom of Zen.

# There Are No Bad People

There is no such thing as a 'bad person.' There are lots of unfortunate people, people who don't know how much grief they are carrying around with them. Sometimes people do terrible things out of pain and confusion. But there are no bad people.

In Buddhism, we train ourselves to see other people, and ourselves, through the eye of compassion rather than through the eye of judgment. Now, that doesn't mean that when one sees someone with a knife going after another person that one takes the view, "Oh, that's a really lovely person there because there are no bad people!" No, seeing with eyes of compassion does not stand against being realistic. You might try to stop the person with the knife, but at the same time you don't have to hate him. It's an attitude of mind. It's the attitude with which we approach others, and it's the attitude with which we would like others to approach us. We can't take this attitude if we go around with a chip on our shoulder feeling abused and knocked down, and looking for ways to do something horrible to someone else.

We tend to think that it is "natural" to want to kick someone who has done something very harmful. Well, there may be a sense in which this is "natural" for the little self. But this way of going about things just adds suffering to the world's load of misery. What we are trying to do in Buddhist training is to *not* keep piling suffering on top of suffering.

If someone is going around killing people, something needs to be done. But one can do that out of *compassion* for that person, as well as for everyone else. Because if you just sit by and do nothing when someone is acting in that way, which is a crazy way to act, you are allowing that person to heap up suffering for himself or herself, not to mention the suffering that he or she causes the victims.

But do we have to do these restraining actions harshly? Can we not take whatever practical steps need to be taken out of wisdom rather than revenge and hate? I think that is the shift that we need to encourage and nurture within ourselves and within society. Today I have been thinking of the Buddha's words, "Hate was never appeased by hate. Only love can appease hate. This is the Law."

Deep within our heart, we all know this. If I come into a situation full of hate, I will just get hate back, and in return I will become more hateful. Even if I cower and retreat on one level, in my heart I will be nurturing hatred. And my heart becomes more hardened. In *What is Truly Meant by Training and Enlightenment,* Dōgen talks about the power of tenderness, one of the means of being a *bodhisattva* in the world. When we speak kindly to those who are our enemies, their hearts are softened. When we speak kindly to our friends, friendship is strengthened. It's just logic really. I think of this as *"responding rather than just reacting."* We are training ourselves not to be 'natural' in the little self way, but to be natural in a *true* way, which is a way that expresses the Oneness of things.

Astonishing things can happen when we do this. We all know about Mahatma Gandhi. He freed his country through not harming others. There is real power in compassion. It's a different kind of power than the 'eye for an eye, tooth for a tooth' kind of power. And it is *true.* It is in harmony with *Truth itself.* There are true stories about monks who meditate in the forest in Thailand. There are stories of their meditating and being approached by tigers, and the monks are not hurt. In their hearts, the monks are not wishing to do harm to other living things, and the animals of the forest sense this.

We can grow, we can live a life of greater harmony and peace, and contentment and joy within ourselves, and we can convey that to others. Reverend Master used to say, "If I can do it, you can do it too." I feel that in some ways I started at 'minus one hundred' rather than 'zero' in my spiritual training. So I can say with heartfelt certainty, "If I can do this, I *know other* people can do it too." It's hard work. I try to convey encouragement to others: "Keep at it, keep at it, do the practice, meditation and daily reflection, setting a regular time for formal meditation, sincerely doing it like any other learning, except that it's a little more subtle, a little less obvious than other kinds of learning." Growth happens. It happens. We have to do our part, and the Eternal will do the rest. We are getting help, we're not alone, we never have been alone.

To know that you're not alone when you're really frightened is astonishing. It changes everything. Well, the *feeling* of reassurance, of being comforted, does not stay forever. Like all feelings, it passes. That's just the way it is. But we can keep training, keep moving in the right direction, and that puts us in touch with that Place again and again, more and more.

# Whatever Happens, Be Still Within

When I first moved to Vancouver Island, after having been in retreat at North Cascades Buddhist Priory, I felt that I was more in touch with this spiritual Place. Call it 'the Eternal,' call it 'Buddha Nature,' or 'Higher Place.' And sometimes suffering itself would become remote—almost theoretical. It was like, "Yes, there's been struggle and suffering, but now I'm just flowing with Life."

Well, if that ever happens to you, remember that all of our states of mind are impermanent. Yes, I had a little honeymoon phase after my very intense and difficult retreat, and it was lovely. But you can't hold on to even the most serene states of mind. There's always more spiritual work to do. I remember Reverend Master would say, "Every morning I have breakfast with Mara, and when I do, I use a long spoon." Mara is the personification of what the little self is trying to get up to at this particular time. Sometimes it is temptation or desire, but, more broadly, it is whatever the spiritual hang-up happens to be *right now.* Even peace of mind is not something that you can hold on to. Right now, I remind myself, "Hey, Meiten, you don't have to act on this thought or impulse. You don't have to act on it!" Let it come up, and let it go. Sit still!

I'm old, and I'm getting older. I often wake up feeling really crummy. My body hurts. For many years, I lived in the monastery and mostly followed the schedule. That was really helpful. But now it is really important for me not to be so dependent on any set way of doing things. I need to trust my intuition about what is good to do from moment to moment.

So I can't structure my day like I used to. That structure doesn't seem to be the way forward right now. So, each day, each hour, each moment, I'm "groping for my pillow in the dark," as one Zen master expressed it. In my old age I'm *waking up* to this way of living! So I get up in the morning, and I sort of ease into the day in a meditative frame of mind. It doesn't mean I'm sitting all morning on my cushion in formal meditation. Maybe some people do. I can't do that for many reasons. And, more to the point really, it wouldn't be *right* for me to do that now. Anyway, I start my day in a meditative frame of mind. I think all that time in the monastery meditating formally with the other monks must have laid the foundation for what I am doing now. Anyway, I can't hold on to the past. I have to train in the present.

And I have to be willing to tolerate the discomfort of Mara, meaning that if there is something spiritually off-balance, I have to be willing to hold that in my 'meditative frame of mind.' Just sit there, having breakfast with Mara, but using a long spoon. The 'long spoon' is not letting Mara get control. And the 'having breakfast with Mara' is not attaching to anything or trying to push anything away—in other words, *meditation*. That 'off-balance' thing can be a mood, a feeling, the memory of something that I did, or that someone else did, that is somehow disturbing. It can be anything. But when that off-balance is going on, I definitely don't feel that everything is flowing smoothly, everything is alright. No, it's not alright for this little self!

The meditative stance is to just keep aware, to keep *listening*. To just be still within whatever is going on. And somehow, as I do this—and again, you can't program it, you can't make it happen—

the 'off-balance' thing dissolves. And then the sense of the presence of Something greater is there. And everything changes! On one level, nothing has changed at all, and yet now I have the sense that, yes, I am really following that Something greater.

If I don't do that listening, that sitting still, I will act out of neediness, I will let Mara get control. And that just makes things harder. When the off-balance block dissolves, I am free to act out of a fullness, rather than a neediness. Somehow, it's not 'me' any more. The *following* is what is real, not 'little self.' And when I find this Place of inner fullness, I know that, fundamentally, *everything is alright*. All is well, all is going just as it should.

# Appendix

# Guidelines for Meditation

The purpose of Serene Reflection Meditation (Soto Zen) is to find within ourselves that which is Eternal and Unchanging, the Buddha Nature, which is the true nature of all beings. Meditation is a practice that enables us to awaken to our intuitive knowledge of the Buddha Nature and, in so doing, to live more in harmony with the source of compassion, love, and wisdom. Meditation is the foundation of Buddhist religious practice.

Here are a few points to remember when establishing your meditation practice:

1. Wear neat, comfortable clothing that does not restrict circulation in the legs. Sit in a room that is well-ventilated and not brightly lit, facing a wall or other surface that is not distracting.

2. Sit in a stable posture, either cross-legged on a cushion, kneeling on a bench, or sitting in a straight-backed chair. The spine should be erect, naturally balanced, with an inward curve at the lower back. Sway gently back and forth and from side to side to find your point of balance.

3. Keep the eyes open, with the ears in line with the shoulders and the nose in line with the navel. The eyes are lowered slightly. Gently focus on a surface within three or four feet in front of you. If you wear glasses, leave them on.

4. To begin meditating, take two or three deep breaths, following the energy of the breath from the base of the spine up the back on the inhalation, over the top of the head and down the front on the exhalation. After setting up this circular breathing pattern, breathe normally and quietly.

5. Keep your lips and teeth closed. Place the tip of the tongue against the back of the top teeth.

6. Rest your hands in your lap close to your body with the left palm in the palm of the right hand and the thumbs touching lightly.

7. Initially, sit only for as long as you can meditate well, with an alert, bright mind, with awareness. Do not attempt to cut off your thoughts; rather, simply be still with an awareness of what is going on in your mind. When you realize that you have drifted off in your thoughts, gently bring yourself back to being aware of whatever is passing through your awareness. Let go of criticizing or judging your meditation as good or bad.

   If you feel too scattered with "just sitting," bring your focus to your breathing, following the in and out motions, and let your mind ride upon the breath. If you still feel unsettled, count your breaths up to ten and then start over at one again. When you feel more settled, return to "just sitting" without a specific focus, because this is the important aspect of Serene Reflection Meditation.

8. Sit regularly, every day if possible, even if only for a few minutes. Do not meditate soon after meals. Meditating with other people

is helpful but does not substitute for doing your own regular schedule of meditation.

For more information about the nuts and bolts of meditation practice, two excellent online publications are available at www.shastaabbey.org through the link entitled “Meditation”: “Introduction to Serene Reflection Meditation” and “Serene Reflection Meditation.” For more information about the Order of Buddhist Contemplatives, its publications, and Reverend Master Jiyu-Kennett, consult the website for the Order of Buddhist Contemplatives: www.obcon.org

# Recollection

Recollection is a very useful *adjunct* to our formal meditation of 'just sitting.' Its purpose is to help us learn from our life experiences by establishing a special time to more actively reflect upon them. When we live our lives more or less on autopilot, more by reflex than by awareness, following old grooves of habitual tendencies long engrained and hence unnoticed, then an unsatisfactoriness, a niggling sense of something not being quite right, can linger, and we may spin around in circles without really coming to grips with it. As one Buddhist master put it, 'This is the habit of the heedless mind.' When we are on our precious spiritual journey, we have the opportunity to do better than that and can make helpful changes to replace old patterns. Daily recollection, it seems to me, helps implement these changes. Otherwise, how are we to know which tendencies are valuable and which have lost their value and keep us from living harmonious, contented lives?

Such is our resolve when we begin a recollection period. Many find it helpful to write down these recollections, something I recommend unless one feels an aversion to doing this. It keeps us honest, so to speak, by allowing us to examine things that come up in meditation or during the day. Some of these things may be disturbing and, because we have to get on with whatever comes next, don't receive sufficient attention at the time. By sitting quietly, we allow things to arise that it may be useful to explore further. We get the hang of doing it through practice.

When something arises that we sense we could learn from, this is where we begin investigation or inquiry—the second factor of the Seven Factors of Enlightenment. We now use our mental apparatus *actively,* as Sherlock Holmes does in solving a mystery, exploring carefully and fully; we don't want to leave anything out because we might miss an important clue about what 'pushes our buttons,' or about what sort of reaction leaves a dissatisfied feeling in its aftermath. Starting at the beginning and going through to the end is probably best, although we don't want to get stuck with any rigid rules. Just take it from the top. Perhaps an unpleasant interaction with someone will come up, or some disturbing situation. Whatever it might be, the important thing is to have a specific, concrete situation to investigate—since we can't solve everything all at once.

Here are some suggestions on how to proceed.

1. Ask how it began—what you were feeling at the time or just before (headachy, cranky, sad, pressured, insecure, happy, pleased, etcetera)? Look back as objectively as you can, because helpful information about our humanity is right here.

2. Look at how the interaction actually took place and developed, paying close attention to those small movements of the little self that can be so easily overlooked. Deep-seated feelings of insecurity can be triggered by someone's manner, facial expression, seeming abruptness, or apparent lack of interest. We tend to gloss over these triggers because they make us feel uncomfortable, but that is exactly the way we allow our 'discomfort zone' to increase. Instead of heeding our longing

to live harmoniously and buoyantly, too often we give in to little self's protests of not wanting to see the way things are—not wanting to face our vulnerabilities. We live in a grand illusion. It doesn't have to be that way, but only we can use the opportunity to change.

3. Review the particular situation as if it were a film playing in slow motion. We can stop at any frame and look more closely. This is informative as an exercise in that it allows us to stand back from what is being investigated and appreciate just what did happen with all its accompanying unsatisfying results. We learn from karmic consequences that our actions leave a wake, not only for ourselves but often for others too. We begin seeing where we simply fall into old careless habits of body and speech, as well as how these can be prompted by habitual ways of perceiving our world, how our mental activities—our thoughts—trigger our actions of body and speech. The opening lines of The Dhammapada now become a truth we know for ourselves:

   We are what we think.
   All that we are arises with our thoughts.
   With our thoughts we [create our] world.
   Speak or act with an impure mind
   And unhappiness will follow you
   As the wheel follows the ox that draws the cart.

   Recording faithfully an earlier played-out life situation can be enormously helpful—but only if we do something with it.

4. The next step is to consider how it could have gone differently. Here it is not helpful to dwell on what the other person might have done; that's up to him or her to look at and is really not our problem. As my Master would say, 'Each man his karma makes and must carry for himself.' It is even more important to stop our painful habit of judging ourselves as terrible for having done whatever is revealed, or justifying ourselves for the perceived lapses in how we 'should' be. The challenge is, without letting the judgmental mind to get in the way, carefully to consider what we might have done differently so as to avoid carrying around the repercussions. This is a challenge because whatever we did at the time was what seemed the natural or obvious thing for us to do. Now we give ourselves the chance to see that such behavior is never written in stone, that we have other options, and that the natural response feels natural only because in the past we opted to do it. We need to examine whether we really need to be defensive, guarded, or whatever. *It is important that we don't get hung up on the past.* The past is of use only when it throws light on the present. We might find that there is something we can do now that will heal the situation for us. If there is and it seems good to do, then do it and let it go. We want to get on with life, not get stuck. If nothing comes up as good to do, be assured that another opportunity will arise. That's just the way life is.

The true wonder is that we really can change, that we can learn to make constructive choices that help us become who we want to be. We consciously choose by our Right Intention to clean up our old karma. The waves from habitual, unhelpful actions and reactions gradually lessen because we no longer stir them up. And we learn to recognize (re-cognize) our Buddha Nature, the still, small voice of our True Self. We experience in our own lives the wonderful metaphor of True Self as the sun that is always there when we allow the passing clouds to float on by without attaching to them. We live a more enlightened life that is indeed a lighter way to live. This effort of daily recollection—which is a companion to our foremost spiritual effort of formal meditation in which we cultivate the pure awareness of being fully present—brings much fruit and helps us to live in the present. More and more, we come to see those subtle movements of the little self as they arise, and in seeing them we pause before reacting. By pausing, we have the opportunity to respond more appropriately to the situation. We let karmic distortions appear without being so threatened by them because we learn how deceptive our perceptions can be and come to know that we don't have to act upon them; they lessen directly by our precious awareness of what is happening. We don't need to read a book about it or go to classes—we just need to do it and learn for ourselves what is valuable for us.

This is very liberating, and we learn we really can, as the Buddhist ordination ceremony tells us, *live in the world [with all its demands and challenges] as if in the sky [of our Buddha Nature]*. We don't need to get rid of anything. There is a natural transformation as our True Self lightens our lives—as the defilements of greed, hate, and delusion, which characterize our karmic little self, gradually and naturally turn into compassion, love, and wisdom, which characterize the true nature of life. It is wonderful! We just keep at it; we keep going in good faith, knowing that this wonderful process of practice and training is working for us all the time. And it is!

# Transitions

To become better aware of the important space between two activities, I find it helpful to remember the Closing Verse of our Mealtime Ceremony. This helps me notice when little mind has jumped forward before that Closing Verse has ended one activity or has lingered back after a new activity has been embarked upon following the Verse. It gives important boundaries within our day their proper emphasis and reminds us to do one thing at a time, not futilely attempting to jump ahead of ourselves or hang on to that which has passed. The transition space provides an opportunity to come back to center and listen to the guidance of our Buddha Nature, or True Self, and to remember that there is much more to life (the Universe) than our little self's karmic tendencies ("unclean water"). This willing awareness also allows us to appreciate how unskillful actions interfere with the freedom of letting go and being in the present moment.

Closing Verse
The Universe is as the boundless sky.
As a Lotus blossoms above unclean water,
Pure and beyond the world is the Buddha Mind of the trainee.
Oh Holy Buddha, I take refuge in Thee.

# The Links of Dependent Origination

### The Twelve Links in the Conditional Arising of a New Being

Dependent on ignorance [of the true nature of existence] arise volitional or karmic formations.

Dependent on volitional-formations arises relinking consciousness [rebirth].

Dependent on consciousness arises mentality-materiality [mental and physical combination].

Dependent on mentality-materiality arises the sixfold base of experience: the five physical sense organs and, the sixth, self-consciousness.

Dependent on the sixfold base arises contact.

Dependent on contact arises feeling.

Dependent on feeling arises craving.

Dependent on craving arises clinging.

Dependent on clinging arises the process of becoming.

Dependent on becoming arises a new birth.

Dependent on birth arise aging and death, sorrow, lamentation, pain, grief, and despair.

Thus does the whole mass of suffering arise.

# Reverend Master Meiten McGuire, M.O.B.C.

Reverend Master Meiten was a monk in the Soto Zen tradition. After many years of training in spiritual and monastic communities, she spent the last fifteen years of her life teaching and writing in Victoria, British Columbia, Canada. She died peacefully in Victoria in January 2018 at the age of 91, surrounded by some of her many students.

Reverend Master Meiten was born in California in 1926 and received her Ph.D. in Psychology in 1952 after majoring in English and Philosophy. In her professional life she practiced clinical psychology; her last position was that of associate professor at the University of Manitoba, Canada. In 1972, following the death of her son, she went to an Ashram for spiritual guidance. This was the beginning of her commitment to finding a spiritual solution to the suffering she had experienced.

In 1978, she continued her spiritual journey at Shasta Abbey in California, and received ordination as a Buddhist monk from Reverend Master Jiyu-Kennett, abbess and founder of the Order of Buddhist Contemplatives. The Soto Zen lineage followed at Shasta Abbey and world-wide at other temples of her Order is known as Serene Reflection Meditation.

In 2000, Reverend Master Meiten was named a Master of the Order. All of her spiritual training helped her to the growing realization of her spiritual quest: how to bring an end to the suffering she lived with much of her life.

In 2003 Reverend Master Meiten moved to Victoria, BC and began fifteen years of teaching the Dharma to grateful students. Through Dharma talks, meditation instruction, study groups, retreats and spiritual counseling, she offered others the teaching and practice that changed her life. Reverend Meiten's first book Reflections on the Path was published in 2008; her second book Reminders on the Way was published in 2012; and her third book Returning to Stillness was published in 2014.

# About Vancouver Island Zen Sangha

The Vancouver Island Zen Sangha is an independent meditation group that practices Serene Reflection Meditation (Soto Zen Buddhism) as taught by the Order of Buddhist Contemplatives. The group is located in Victoria, British Columbia, Canada, and was founded by Reverend Master Meiten McGuire. The Sangha's work and publications are not financed by any organization and are entirely supported by donations.

We are grateful for all donations received and, being a recognized charitable organization, are happy to provide Canadian tax receipts upon request.

If you would care to make a donation please go to our website:

**www.vizs.org**

Manufactured by Amazon.ca
Bolton, ON

31567671R00314